PERSONALITY
IN
HANDWRITING

D1621529

PERSONALITY IN HANDWRITING

A Handbook of American Graphology

by

ALFRED O. MENDEL

With a Foreword by
RUDOLF ARNHEIM, Ph.D.
Member of the Psychology Faculty
Sarah Lawrence College

NEWCASTLE PUBLISHING CO., INC.
NORTH HOLLYWOOD, CA
1990

Copyright © 1990 by Newcastle Publishing Co., Inc.
All rights reserved.
ISBN 0–87877–153–0

To the Reader:

The author and editor of this manual have taken painstaking efforts to maintain the anonymity and rights of privacy of all persons whose handwriting samples appear herein. With respect to the handwriting samples of any person who is not a public figure, such samples may in fact have been altered, for purposes of concealing their identity, and will not necessarily be actual examples of any person's true penmanship. Notwithstanding this, if it occurs that any person is thought to be identified, on the basis of any handwriting sample contained herein, the reader should bear in mind that the text accompanying each respective sample represents only the author's analysis of said sample, based on generally-accepted graphological principles, and makes no comment on the character of any real person.

A NEWCASTLE BOOK
First Newcastle printing September 1990
1 2 3 4 5 6 7 8 9 10

Printed in the United States of America

ACKNOWLEDGMENTS

I wish heartily to thank Alfred Baer, M.D., for his expert advice, and my good friend, Joel Shor, for his frequent comment and lively encouragement.

For their permission to quote and otherwise reproduce material they own or administer, I am indebted to The New York Public Library (particularly its Manuscript Division and its Berg Collection), to Alfred A. Knopf, Inc., A. N. Palmer Co., Inc., Doubleday and Company, Inc., and George S. Kaufer, M.D., of New York; to W. B. Saunders of Philadelphia; to George Allen & Unwin, Ltd., and A. M. Heath & Company, Ltd. (acting for the executors of the late Robert Saudek), of London; and to Orell Füssli Verlag, Zürich.

Above all, without the unstinting help and open-mindedness of Lillian, Wilma, and Jesse, and a score of other friends and acquaintances who provided me with "case histories," this book could not have been written.

ALFRED O. MENDEL

TABLE OF CONTENTS

CONTENTS

CONTENTS

FOREWORD

What is the nature of the hidden motor which makes people love and hate? We listen to people's voices and grasp their language. Their faces tell us a good deal. We see our neighbors rush and fight and hesitate and sit down for food and rest. Roughly we understand. Yet we know that human bodies are but puppets, pushed and pulled by the central force which makes for desire and fear, receives images, thinks and wills, and still cannot be found in the world of tangible things.

No microscope will ever show us the other fellow's mind, and even in ourselves, more often than not, we experience drives, capacities, moods, without being able to trace their origin and hence to understand, to predict, to control them. This blindness for the mechanism which concerns us most makes us search constantly for the physical reflections of the invisible. By watching the small muscular changes in his mother's face, the baby distinguishes friendliness from impatience. The modern psychologist observes the way people handle toys, improvise on the stage, draw a man on paper, invent stories to fit pictures, discover images in amorphous ink blots. These are "projective techniques"— methods to obtain physical imprints of the intangible, the unknown.

Graphology is such a projective technique, and the physical imprints which it uses are among the most abstract: mere line-patterns, whose verbal meaning is ignored. It is true that there is abstractness also in the Rorschach test in that it

11

removes the subject from everyday life situations by asking him to find meaning in a shapeless spot; but at least it yields descriptions of concrete objects: rabbits, flames, fighting dwarfs. On the contrary, handwriting—as O. Diethelm has pointed out—does not reveal the content of mental activity, but the "formal aspects of the driving forces." Handwriting is an abstract diagram of the strength and direction of vital energies, of the degree of balance, harmony, rhythm, control, inhibition, spontaneity, etc.—central psychological factors, from which practical, external attributes can be derived only secondarily. It presents an image of man likely to be appreciated by the generation that produced "abstract" art.

Two psychologists, Allport and Vernon, have aptly defined graphology as "the art (and perhaps the embryo science) of determining qualities of personality from script." They speak of an art because the main business of a handwriting analyst consists in observing and interpreting perceptual patterns which resemble those of a painting or a symphony in that they are complex and, for the most part, not approachable with our present methods of measurement.

Whether "intuitive" statements of the type used in graphology as well as in the arts differ in kind or only in degree from scientific ones is open to question. Whenever he can, the scientist reduces the investigation to perceptual situations which are so simple that they can be identified without ambiguity: the position of a hand on a dial, the difference between red and blue observed on litmus paper. However, in doing so the scientist must make sure that the essentials of the phenomenon he studies are adequately reflected in the simple, measurable symptom. Can the difference between pleasure and pain in an infant's cry be measured in the volume and pitch of the sound? Are the feelings and opinions of an adolescent truly recorded by the "yes" and "no" answers to a questionnaire? And, on the other hand, are the reactions which the psychoanalyst obtains from his patient clear-cut enough to warrant the bold inferences so eagerly accepted by many a scientist?

Graphology offers a dramatic example of this battle for scientific truth. Its students range from the soothsayer in the night club to the experimentalist who measures pen pressure in the laboratory. A creditable desire for precise identification led the graphologists of the nineteenth century to initiate the futile search for correlations between isolated character traits and specific graphic signs in handwriting. Some modern research workers, contemptuous of the Abbé Michon and his followers among the popular graphologists of our day, nevertheless emulate his method by measuring the height of letters in millimeters and correlating the result with isolated personality factors defined by tentative tests. In contradistinction to this approach, philosophers, visionaries, essayists, and zealous practitioners produce detailed personality portraits by merely looking at a handwriting, often with astonishingly accurate results. Most of them are able to point out specific indicators which they consider useful, but are at a loss to describe in general terms their method for the essential process of evaluating such detail in the context of the whole.

The methodologic struggle in graphology is only a special case of the more general problem formulated by the Gestalt psychologists. They assert that natural phenomena can be described adequately only if the analysis refers to their whole-structure rather than to a sum of artificially isolated elements. They have shown that the atomistic method affords at best a first approximation, which must be overcome if the scientific description is to do justice to the living core of its subject. It is too early to tell whether the exactness of measurement can be achieved in the analysis

13

of whole-contexts. But it has been demonstrated, for instance, in the field of learning and thinking, that the Gestalt method is capable of grasping central aspects of psychological processes more essentially and truthfully than the highly exact traditional procedure of counting repetitions.

For graphology this means that, while numerical exactness is desirable as a final aim, limitation to the measurable would at this time be fatal to progress. The graphologist may be pleased to notice in a recent authoritative statement by F. A. Gibbs on brain waves, a field of research quite safe from the suspicion of intuition and Gestalt heresy, that the criteria used in the classification of the electro-encephalograph are "necessarily subjective, for only an exceedingly cumbersome object method can integrate and weight the many significant aspects, such as frequency, amplitude, waveform, variability, etc."

At the present stage of graphological affairs an open-minded and at the same time critical consideration of all available resources is necessary. The traditional interpretations, the rules of thumb, the hunches, the speculations, the intuitions, are all needed as working hypotheses to guide the experimentalist in setting his problems. The psychologists, newcomers in the field of science, can well afford the humbleness of their older colleagues, such as the physicians, who have profited from a careful study of medieval treatises, the practices of peasant grandmothers and tribal medicine men, and—more reluctantly, it is true—from the findings of explorers who do not hold an M.D. degree.

Many fundamental graphological tasks are yet to be accomplished. Methods of analyzing the structure of a handwriting "from above" have to be worked out. Atomism is not overcome by the mere consideration of "relations" between single traits. Much research is needed in order to determine which aspects of personality are reflected in handwriting and whether or not the hierarchy in which they appear corresponds to what is actually accentuated in the person. The causal relations between the structural features of the script and those of personality must be explored. And superstition must be vigorously separated from truth.

In the search for graphological method, Mr. Mendel's book will be helpful. The author combines sensitivity and imagination with experience. He uses much valuable European material not yet translated into English. He presents some stimulating case material. He likes to speculate, to attempt generalizations, to explore dark areas. With all his enthusiasm and confidence, he is aware of the fact that in his field every assertion has still to be accepted with a grain of salt. And I am sure that he expects watchful interest and critical co-operation rather than blind belief from the reader who opens this book with the desire of increasing his understanding of himself and of others.

RUDOLF ARNHEIM

Bronxville, New York
December, 1946

SOME GENERAL REMARKS IN THE GUISE
OF AN INTRODUCTION

What is Handwriting?

If someone with no notions of writing, a savage, for instance, observed a man writing a letter, he would think him given to strange motions. Writing is gesturing, and expressive movements have always had their meanings and interpretations. There are conventional gestures, and they have conventional meanings. There are also very individual expressive gestures, and they tell their particular stories. Both the copybook models we were taught to follow in school and the changes we make in them are gestures that can be analyzed and interpreted. *Graphology,* we shall see, *is the psychology of man's finest expressive gestures.* As such, graphology is part of the science of psychology, one of its tools.

"Brain Writing"

Though we write with the hand, writing is certainly not only a physiologic muscular activity. It is an expression of the whole personality,* both in form as well as in content. We can learn to write without the hand, but we lose much of our writing ability if our brain has been seriously injured. The foot or the mouth might do the work of the hand; nothing can replace the brain that guides the hand, the foot, or the mouth, and that centralizes the personality.

---

* By personality we mean here the total pattern of a person's distinctive ways of facing life.

Handwriting may actually be called "brain writing" (Preyer).

Yet even with such concepts at our disposal we must realize the complexities and the perhaps insuperable limitations in fully interpreting an adult handwriting unless we first know the style and the penmanship models taught to him as a child. For without this knowledge we cannot definitely recognize what, in the handwriting before us, is copybook imitation, and what are the personal changes, additions, and omissions.

This is not to say that the "imposed element," the copybook imitation, does not lend itself to interpretation. Since imposed elements are the result of a national, systematic instruction over a number of years, their analysis is the analysis of a nation's educational aims as manifested in a person's handwriting.

We must now look more closely at school norms and the ways of American instruction in penmanship.

Too Much Penmanship

We read in the preface to *The Palmer Method of Business Writing:* ". . . freedom of movement is the foundation,

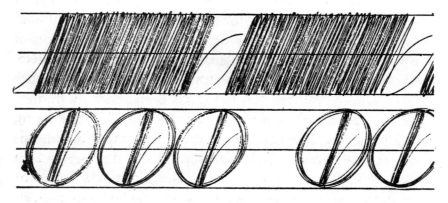

and through constantly repeated series of rapid drills, the application of movements becomes a fixed habit of the learner."

The child of school age is subjected to copy drills and exercises, to a disciplined course of writing. For many years he is painstakingly taught to achieve a reasonable facsimile. This process of learning to write may be seen as a character-forming situation. Apparently, a particular method of handwriting instruction has been elevated by American educators and given almost full control. Thus the handwriting of American adults more or less conforms to or deviates from this standard. (It is for this reason that I subtitle this book, "American Graphology.")

The degree to which a person conforms to the instruction and drills of his penmanship teachers is one indication of his character. From conformity to school norms (American or foreign), or, to put it differently, from failure to exhibit individual deviations, the graphologist can draw conclusions as to the general immaturity of the writer and his civic virtues, to mention only two obvious interpretations.

Your Individual Handwriting

However, very few people submit completely to school drilling. Almost no one can help introducing some individual variations, and a few do this to a remarkable degree. It is these additions and simplifications of the models, both deliberate and unconscious, which form the second and richer source of clues for the graphologist.

This, therefore, is the way an individual handwriting style comes into being: The child, after experiencing his years of schooling, enters adolescence, usually a turbulent period, reproducing many of his infantile conflicts. What he is essentially *striving for,* together with his developing character traits, inevitably begins to express itself in his

19

script. At the same time, he becomes conscious of many impressions he would like to create.

His handwriting, consequently, undergoes two basic and final changes: he *deliberately* introduces variations, which he hopes will achieve a certain effect; and his re-emerging basic character shows itself in the *unwitting* peculiarities of his script.

The reader will, in the following pages, recognize these life-history aspects as they are considered in the system of graphology here proposed. Yet I shall refer repeatedly to the Palmer Method as the model which has been impressed upon most American school children for decades. I shall refer to this model as the norm from which each of us, as an adult, tends to deviate according to the dominant personality factors within us.

The Pen in Graphology

The appearance of a handwriting is to some extent dependent upon the pen used. Most people are instinctively aware of this fact. They give much time and thought to the selection of a pen that suits their hand, a pen that permits the hand to perform the writing that is quite natural or most pleasing to the writer. The "writing" is the individual variation of the copybook norm which the writer likes best. It may therefore be safely assumed that most pens and every individual style of writing are rather deliberately selected; once a person has found "his" pen and "his" style, he will not freely part with either of them.

Yet the same person with the same pen does not write the same word or single letter twice in exactly the same way. "Life resists rules," Klages remarks in this connection. The person who could repeat himself exactly would not be a human being.

20

Graphological Interpretation is Logical

Graphological interpretation proceeds logically. A person of many handwritings is a person of many moods.* He is lively and impressionable. He may start writing with considerable pressure and rather small, narrow letters that stand upright, sloping neither forward nor backward; he concentrates completely upon his writing, and his hand works coolly, systematically, leaning rather heavily upon his pen.

The further he advances, the freer and easier he feels, and the more he is carried away by his deeper enthusiasm, the more his letters grow in height and width; the pressure decreases, the handwriting tends to slope forward. Now and then, especially when he feels the need of returning to more detached writing, the slant of his letters may lose its forward slope, their height and width may shrink again. Change of character? No. Within a quarter of an hour, in one piece of handwriting, an impressionable man may produce a number of variations of his handwriting—variations, but not different handwritings.

It has been considered advisable to discuss this phenomenon in the introduction because the beginning graphologist, eager to display his new skill, runs the risk of losing confidence in his newly-found abilities and interpretations if not properly cautioned. His friends and first clients are not always ready to encourage him; on the contrary, even his friends are usually eager to prove him wrong. Quite naturally, a person's handwriting does show some variations from one writing situation to another: filling out a formal application or scribbling personal notes for the use of no one but the writer.

---

*On close scrutiny, the seeming differences in these "many" handwritings can be boiled down to five basic features: change of margin, slant, pressure, height and width of letters. They indicate a change of mood rather than a change of character. But schizophrenics and pathological liars may habitually produce "different" scripts.

However, let us take a fairly typical and normal writing situation as the standard, that of a letter to a friend. We speak and gesture quite freely in addressing a friend; so also do we "yield" ourselves in a written communication to him.

Know Thyself!

Much as man yearns for complete knowledge of himself, he actually dreads the lifting of the last veil. This, at least, seems to him an indispensable protection, and he hates and restrains anyone who attempts to pull it aside. So there may be valid reasons of self-interest to explain why many people are satisfied with only a rather hazy and superficial knowledge of the persons they are supposed to know and firmly assert they know well. They do not know them, and only rarely can they objectively affirm or deny that which a thorough analysis of a handwriting may bring to light. There is much evidence in current psychological thinking to suggest that only a few of us are the best judges of our own deeper personality traits.

Even if only to avoid hurting his client's feelings, no graphologist should ever appear to be too sure of his findings. In this respect the experienced clinical psychologist or psychiatrist ought to be his model. In spite of the tremendous advance of psychology in the last fifty years, most psychologists know and freely admit that they have merely begun to feel their way into the "Abyss of Human Illusion."

Art or Science?

Ought graphology to be practiced as a science or as an art? Strangely enough, the answer received often appears to depend on the questioner. Two eminent psychologists, Allport and Vernon,* who are sympathetic toward modern graphology, have stated: "In contrast to skepticism and

---

* Allport and Vernon, *Studies in Expressive Movement* (New York: Macmillan, 1933).

neglect in this country we find alert and sympathetic interest in Europe . . . capable of revealing to the initiated the "essence" of personality; but it is only by intuition and not by analytical or statistical techniques that the essence is grasped. American critics, with their leaning toward specificity and objectivity, regard all methods excepting the quantitative with suspicion."

In addition to these national differences, the answer to the question, "Art or science?" comes through the approach of the individual graphologist to his task and through his personality. The Psychology Department of the University of Göttingen (headed by Professor Ach), after studying a number of graphologists, reported that the "cyclothymic type" always relies on his intuition, the "schizothymic type" (who has no intuition), on his scientifically inclined mind. The "ideal" graphologist, concludes Professor Ach, appears to be a "cyclothymic" with scientific training—the basically intuitive person guided by logical methods.

Gardner Murphy, a past president of the American Psychological Association, whose progressive approach to the psychology of personality is well known, implicitly agrees with Ach in an evaluation of the position of graphology today: "It is only fair to add that most psychologists, remembering its unsavory past and witnessing the quack methods to which it is still largely a prey, have exhibited a cultural lag in their attitudes toward the more careful recent work. To say this is not to maintain that the interpretation of character by handwriting is a science; its most devoted adherents would make no such claims. It is to be used . . . as a source of reasonably dependable clues which demand considerable experience and insight before they are of much value.*"

To analyze handwriting, we need scientific methods; but

---

* G. Murphy, L. B. Murphy, and T. M. Newcomb, *Experimental Social Psychology* (New York: Harper & Brothers, 1937).

the integration of the results of the analysis, defining man's complex personality, must also use intuition: "immediate apprehension or cognition; the power of knowing or the knowledge obtained without recourse to inference or reasoning; insight . . ."*

On the other hand, we cannot begin to inquire into such problems as how the individual handwriting style comes into being unless we do so systematically and scientifically. An integrating system of graphology is a basic need today. However, while employing this method, the graphologist would also avail himself of the intuitive method of retracing the writer's gestures, and so re-experiencing the movements— and possibly some of the emotions—of the writer.

Graphological Knowledge

The story of how one graphologist made up his mind to study graphology well demonstrates how graphological knowledge was and still is collected. This graphologist relates how, as a boy, he had several times chanced, in letters or in his classmates' notebooks, upon handwritings that reminded him, sometimes strongly, sometimes faintly, of other handwritings and people he knew. During these initial studies he became convinced that people who have similar handwritings must also have similar character traits. So, after some further pondering, he boldly offered to describe the personalities of those who had written the letters and notes before him, and he was acclaimed for his amazingly accurate characterizations.

All early and fundamental graphological interpretations were based upon such rather crude observations and superficial conclusions. Yet the most scientific and exact tests of

---

* *Webster's New International Dictionary* (Springfield, Mass.: G. & C. Merriam Co., 1942), p. 1304, col. 2.

the twentieth century have mostly reaffirmed and refined these intuitive interpretations.

Tested Knowledge

Using scientific tests to establish norms and averages, the size of letters in thousands of handwriting samples was measured in millimeters, and the pressure of the pen was measured in kilograms and grams. People who habitually connected their letters or characters by means of "garlands" were asked to use "arcades" for a while instead, and vice versa, and to describe their impressions and feelings; others, who perhaps preferred "threads" in their writing, were induced to adopt "angles" temporarily and to tell what they felt during the tests. This was done in order to re-examine the established interpretations of garland, arcade, and angular connections.* Then, to find out which features of our handwriting are performed automatically, and which deliberately, extensive writing tests in darkened rooms were conducted.**

Still more research work remains to be done. For instance, whereas centuries of medical research and teaching have given psychology some framework within which the student can move rather methodically, instruction in graphology, a relatively recent development, starts and stops almost anywhere.

The capable Jacoby, in his *Analysis of Handwriting*,*** starts his teachings with "Degree of Legibility"; Pulver, whose fame goes far beyond his native Switzerland, begins his *Symbolik der Handschrift**** with a chapter on "Rhythm

---

* Johannes Walther, *Die psychologische und charakterologische Bedeutung der handschriftlichen Bindungsarten* (München: Neue psychologische Studien, 1938).

** Rudolf Werner, *Psychologie des Schreibens* (München: Neue psychologische Studien, 1937).

*** London: G. Allen & Unwin, Ltd., 1939.

**** Zürich-Leipzig: Orell Füssli, 1940

in Handwriting"; the prolific Saudek* opens his instruction with the "Relative Speed of the Act of Writing," and Klages, without whom graphology would still be a pastime, starts his basic book, *Handschrift und Charakter,*** with "Symmetry and Regularity." For a while the eager student will read through any of these valuable books on the strength of their merit and his own enthusiasm. But as soon as he pauses to take stock, he is in danger of losing his way. Graphology and graphological instruction do not yet possess a clearly defined system.

Graphology's Functions

The question is often asked: "What uses does graphology serve?" It is clear that graphology has at least two functions. One is purely practical, the prediction of an individual's behavior. Business and government, for example, have profitably used graphological interpretations as guides in the selection of employees and credit risks.

Another function is the elaboration of knowledge concerning the human personality. Whatever it adds to the theories and facts in psychology brings us further along in understanding ourselves and others. The psychologists, who approach the problem of human motivation and character structure, often must laboriously fit together clues from many sources: what a man says, his facial and body movements, his life history, and so on. Graphology can be a valuable supplement and often a short cut in delineating trends in the personality of an individual. It is a series of interpretations based on a *permanent, graphic record* in which the writer has revealed himself—deliberately or unwittingly. The most gifted graphologists have time and again demonstrated what to the uninitiated seems an almost uncanny ability to

---

* *What Your Handwriting Shows* (London: T. W. Laurie, Ltd., 1932.)
** Leipzig: J. A. Barth, 1940.

interpret and predict the most concrete aspects of a person's thinking and behavior. And this from only one of his expressive gestures.

A few graphologists have gone even further in adopting the idea of drills and exercises and giving it a new and more promising twist. The late Dr. Eric Alten, a serious graphologist, worked with the theory, based on assumptions accepted among European graphologists, that a person could rid himself of certain bad habits or shortcomings by systematically omitting those features from his hand which pointed toward these habits and shortcomings. I have no firsthand knowledge of the success of such drills, and I would not expect them to produce results in basic faults. Unfortunately, in this country the first people to exploit this idea were not psychiatrists but quacks.

Presenting a System of Graphology

Graphology is neither an uncanny nor a miraculous skill. As this book undertakes to demonstrate, there are sound and tested methods and rules that can be studied and used by anyone who will take the trouble to learn them. For this work introduces an innovation in writing on graphology in that a first attempt is made to systematize the approach to handwriting interpretation. In order to establish a system, a central point, a focus, had to be chosen. I might have begun with the pen, the paper, or any other essential element in handwriting. But in this handbook the eye has been chosen as the starting point. Obviously, the eye is an essential instrument for both the writer and the graphologist. Before we can analyze a specimen of writing, we must see it.

However, we do not see all of the handwriting at first sight. We progress gradually, step by step, from the most obvious to the most hidden. At first sight, or at a distance, a letter may appear only as some grey, irregular quadrangle, superimposed upon a larger and more regular white quadrangle, the sheet of paper. All that we can see are the margins of the letter. Therefore, my first interpretative chapter is on "Margins." Then, upon closer scrutiny, we perceive the space between the lines, how far apart the lines stand each from the one above or below, then the space between words, the slant of the writing, the pressure, and so on.

The interpretative chapters in this book follow the Eye System. There are nineteen such chapters, and in each chapter the reader is enlightened as to *what aspect* of writing is being interpreted, the *interpretation itself,* and the *reasons* for the judgment. Further, he is provided with a *systematic guide* on how to proceed logically in this direction. We have borrowed heavily from the insights of other psychologists where applicable—notably from Freud as regards *development and motivation,* and from the gestaltists as regards *perception and learning.* There is also a chapter on "Style Evaluation" according to Klages, and a chapter on "Pressure" mostly based on findings reported by Saudek; in the chapter on "Zones" I have drawn on the findings of Pulver.

Most of the interpretations and theories presented are quite logical, almost self-evident. Others may seem to lack the force of logic, but since they have shown themselves to be reliable, I cannot, in the interest of the readers, simply ignore them. Their logic may merely go beyond our present understanding. Nature, always logical, is not always obvious.

The reader who, for the first time, is acquiring information on graphology, or the experienced graphologist, for whom this handbook will serve as a reference book, may find this attempt at systematization of graphological knowledge, and especially the summaries at the end of most of the chapters, as useful as they were to me. In manuscript form, they served me as a quick and ready reference in my work as a practical graphologist. Whenever a script turned up that was either quite unique or else devoid of clear, personal deviations from the copybook, and which had to be analyzed promptly, I proceeded along these lines:

First, I would try to form a general impression of the sample—Chapter 1 presents clues for a summary evaluation of the style. Then I would approach the margins (Chapter 2), the spaces between the lines and words (Chapter 3), and the direction of the lines (Chapter 4).

In studying the slant of the script, which is the subject of Chapter 5, a ruler and angle-meter were sometimes found to be useful, particularly to judge increasing and diminishing slant. When, as a practical graphologist, I had also examined the quality of the pressure in the handwriting, I had seen and considered everything that was apparent at first sight.

A similar methodical procedure was followed with those features of handwriting that can be seen only at second and third sight. These less obvious qualities include such minute details as concealing strokes, and initial and end adjustments. Thus, by following the nineteen chapters of this handbook as nineteen signposts, one may arrive at a practical analysis of the sample, which can be integrated into a portrait of the personality within a reasonable time, whether the sample is "yielding" or "resisting."

The psychologist, accustomed to being "objective" and "relativistic" in his study of personality, may take exception to the frankly ethical view which I assume in my personality interpretations. To this I can only state that human relationships are based on ethical values. Graphology, in characterizing human beings, cannot, nor, indeed, should it, avoid expressing the accepted judgments about their general worth and soundness.

A FEW PRIMARY PRINCIPLES FOR
GRAPHOLOGY STUDENTS

The concept of graphology as the psychology of man's finest gestures permits us to establish certain fundamental principles that are of definite importance to anyone bent on interpreting man's handwriting.

To move our hand, or even our eyebrow, our *brain* may have to give an order which, in turn, may have been suggested by an *impulse,* conscious or unconscious. Then the *muscles* do the actual work: they lift the hand or the eyebrow, as the case may be.

Every gesture, therefore, may fuse three currents in man: the *emotional,* the *intellectual,* and the *physical.* Likewise every stroke of his pen. Our interpretations, consequently, operate on these three levels.

Pressure, for instance, is indicative of vitality, delight in asserting oneself, and preference for bodily exercise, from mere walking to polar expeditions. However, it would be erroneous to think of the pressure writer as only lively, or self-assertive, or athletic, for he may be all this in one: the lively *and* the self-assertive *and* the athletic may have been wedded in his person to form one whole that has something of each and is none of them completely and exclusively.

Such a situation would be hopeless for one who tried to describe it if our language did not also have literally dozens of different expressive terms for just such a man—and if those who want their handwriting analyzed were not willing to listen for hours. Therefore, in graphology it is neither possible nor advisable to be brief: man is not simple, and to

30

be brief may be an improper attempt at over-simplification. A graphologist, after having analyzed a man's hand for a whole evening, was asked by the subject to summarize his personality in one word. He answered: "You ask for too much," and the man's wife thanked him with her eyes.

Yet with all his thoroughness, there will be personalities whose "ways of facing life" no graphologist can describe because they could not be known even to those who have associated with them for a lifetime. This will be freely admitted. But in spite of this, handwriting is a more natural and more intrinsic expression of the personality than direct personality testing. Graphology, therefore, is superior to questionnaires (or tests based on questions and answers) for analyzing and portraying a person's personality.

The following nineteen chapters, arranged according to the Eye System, permit the student to examine and analyze a handwriting sample by a running comparison of its characteristics with the headings and interpretations offered in each of the chapters.

A general style value must first be established. It will guide the reader to correct conclusions where several mutually exclusive or contradictory interpretations present themselves; also, where interpretations are suggested that are not contradictory, but different in degree.

No device or formula can ever be as subtle and fine-grained as a person's mind. But, on the whole, people are not quite as different from one another as they would like to be, nor as complicated as they sometimes pretend. Therefore, in the majority of cases the knowledge presented in this handbook will suffice, provided these primary principles are observed.

All the interpretations offered here, and current for the most part among leading graphologists of all countries, are based on ink-written handwritings. Qualities such as pressure, the connection of letters, and even legibility, may be strikingly different in pencil-written samples.

The sample must be at least one full page; smaller samples have inconclusive margins. Insistence on full pages made in several different writing situations prevent basing one's analysis on a hurriedly written or on an unusual or distorted sample.

There are a number of graphological means to differentiate the mental age and the sex of a handwriting; yet the age and sex of the writer may differ from our finding. This is the reason why experienced graphologists ask for age and sex. If, then, the handwriting tells a different story, it yields a number of important clues.

Even experts study a sample thoroughly before they answer questions. A close examination may reveal details that escape the first impression. But first impressions are also important; they can tell more about the person as a whole than any detail. In short, it takes both, the over-all impression and methodical thoroughness, to arrive at a true-to-life picture.

As a rule the people one meets impress one as integrated wholes, not as senseless sums of traits. Therefore, after the analysis there must follow a synthesis. Especially the individual traits one has discovered can be related to the over-all pattern, and thus made to yield new and often very characteristic traits. In fact, every trait is influenced by every other trait and cannot be judged by itself.

For instance, in the chapter on "Margins," I discuss two different possibilities of "no margins": the prodigal and the egoist. Now, suppose one meets a Style Value positive, No Margin case (female), *quite sizable hand, garlands, and over-all pressure.* The interpretation must be: prodigal. Yet this is a prodigal of quite a peculiar kind. The pressure, the garlands, and the size (see 'Pressure," "Connection of Letters," "Size of Letters") give to the word "prodigal" a special connotation. Such women are prodigals in love. They win and hold their men by lavishing on them all their innate warmth and sympathy, by loving them without stint or reservation.

Sometimes a handwriting sample is so close to the copybook model that it seems to lack analyzable peculiarities. To discover these, it is advisable to place a copybook page next to it; all of a sudden the deviations will become apparent.

Even though man is an integrated whole, he is not free from inner conflicts. Two opposing traits may exist within one and the same mind. Or a person may long to do a thing and never do it. Altogether, he is not always what he seems to be. In speech, a slip of the tongue can reveal the speaker's true intentions; in handwriting, it is the insignificant-looking middle zone, and the initial and end adjustments that may give the writer away.* A "Yes" all over the capitals is a mere boast concealing the middle zone's "No."**

More and more, original, intuitive interpretations of the early French and Italian graphologists are being methodically re-examined; wherever such a re-examination exists, I have quoted it. In some instances I have conducted such re-examinations myself, but in most cases I have had to rely on interpretations current among thousands of professional graphologists in this country and elsewhere. In the process of fitting them into the system of this book, however, I have sifted and compared them with the results of my own experience. What is given here, I believe to be well founded. I hope the experimental psychologist will take my hunches, examine them, then reject or verify and refine them.

---

* Chapter 20, "Analysis and Synthesis, Including Initial and End Adjustments."
** Chapter 7, "Zones and Their Meaning."

I

AT FIRST SIGHT

Chapter 1

STYLE EVALUATION

In the introduction I stated that early graphological interpretations were largely based on the assumption that people
with similar handwritings have similarities. Then the rather
striking and obvious "signs," for instance t-bars, i-dots, and
capitals, especially the capital letters in a person's signature,
were made the basis of comparison between two or more
handwritings.

Treacherous Pitfalls

It may be safely assumed that people who carefully select
hats, gloves, ties, and shoes will not allow their handwriting
to escape scrutiny. In the course of the years they will discipline their hand so as to make it appear as they wish; and
not infrequently another person's handwriting will serve as
a model.

The capitals especially are likely to be affected and
shaped to impress others. Hence, the most striking and obvious "signs" in a person's handwriting are not always the
most revealing ones. (Forgers, too, concentrate on copying
obvious characteristics, such as capitals, t-bars, loops, and
flourishes; the inconspicuous smaller letters—*a, c, e, i, m, n,
o, r, s, u, v, w, x, z*—often escape their attention and may
betray forgery.*)

---

* The ways in which signs can aid the graphologist are discussed in
sections below.

While there are graphologists who can see through "disciplined," artificial writing, the simple comparison of "similar signs" in different hands has still other and more treacherous pitfalls. To have discovered and defined the pitfalls of the old, but not yet completely discarded, school of "sign interpretation" is one of the merits of Klages.

In the seventeenth and eighteenth editions of his *Handschrift und Charakter* Klages presents, as an example of what he means to convey, two boys before a tulip bed: the one, *A,* immediately picks a few tulips; the other, *B,* does not do so. Is the conclusion to be drawn that *A* has a stronger urge toward flowers than *B*? Not necessarily! *A* may have the stronger urge; or they may both have the same urge; or *B* may have the stronger urge. But *B,* in addition to his urge, is twice as much afraid of punishment as *A* who, only half as fearful as *B,* quickly stoops and picks the flowers. In other words, *A* may be said either to be less inhibited or to possess a stronger urge than *B.* We cannot, from an onlooker's standpoint, assert the one or the other with certainty.

Ambiguity in Interpretation

In graphology, pressureless handwriting, for instance, may indicate a number of personality traits from superficiality to idealism. Graphologists know this very well, and one of their most important tools is a well-balanced vocabulary.

But instead of giving their interpretation color and subtlety, this vocabulary and the wide range of traits are often the source of unintentional ambiguities and consequent bewilderment.

In his book, *Mind Your P's and Q's,* Jerome S. Meyer* gives the following interpretations for "fine writing": "highstrung, sensitive, unassuming." The question remains un-

---

* New York: Simon and Schuster, 1927.

38

answered as to when "high-strung," when "sensitive," when "unassuming" would be the fitting interpretation—in short, when a *negative* or *positive* expression of motives is present. For, most probably, one and the same person cannot be both high-strung as well as unassuming.

Sizing Up a Style

The clarity we need comes from Klages' "Formniwo," which is translated as "style value." Klages established the style value in order to give the graphologist a yardstick in his continuous quandary over what was often two possible contradictory and irreconcilable interpretations. Before the discovery of style value, the graphologist's decision between "high-strung" and "unassuming" was a matter for his intuition, and those who had none dismissed all the results obtained as "pure guesswork." Style evaluation narrows and defines the field in graphology in which only intuition can produce satisfactory interpretations.*

The procedure to be followed is a general evaluation of a person's personality on the basis of *whole aspects* of his handwriting, even before we enter into its more detailed analysis. We would, then, once and for all know in ambiguous cases of ethical implication whether specific interpretations should be *positive* or *negative*.

Graphology, in sizing up a person's character (as manifested in his handwriting), dissects the whole on three levels: (1) man's drives and motives, (2) man's creative and intellectual capacities, and (3) man's social and civic virtues. Klages has proclaimed his conviction (and forty years of experience have not contradicted him) 'that if we know how

---

* It has seemed to me that the concept of style evaluation is more appropriately applied to the handwriting of men than women. The reason may be that men more generally can face scrutiny as to their positive or negative position toward society; yet some women, who apparently have risen out of their traditional and passive secondary role in society, also manifest style value in their scripts.

a person thinks and feels, the degree to which he can measure up to society's hopes and expectations, and his capacity to add to humanity's values, then we can predict how he will act in many specific situations.

A good way to judge a person's capacity for thinking and feeling is through the *rhythm* of his handwriting. Rhythmic harmony in forms and spaces, such as margins, spaces between lines, words, letters, shows us the richness, variety, and organization in a person's thinking and inner life.

The *symmetry* of a handwriting reveals what a person may have done with the education society has bestowed upon him, whether or not he can take care of himself, whether he is willing and able to fit himself into society's frame—his inner balance.

A person's creative qualities may be seen in his success with *simplification* and *improvement* of the script. Most people accept penmanship instruction at its face value, but some do not. Just as they ceaselessly try to improve themselves, so they try to improve their "tools," from their methods of thinking down to writing *A B C.* (Humanity is dependent upon people who improve humanity's tools and enrich our life by simplifying its technicalities.)

In addition, we check the *legibility* and *fluency* of a person's hand because legibility, without which handwriting cannot function, is a gauge of the writer's purposefulness and social co-operation; *fluency* in handwriting is a measure of both a person's clearheadedness and his sincerity. A limping speech* not only permits the conclusion that the speaker is mentally deficient or muddleheaded, but also that he is not telling all.

Once we have received a person's "answers" to these

---

* Speaking and writing parallel each other in many respects. See p. 111.

five pertinent lines of inquiry, we may be assured against surprises as to the subject's character in a detailed analysis of his handwriting. Now we know him, not in part, but as a whole; the details, as details go, will round out the picture of the person; but in this they will follow the style evaluation, not determine it.

To grade the handwriting in accordance with its style value, I use a scale of seven figures, 1, 1½, 2, 2½, 3, 3½, 4. At first we shall have to proceed by steps, as suggested under "Method of Determining Style Value" at the end of this chapter. Later on we shall be able to establish the style value of a sample almost at sight.

THE FIVE KEYS TO STYLE EVALUATION

1. *Rhythm.*—What is rhythm? Webster gives a definition that does not help us much: "Movement marked by regular recurrence of, or regular alternation in, features, elements, phenomena, etc.; hence, periodicity." Klages' definition of mechanical rhythm, even in the abbreviated form presented here, nevertheless tells us what he means to convey: "The entire universe is rhythmically organized. Science has rightly discovered, even though it has understood with difficulty, the rhythmic nature of sound, heat, electricity, and light. Every song has both its rhythm and time. Perhaps it was necessary first to confuse them with each other in order to learn how to keep them strictly apart. Although, in poetry and song, for example, they seem as intimately linked as a pair of dancers, they are opposites. The flapping of the wings of birds in flight is rhythmic, as is the stamping of wild horses, and the gliding of fish through the waves. But animals cannot run, fly, or swim according to time, just as we cannot breathe according to time. Beating time always

produces the same results in the same periods of time; free rhythm produces only *similar* results in *similar* periods of time."

We can immediately recognize and measure the *rhythm in space* of a handwriting by looking at its space pattern: whether the *margins* are harmonious among themselves, whether they are in harmony with the *spaces between the lines, between the words,* and *between the letters.* Disharmonies have the peculiarity of catching the eye; it is therefore not very difficult to establish the grade of space rhythm in a handwriting.

To establish a handwriting's *rhythm in form* is a matter of a more artistic examination in detail. Oscar Wilde's handwriting sample shown on the following page gives us ample opportunity to discuss this aspect of rhythm.

Though narrowly spaced, handwriting may nevertheless also have space rhythm; it makes a difference in evaluation whether the spaces are wide or narrow, for wide spaces may "contain" more and deeper thoughts and emotions. But too wide spaces (in comparison, for instance, with the spaces between the letters) must strike us rather as emptiness. To steer clear of "too narrow" and "too wide" spaces sounds like a nightmare, but actually is quite easy if one has a sense of beauty; insight helps, too.

This sample is part of a letter by Oscar Wilde to John Ruskin. The spaces between the letters, the spaces between the lines, and the margins are neither too large nor too small; at any rate, they are harmonious. For instance, as befits a thoughtful, contemplative writer, the intervals between words are of special importance to him; he must maintain them in their full width however long or short the words are. Therefore, we see him move to the right the beginning of the word "be" (in the eighth line) because he obviously considered the space between "how" and

42

"gratified" (at the beginning of the preceding line) as a bare minimum.

So far we have spoken of space rhythm; Wilde's form rhythm is equally remarkable. His *I* returns in his *H*

(Happy), in his *P* (Prince), and, inversely, in his *v*; it returns, not as a repetition of itself, but as a variation. The seven t-bars in this sample fit so perfectly their *t*'s and the position each *t* has within its word that even though they obviously are brothers, they could not be interchanged without profoundly disturbing the rhythm of form within this handwriting. Whether two letters are connected or not, they follow each other with perfect rhythm.

Rating a handwriting's rhythm is a matter of insight and sensitivity as well as reason and expertness. Klages rated Oscar Wilde's total style value (mostly on the basis of his rhythm) no higher than 3, but I believe that the above sample is much better in quality and more typical of the writer than the one Klages used. Moreover, a rating of 4 in rhythm does not in itself mean an all-round style value of 4. Many a writer with a first-rate rhythm writes, for instance, with second-rate legibility.

2. *Symmetry.*—Symmetry in handwriting exists if the *l*'s are about three times, the *g*'s two and a half times, and the *f*'s four times as tall as the minimum *a*, and all of them are equally well developed. This proportion of $1:3:2\frac{1}{2}:4$ is more or less the basic proportion of the Palmer Method models, considered the most widely used models for writing. In Palmer models the minimum *a* is 1/16 of an inch high.

Do not fail to see

Obviously the Palmer copies were written by a man. The proportion of $1:3:2\frac{1}{2}:4$ may be assumed to be an American man's proportion in handwriting. A woman's hand, for reasons given in the chapter on "Size of Letters," has slightly different proportions. A ratio of $1:2\frac{1}{2}:3:3\frac{1}{2}$ may be about normal within Palmer Method patterns.

All these proportions are copybook and therefore theoretical proportions. They are as important as textbooks and schoolteaching in general. Many believe that life would be pleasantly different if everyone followed textbooks and law books, but we are prepared to compromise. It is the same with handwriting. We are taught to follow Palmer rules and proportions, but sooner or later we develop our own peculiar proportions, the proportions that characterize us

44

for the graphologist and that, incidentally, may be more beautiful and natural than Palmer's. We therefore cannot

assign such deviations a lower grade as long as the new proportion *does not overdevelop one zone at the expense of another.*

It may be noted here that the above-quoted Palmer proportions are similar to writing proportions established in other countries. Not so the actual heights. Pulver comments that the height of a minimum *i*, the "i-height," of 3 mm., seems to be international, but on closer investigation it seems rather to be European. The Palmer *i*'s vary from 1 to 2 mm.; like all Palmer minimum letters they are supposed to be "about one sixteenth of an inch" high (which is 1.75 mm.).

The above proportions were found by measuring the *a*'s, *l*'s, *g*'s, and *f*'s within a word, if possible, within the same word. No initial or end letters were included in the survey because they tend to be somewhat out of proportion. And because, in many hands, every word has its peculiar dimensions (even though not its peculiar proportions), it is advisable to remain within one word when measuring letters.

The harmonious proportion in the height of the characters is not sufficient basis, however, for speaking of a handwriting as symmetrical. Excess in width, pressure, slant, loops, bars, dots, flourishes, or any other excess in a handwriting disturbs its symmetry. To be called symmetrical, the letters, whether they are capitals or minimum letters, must be gradually well developed, neither too narrow (deflated) nor too wide (inflated). For a character, when measured as a whole, is measured not only by its height, but also

45

by the space it covers. Wide lower loops in a generally narrow hand, or together with deflated small letters, to mention but two frequent types of disparity, contradict the idea of symmetry. Unevenness in slant or pressure belongs to the category of disproportions. These are dealt with later under such headings as "Lower Zone," "Size of Letters," "Slant," "Pressure," and so on.

It is true that very few hands can be subjected to such scrutiny and still be considered symmetrical. But perfect symmetry, if it could be achieved, would surely be superhuman.

3. *Creativeness.*—If it is a fact that very few handwritings can be considered more or less symmetrical, it is also a fact that still fewer show creativeness. The average person will not complain about this; he likes being one of a crowd, following the traditional pattern. He really dislikes being different, not "regular," even in his hand.

The patterns our boys and girls are taught to follow in school in their writing drills are the result of many centuries of work. Originally based upon European, especially British, models, they now embody probably everything that is called American. To break away from this common standard, to follow one's own bent, is well-nigh heresy. Only one in a thousand has the boldness and independence it takes to be a heretic, to write his own individual hand. To go further, replacing some of the generally accepted and therefore almost sacred models with one's own creations (which may actually make for easier writing without impairing the legibility of the hand) calls for the boldness of an independent person who is also well-educated, discriminating, and creative. To invent and use new *and* better characters or connections of characters is a feat that perhaps only a genius can achieve.

46

An original hand and a creative hand are two different things, inasmuch as an original penman is not always a creative person, whereas a creative person always writes an original hand. To be original, to have an individual hand, means to be unusual, free of copybook fetters; to be creative is to be able to add something to existing patterns. (Banal and schoolboyish handwritings cannot be evaluated as positive in creativeness. To be evaluated positively, a handwriting must show a certain degree of deviation.)

I said above that "one's own creations" must "really make for easier writing without impairing the legibility of the hand." A creation in writing must facilitate writing. It must be easy to do, or take less space, or move the hand in the direction of the writing movement, that is, to the right. Only one who does a great deal of writing, who is daily confronted with the task of noting down thoughts and ideas as they come and go—only such a person will feel the need of more easily executed characters, and the urge to create them for his own use; by all indications he must be a well-educated person. Furthermore, he will never stop improving his creations because he is demanding, discriminating. And if he can produce a better character that suits his needs, then, indeed, we may call him creative.

Au sujet de Freud, ne trouvez-vous pas que ce serait un

The *et* is one of the most frequently used letter combinations in French. We know, for instance, *Poiret, Dubonnet,* and *et* which is the French equivalent of the English "and." Romain Rolland, author and winner of the Nobel Prize in literature, and a courageous political writer, used an abbreviation for *et*. His abbreviation combines the *e* and the *t* into one very simple, easily written, and legible letter. It is a prolongation of the t-bar to a new character without the *t*. A *t* without the bar would not have done as well, for it looks somewhat incomplete and can be mistaken for an *l*. Rolland's *et* is unmistakable, easily written, and it moves the hand to the right; it is a true innovation. Natural and self-evident as it may look, it took a Romain Rolland among forty million Frenchmen to create this abbreviation.

Unusualness by itself is not sufficient. The *p* in this word "*Septiembre*" is unusual in appearance; but it is neither simple nor more easily written; moreover, it moves the hand in the opposite direction from the writing movement. With regard to individual writing and creativeness, this *p* rates 0. (We must beware of innovations in writing that are not simplifications of the writing process.)

True individuality is not demonstrative. This specimen, written by a young and well-read girl with literary interests and abilities, is quite undemonstrative and very purposeful in almost every detail including the most minute; it also shows intelligent simplification of a *g*, two different *h*'s,

48

each quite legible and sensibly varied according to its place, one within, the other at the end of the word; and a practical connection of an *o* with a *b* in "job."

4. *Legibility.*—(See also the chapter on "Legibility.") We write to be read. A letter that cannot be deciphered by the addressee has failed in its purpose. A legal document is invalid if it cannot be clearly read and understood by everyone concerned.

To establish the degree of legibility, we must try to read the individual words of the sample out of context. Normally, we do not read word-by-word. Rather, we guess our way from word to word, and unless we stumble over an unexpected expression, we prefer to believe that the writing runs smoothly and is easily decipherable. Therefore, the only way to establish objectively the legibility of a sample is to take words at random out of their context and examine them. The result of close and unsentimental scrutiny is sometimes quite unexpected; very intelligent writers cannot always pass it.

5. *Speed.*—The sample under scrutiny must also show that it was written spontaneously. If "creations" need time to be produced, they contradict the most elementary graphological law of creativeness: time-saving simplicity. In addition, slow writing is almost always suspect. Although fast writing is a matter of experience and manual skill, and many slow writers are merely inexperienced writers, haltingly produced script is nevertheless typical of many individuals with criminal tendencies. Conscious of the genteel values of a legible and conforming handwriting, but unable to produce it spontaneously, they "patch up" their first efforts by straightening out the strokes, closing the open *a*'s and *o*'s, and improving their t-bars. The result is an unclean hand. There are a number of features that tell us whether a writing

49

was produced fluently. They are right-slanted writing with growing right-slantedness, inexactly placed i-dots with most dots in the form of minute lines or curves placed ahead of the letter *i* itself, letters and letter connections in garland forms rather than angles and arcades, left margins widening toward the bottom of the sheet, more and longer finals, wide script, smooth and unbroken strokes, light, not heavy writing.

Method of Determining Style Value*

After discarding handwriting samples of clearly infantile or schoolboy character, we examine each of the remaining samples for its rating in rhythm, symmetry, and creativeness. The following Table of Ratings lists the characteristics a handwriting must possess to be rated at all. If the 4-point description fits the sample, it has earned a rating of 4; if the 3-point description applies, it has earned a rating of 3; and so on. If none of the descriptions is appropriate, the sample rates 0.

We use half-points to rate samples that only partly fulfill the requirements for any given score. For instance, if our sample does not fully come up to the 2-point description, we can score it 1½. To the sum of the ratings for rhythm, symmetry, and creativeness a point or a half-point is added for legibility plus speed.

As a result we have four factors, each with a possible score of 1 to 4. To arrive at the final rating, the average of the four individual ratings is calculated by adding them together (the sum cannot exceed 16) and dividing by 4.

---

* In his writings on script value (Formniwo) Klages gives the reader an idea of what he means, but no exact advice as to how to establish it methodically. I have therefore acceded to the requests of friends, interested in graphology, to formulate a process of evaluating handwriting. For this formulation Klages is not responsible.

The result—which cannot exceed 4—is the style value of a handwriting.*

A style value of *1½ or less* implies a generally *negative* interpretation, a rating of *2 or better,* a generally positive interpretation.

An example of the practical use of the style evaluation in reducing ambiguity may be seen in the case of a handwriting revealing "much pressure." Does it mean rudeness or an alert spirit?

Style Value	Interpretation
Less than 1	Rudeness, aggressive attitude
1 to 2	Argumentativeness, opinionatedness
2 to 3	Alertness, independence
3 to 4	Free choosing of ideas, fighter for the oppressed and weak

TABLE OF RATINGS

I. *Rhythm*

To earn a full score of 4, 3, 2, or 1, the handwriting must:

4   look well balanced, without "holes" or "crowded spots" in the spaces, or excesses in height or width of letters; in addition, the general impression must be pleasing; our examining eyes must nowhere feel retarded or arrested; the sample must show a soothing equilibrium of black and white; show especially aesthetic forms of letters which are repeated as variations.

3   show that all spaces *and* most letters are evenly developed (watch the spaces between lines and words!) and in rhythmical balance among themselves.

2   show rhythmical balance among the margins on the one hand, and the spaces between lines and words on the other.

1   have only three of the four margins in rhythmical balance among themselves.

Deduct one point if the description does not fit your sample at all, a half-point if it fits halfway.

---

* Tests conducted by the writer indicate that there is close agreement between results obtained by untrained persons using this scale and the ratings of professional graphologists. Differences did not exceed a half-point.

II. *Symmetry*

To earn a full score of 4, 3, 2, or 1, the handwriting must:

4   be equally well developed in every letter of the upper, middle, and lower zones of the writing (watch excesses in lower and upper zones, insufficient development in middle zone); the proportions maintained must be 1:3:2½:4 for a man and 1:2½:-3:3½ for a woman (watch excessive capitals, loops, inflation or deflation); pressure pattern must be symmetrical (pressure in downstrokes only); show no excessive use of accessories as t-bars, finals, commas, and only slant between 55° and 90° from the horizontal.

3   be equally well developed in every letter and zone, but in slightly different proportions, which, however, do not permit the development of one or two zones at the expense of another or others; pressure pattern must be symmetrical (pressure in downstrokes only); show no excessive use of accessories, and only slant between 55° and 90°.

2   have most letters and at least two zones well developed; good pressure pattern (in downstrokes only), most accessories evenly used.

1   have a majority of letters and two zones sufficiently developed; a good pressure pattern (in downstrokes).

Deduct one point if description does not fit your sample at all, a half-point if it fits halfway.

III. *Creativeness*

To earn a full score of 4, 3, 2, or 1, the handwriting must:

4   be in all details a completely individual hand, with all letters more or less simplified: use of printed letters where they represent the simplest form (the Greek ε is not simpler than our *e*!); no left-tending strokes where right-tending strokes are supposed to be and are more practical; in addition, occasional original and useful letter combinations.

3   be an individual hand, with use of printed letters; no unnecessary left-tending strokes; generally simplified writing.

2   be an individual hand, without left-tending strokes at the start of capitals and the end of middle zone letters.

1   be an individual hand, simplified in parts.

Deduct one point if description does not fit your sample at all, a half-point if it fits halfway.

52

STYLE EVALUATION

IV. and V. *Speed and Legibility*

Give 0 points for slowly written handwriting
    1 point for fluently written handwriting
plus

    0 points for practically illegible handwriting
    1 point for not easily readable handwriting
    2 points for handwriting legible in context
    3 points for legible handwriting even out of context

Chapter 2

THE MARGINS

THE PLACE THE WRITER WANTS TO OCCUPY AMONG HIS FELLOW
MEN, AND THAT WHICH HE REALLY OCCUPIES

Motion pictures* taken of people writing revealed that
for a fraction of a second the writer pauses at the beginning
of every line, and, circling with his pen above the paper, he
starts or resumes writing at the point he considers sufficiently
distant from both the left edge of the paper and the preceding line. Moreover, when tested in darkened rooms, subjects,
even though they knew the shape and size of the sheet, could
not keep to any marginal pattern; the lines ran criss-cross
over the sheet. Consequently, testers drew the conclusion
that the left margins (and at the same time, the upper and
lower margins) are chosen deliberately, with the open eye.

Some writers know very well that their letters present a
definite and characteristic picture; they even speak of
"their" margins. And a majority of writers will admit some
deliberation in the choice of the width of the left margin.
But only in exceptional cases is the right margin developed
with similar deliberate care. The reasons for these different
attitudes toward what seems to be equally important aspects
of writing probably has something to do with the process of
writing.

After the writer has arrived at the end of the first line,
his first goal, the right, not the left, margin assumes for him

---

* Rudolf Werner, *Über den Anteil des Bewusstseins bei Schreibvor-
gängen* (München: Neue psychologische Studien, 1937).

the role of a front toward the addressee and the world. The left margin remains the "face" that even writers of questionable writing manners insist on "showing" to a certain extent; the right margin betrays the distance which they then really maintain. At the first line the relation between left and right margins is like that between a plan and its realization.

Does this relation change in the course of writing? At the end of the first line the writer stops where it seems to him most appropriate and returns to the left margin to start a second line. While I concede that a few writers will deliberately choose, point by point and line by line, a straight left margin, others are carried away by their enthusiasm, their impatience, or whatever emotion accompanies the writing; they move the starting point of the written lines more and more to the right, toward the right margin—the left margin widens.

Or a few writers, also fully conscious of the implication of the left margins, nevertheless cannot entirely fight off their prudence or shyness, and therefore with every line move

the starting point further and further back to the left—
the left margin narrows.

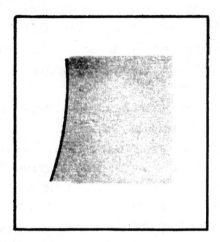

In both these cases the writer abandons his original plan
to show distance and reserve and develops the left margin in
full accord with the right, the "real" front.

The starting point of the last line, then, begins to establish the lower margin, half deliberately, half spontaneously.

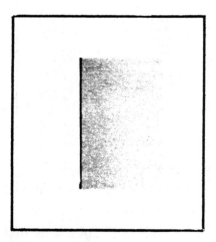

If the left margin is the face we show, then its width
might well be regarded as a demonstration of the distance

we wish to maintain between our neighbors and ourselves. I say "demonstration" because only the non-deliberate right margin betrays the distance which we then really assume.

Wide left margins may therefore be interpreted as an indication of the writer's respect or reservation toward others. They are found in the letters of shy or proud people. Well-to-do people and those who want to be taken for such, also often exhibit wide left margins. If these margins are at the same time very regular, the suspicion of a certain anxiety of neurotic or snobbish origin cannot be dismissed.

Only this concept of the origin of the left margin as a "show window" seems to explain why, for example, a diminishing left margin may not indicate sociability but rather removes the writer further and further from his aim, the right margin.

Only the profoundly and pathologically self-conscious person will watch and control not only his left, but his

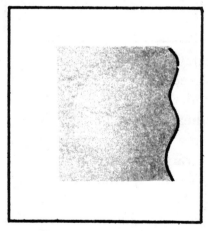

right margins as well. For, as can be imagined, right margins, unlike their left counterparts, are quite ordinarily irregular, plainly not deliberate, and in general as disarranged as one's bed in the morning. Following their irregularities actually means retracing the writer's mind in his relationship to his surroundings and especially to the addressee. Such a source of information is inexhaustible, and the interpretations suggested in the list at the end of the chapter are merely clues that must and can be further developed. By describing the right margin as one would a landscape, it is possible to re-create the exact position a writer occupies among his friends and foes—notwithstanding the pretenses of the left margins.

The interpretation of the *upper margin* has not been sufficiently explored. Most graphologists take the position that it is mainly determined by external reasons, such as the size of the letterhead and the address. One tentative assumption is that narrow upper margins betray informality; wide ones, on the contrary, withdrawal.

How deeply we permit ourselves to penetrate the *lower margin* seems to be a good indication as to how much we concern ourselves with the mystic, emotional, sentimental, sexual, and material. A wide lower margin may be interpreted as superficiality as well as fear of a sexual or emotional trauma. A narrow, lower margin has been found to be characteristic of dreamers who let themselves go, and of materialists and sensuous persons.

Letters *without margins* have been quite thoroughly explored. "No margin" obviously is characteristic of the writer who does not want any "distances" between himself and the rest of the world, who wishes, rather, to be one with it. Why? Again, there may be two incompatible groups of reasons for such gregariousness: boundless sympathy or intrusion, kindness or tactlessness, generosity or greed, sincere interest or idle curiosity.

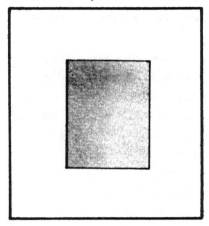

The letter with the wide or fairly *wide margins all around* is that of an aesthete or a withdrawn person. To place one's text right in the center of the sheet is both an indication of the importance we attribute to it and an aesthetic act; the margins here have the function of a picture frame. But they also are deliberate walls against intruders. (A wide-margin writer would probably try to flee the advance of a no-margin writer; but the latter would pursue, surround, and catch the fugitive.) Wide margins have been found in letters of people who avoid the world because it fails to come up to their aesthetic expectations, and in individuals with phobias and fears.

The aesthetic element must not be neglected in the interpretation of margins. For margins are appropriate aesthetic devices in letter writing, and the more artistically inclined the writer is, the more deliberately the margins are spaced. The fact that margins (with the exception of the right margin) can be established and chosen deliberately underscores this concept.

Some people write their letters with margins only to fill them up with pieces of last-minute news or other remarks. It is obvious that such an ill-placed urge for economy reflects rather unfavorably upon the writer's management.

Has the text of a message an influence upon the handwriting? Upon the margins? A sensitive and intelligent writer probably cannot avoid being affected by the message; therefore, the margins and the handwriting tend to express his position toward the addressee; the insensitive dullard probably can put any message on paper without thought or fear. Hence, a sensitive person's letter will show the mood in which it was written; a thick-skinned person's letter will permit a more general and lasting interpretation. It is therefore always advisable to examine several letters written at different times before making an interpretation.

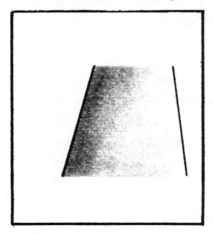

Because they are silently planted on the page, margins sometimes seem to be used by people as a means of expressing their silent sufferings. I have recently examined a rare margin pattern. The left margin, having started as excessively wide (flight from oneself!), grew smaller, while at the same time the right margin also diminished. The writer then explained what these painfully contradictory margins hinted at. Suffering from an inexplicable fear, she could not stay alone but was also afraid of company; since she could sleep only if the lights were left on, she needed sleeping pills, which in turn made her sick.

Thoroughly explored, margins, like any other feature in handwriting, reveal a wealth of characterological information about the writer. As with all other features, I limit myself here to exploring the basic issues, leaving it to the reader to exploit and apply them properly.

Note: To be interpreted positively, margins must be in harmonious agreement with the spaces between lines, words, and letters; excessive, unharmonious development (too wide or too narrow) of one or all margins is probably of compulsive origin, or indicative of mere pretense.

MARGINS

Upper Margin:	Wide:	Formality, reserve, modesty, withdrawal
	Narrow:	Informality, direct approach, lack of (proper) respect, little sense of beauty
Lower Margin:	Wide:	Superficiality, aloofness, idealism (P*), sexual or emotional trauma
	Narrow:	Dreamer, mystic, sentimentalist, sensualist (with pressure in script), materialist
Left Margin:	Wide:	Self-respect, richness, generosity, good cultural background, consciousness of one's own values, aestheticism, reserve, shyness
	Too wide:	Pretense to or caricature of above, or pathological shyness, flight from oneself
	Narrow:	Familiarity, desire for popularity, thriftiness, little sense of beauty, unceremoniousness, free and easy manner
	Widening:	Haste, impatience, enthusiasm, obliviousness to economic necessities, lavishness; attempts at thriftiness fail, innate lavishness breaks through
	Narrowing:	Attempts at lavishness fail because of innate economy; cautiousness, prudence, shyness, suspicion, fear of fellow men.
Right Margin:	Generally:	One's real position with reference to others
	Wide:	Reserve, fear of the future (P), over-sensitivity, impressionableness or neurosis with desire to keep world at safe distance, aesthetic restraint (S**); subjects are bad mixers, not willing to face reality

---

* P = Pulver's interpretation.
** S = Saudek's interpretation.

Right Margin:	Narrow:	Loquacity, gregariousness, vitality, courage to face life, predilection for joining and mixing, lack of aesthetic inhibitions, tendency to act hastily
	Widening:	Shyness, suspicion, fear of fellow men
	Irregular:	Lack of a sense of economy, unwise thriftiness (K*), love of adventure and travel (P), reserve alternating with loquacity, gregariousness alternating with desire to remain undisturbed, ambivalent social attitude
No Margins:	Generally:	Want of taste and morbid curiosity, or wide interest and little reserve
	Positive interpretation:	Unlimited sympathy, kindness, readiness to assist the needy, generosity, sincere interest in mankind, liberalism, prodigality, hospitality, fondness for splendor and luxury
	Negative interpretation:	Egoism, intrusion, curiosity, tactlessness, obtrusiveness, parasitism, tendency to preach thrift but to spend freely for oneself, little concern for propriety or for other people's privacy, garrulousness
All-around Wide Margins:		Voluntary isolation, aloofness, philosophical mind, spiritual independence, xenophobia, secrecy about one's own affairs, delicate taste and sense of beauty, good sense of color, conviction of one's own value, little disposition to join or mix
Left and Right Margins Narrowing:		Marked, perhaps hysterical, conflict between fear of people and the inability to remain alone

---

* K = Klages' interpretation

Chapter 3

SPACE BETWEEN LINES AND WORDS

Space Between Lines

A Picture of the Organization of the Writer's Mind

The striving for order and understanding is characteristic of the mature person. Its visible precipitate in handwriting is the distribution of the space between the lines.

According to tests conducted in darkened rooms, which have been mentioned previously, the *space between lines* probably is *deliberately planned.* This is in accordance with the fact that sensitive writers are fully aware of the individual distribution of space in their letters. W. H. Auden once gave me a sample of his handwriting, but added that neither the margins nor the space between the lines (he expressed himself differently, of course) in the sample showed his "usual" space pattern. He made no similar "apologies" as to the space between words; this, too, is in accordance with the dark-room tests, which established that *spaces between words are non-deliberate.*

The distinction between deliberate and non-deliberate features in handwriting is important. For instance, the space between lines, as a "picture of the writer's mind," has been recognized as dependent on his temporary state of mind. Overlapping lines have been found to be one of the signs of mental disorder; extremely wide space between lines has sometimes appeared in the hands of people who have a premonition of impending insanity.* A sample of Leo Tolstoy's handwriting made in his last days shows such an overlapping of lines that it is practically impossible to read it. (Tolstoy must have thought so, too; the overlapping lines in the sample are crossed out, and it seems to me, who knows no Russian, that Tolstoy repeated their contents below in widely spaced lines.) But even in this remarkable sample of lack of space between lines, the space between words can still be distinguished.

The space between lines is one of the features of a script that can be seen and analyzed at first sight and even from afar. Wide spaces between lines must impress us as a picture of system and order, of executive ability and reasonableness.

But there are wide and too wide spaces. As soon as they become too wide, we revise our favorable first impression and recognize the pedant or the person who keeps at a safe

---

* According to Pulver.

distance from us in order better to maintain his preferred
blasé attitude.

Trouble to be so helpft

With sincere appreciation.

Yours very truly,

Small spaces between lines, on the other hand, tell us of
genuine spontaneity, perhaps also of a lack of reserve, and

since she was 11 mos.
awfully hard to talk and
believe it will be much
She doesn't like her face
and when she sees me c
with the wash rag she —
hides.

some muddleheadedness; too narrow spaces stress the muddleheadedness to an alarming degree.

The fact that the spaces between lines are not hidden but very obvious to everybody, and that they represent a picture of the organization of the writer's mind, seems to suggest that some intelligent watchfulness in schools and offices would be valuable to those who favor early treatment of mental disorders, and to the patients as well. Parents would not permit a child with a fever to go to school, and if they did, the teacher would send him home immediately; but early indications of habitual "muddleheadedness" are too often disregarded.

To the simple and sane person it may seem unbelievable that certain people should have real difficulty in keeping their written lines apart, and that overlapping lines should betray a mental disorder; he himself puts his script on paper, legible and well spaced, as he purposes to do. But it is a fact that mentally disturbed persons, try as they may (and many are indefatigable in their endeavors to bring more order in their minds), cannot always keep their lines apart. Overlapping lines, therefore, are an unmistakable warning to the graphologist.

In the above sample, for instance, the lower zone descends into the following line's upper zone; this subject suffers from a lack of inhibitions and inability to control his sex impulses. Here it is the upper zone that reaches into the preceding

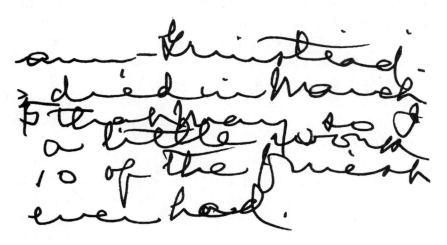

line's lower zone; this is interpreted as an indication of erotic fantasies which, however, are usually not acted out.

Sometimes we meet people who seem completely "normal" until an emergency or other unexpected occurrence reveals them as quite irresponsible. In this script, as in the above sample, we would find that the middle zone remains

68

fairly clear but that the letters of the lower zone crowd the capitals in the next line or vice versa. Such people are quite able to manage the daily routine, but they are not what one would call sane persons.

SPACE BETWEEN WORDS

THE EXTENT OF THE WRITER'S INTROVERSION

The space between words is non-deliberate. Even very sensitive writers have no idea whether or not they leave space between the words they write, or whether this space is large or small. When I drew a well-known musician's attention to the wide spaces he left between words, he was astonished for he had never before "seen" them.

(Tchaikovsky)

The words on paper follow one after the other as they do in speech. A person who speaks with pauses may do so be-

cause he is accustomed to pondering, considering and reconsidering before he acts; or because he wants to stress each
word of his well-calculated speech and let it sink into his
audience's consciousness; or because he does not know what
to say, or is overcome with emotion. In short, he may pause
after his every word because he is cautious and calculating,
or because of a wealth of thought or a lack of it, or because
of his depth of feeling. But if the pauses outweigh the importance of the speech, we must conclude that the speaker
is conceited, affected, and probably inhibited. The same conclusions must be drawn from wide spaces between written
words.

If, on the other hand, there is little or no pause between
the writer's words, he may be a man of action, not accustomed to pondering or even loath to do so; or he may be

impulsive and garrulous; or rather superficial and incapable
of any introspection. But he is natural, self-confident, and
therefore uncritical.

Sometimes the space between words may grow to such
an extent that it gives the impression of excessive emptiness.
70

Whereas well-spaced words reveal the aesthete, the poet, and the musician, those excessively spaced are indicative rather of the spendthrift and the empty head assuming the pretense of mental profundity.

There are those who waste paper and our time quite recklessly: three or four words per line on good-sized letter paper is the best they can do. Pulver calls such writers prodigals, egotists, and semi-gods; he is convinced that they also are little concerned with other people's rights, that they are very inconsiderate.

All the interpretations in the preceding paragraphs are based on the assumption that the unusual spaces between words, wide or narrow, occur regularly. But just as there are writers who space their lines sometimes widely, sometimes narrowly, so there are writers whose words are sometimes widely, sometimes narrowly, spaced. The only conclusion is that such a writer is rather unstable both in his thinking and in his emotions; that he presents sometimes the one, sometimes the other, picture and impression.

The equally meaningful space between letters is treated in Chapter 12.

SPACE BETWEEN LINES

Wide Spaces:

Analytical mind, stands on hard facts, has good manners and is appreciative of good manners, cleanness, considerateness, reasonableness; good executive; capacity for clear presentation of complicated facts; good organizer, sober pedagogue; lack of spontaneity; striving for logical certainty

Small Spaces:

Lack of reserve; spontaneity, muddled thinking; unclear about himself

71

Too Wide Spaces:

Incoherence, fear of logical mistakes characteristic of persons with a premonition of impending insanity, feeble-mindedness; blasé attitude (P)

Too Small Spaces:

Inability to see things as they are; regression, infantilism

Lines Overlap:

Lower zone descends into next line's upper zone: Lack of inhibitions, inability to control sexual impulses, overoccupied with instinctual life
Upper zone reaches into preceding lower zone: Erotic fantasies, usually not acted out
Lower zone crowds capitals of next line while middle zones remain clear: Capable of managing daily routine but incapable of reasonable thinking and proper emotional life; loses head in emergency

SPACE BETWEEN WORDS

Small, Even Spaces:

Activity, reasonableness, self-confidence, thriftiness, good balance, talkativeness, lack of criticism; good homemaker, "extrovert" personality

Sizable, Even Spaces:

Interest in literature and poetry, fondness for music, talent for poetry, philosophical turn of mind, caution and criticism, deep feeling, firmly rooted convictions; "introvert" personality

Small, Uneven Spaces:

Chattiness, gullibility, inharmonious personality, little or no musical sense

Sizable, Uneven Spaces:

(With low style value) hesitation, confusion, empty-headedness; (with good style value) trickiness, very critical mind and way of reasoning

Sizeable, "Seemingly" Evenly-Spaced:

Balancing his feelings of instability, he poses with an air of certainty and so deceives us (fast talker)

Chapter 4

DIRECTION OF LINES

THE WRITER'S MODE OF PURSUING HIS AIMS

Instruction in penmanship insists on writing in straight lines. At first we are given lined paper. But even after years of practice only a comparatively few persons can maintain an almost straight line (parallel to the upper and lower borders of the paper). This almost straight line I shall hereafter call a "straight" or a "regular" line.

It must be admitted that it takes quite an amount of equanimity and steadfastness, or rather self-discipline, continuously and simultaneously to think, write, and maintain a straight line on an unlined sheet of paper. Deviations from the line, therefore, cannot be the exception, but must be fairly frequent.

Fatigue must be considered a most plausible cause for *descending* lines. A tired hand and arm quite naturally retire slowly toward the body of the writer; at the same time the lines of writing slope downward. Yet, for the normal person writing is no tour de force; experienced writers can write for several hours on end without tiring.

We speak of "hanging one's head and ears," of being "downcast." Indeed, when the first lines of a person's writing show a descending tendency, he probably is downcast rather than physically tired. Or can physical exhaustion be at the same time not so great as to prevent a person from starting a letter, and yet great enough so that even his first lines descend?

73

Generally speaking, descending lines are interpreted as caused by depression and pessimism. This concept of an

almost wholly psychological cause for the direction of lines is supported by tests. Lines written without the help of our eyes may be quite generally as straight as usual. I mention these tests, too, because if it is not the tired arm, it may be the tired eyes of an exhausted writer that cause him to write in descending lines. But, again, even blindfolded he writes a straight line—if he ever wrote one.

Some people never learn to write in straight lines. Inasmuch as we understand the straight line as the purest manifestation of the educational ideal with which we are imbued in school, those who abandon it in their later life probably are not too respectful toward the community's educational ideals for the following generation; they prefer independence to civic virtues.

Whether or not the first straight line is followed by a second and third depends on our vision; for whereas each line is executed automatically, its parallelism with the rest of the lines depends on our eyes. In the dark-room tests no one could produce parallel lines; the lines ran criss-cross over the paper.

Experience shows that a depressed mood temporarily manifests itself in descending lines. So does a basically pessimistic and resigned disposition; only this disposition will not permit the lines to regain their straightness. The question whether a mood or a basic disposition is exhibited is reliably answered by other features of the hand: for instance, a person with right-slanted writing will be less self-conscious and secretive about his moods than a writer with an upright or left slant. By the same token, if a person who can produce a straight line permits his moods to show up in his writing, we must pronounce him demonstrative, self-indulgent, and oversensitive, hence generally weak as well as moody.

A special case is the straight line with a *curved, descending end.* It is the result of writing with the hand firmly rooted in one spot. The line, then, is practically part of a

curve that becomes evident only at the end of the line. (This is not a usual way of writing; most writers follow with their hand the forward-moving fingers that hold the pen.) Such partly curved lines have been observed in writers of considerable manual skill.

What may seem to be a variation of this special case, the *squeezing of words* into an inadequate space at the end of a line, really is not a variation at all. It is untimely and spotty

economy, well illustrated by the writer's determination to utilize, at the very end of the line and almost too late, every bit of paper at his disposal.

A good way to examine the direction of lines is to look at the handwriting from one of its margins by raising the sample almost to the level of the eyes. We can then perceive even that miscroscopic descending tendency of lines that has been found to be characteristic of a *not fully overcome inferiority complex.*

Ascending lines, again, are caused either by a mood or a disposition. The mood is *optimism,* the disposition, logically, *ambition,* zeal, restlessness, and an aggressive, pushing, and buoyant spirit.

When we write, we move our hand from left to right. We progress, advance, have an aim toward which we strive. The writing movement, therefore, is interpreted as a movement toward the future and our hopes and aims. (The reasons are more fully treated in the chapter on "Zones.") We can follow this movement in a person's handwriting, and scrutinize it on the basis of every word and even every

76

letter. Merely from tracing a person's written lines we can interpret and predict his *working manners,* his attitude and approach to the practical problems of life.

For instance, we can tell that a person who writes a straight line from the left margin to the right can also *go straight toward his daily aim* unhesitatingly and without much ado, for he is an orderly and reliable, though not a very sensitive or very lively person. If this straight line happens to coincide precisely with a ruled line, we may be sure that our subject is also unswerving, even unyielding. If slightly above the ruled line, the handwriting may be interpreted as indicating *habitual lightheartedness,* and even looseness, whereas the writing that remains slightly below the ruled line is indicative of too much *realism,* in other words, sobriety. (For all these reasons it is advisable to use lined paper for employment applications.)

I stated above that we can interpret and predict a person's working habits on the basis of his lines, words, and even his every letter. In this I have followed a school of thought in graphology, brought to perfection by Klages, which has proved its practical value time and again. The underlying idea is to follow the lines and letters of a handwriting sample as though we were trying to copy or imitate the gestures that brought it forth. With sufficient imagination and sensitivity we can then relive something of the emotions that inspired the original writer.

This approach is more generally accepted and practiced than many educators realize. Education encourages imitation and implies that through imitation we, too, shall reflect the spirit that inspires the teacher. Expressive movements, in particular, are best understood if relived. No gesture could mean much to the onlooker if, while observing, he could not reproduce in himself the tensions and urges that express themselves in the gesture. (Certainly much of the training in dramatics follows this principle.) In fact, practically all scientific tests of graphology have consisted of the strict imitation of certain manners of writing and the recording of the feelings the imitators thereby experienced.

I therefore urge the reader to retrace and imitate, with or without a pencil, the lines of a handwriting sample he wants to analyze. He will quite naturally be able to follow the interpretations of the slightly *convex* lines we see quite

often. Obviously, such a writer approaches his aim with ambition and a pushing spirit (as indicated in the ascending beginning of the line), but too soon his *zeal declines;* having started with much, probably too much, self-confidence and hope, he loses interest and gives up before the task has been completed.

On the other hand, the writer of *concave* lines approaches his task with little optimism but *reaches his goal* once he has overcome his initial lack of self-confidence. This cautious

working manner seems well adapted to a person whose goals are high and who wants to explore them fully before undertaking to achieve them. Klages observed convex lines in the handwriting of the philosopher Schopenhauer. But among one thousand samples, only three instances of concave lines were found.

In addition to the lines described above, there are also ascending and descending *steplike* lines. Lines that are broken into *ascending* steps are found in the handwritings

of people who have little stamina, but who are inclined to be *overoptimistic* so that they constantly have to recall themselves to reality. The *descending* steps, on the other hand, are characteristic of writers who bravely *fight against*

depressive moods and an inner resistance to writing in general which they overcome, only to be defeated again. Oddly enough, descending steps have been observed in the handwritings of well-known professional writers, such as Thomas Mann.

That *wavy* (meandering) and constantly shifting lines are indications of *moodiness* and unsteady working habits cannot surprise us. Schneidemühl reported that he found such lines in the hands of members of a family who had suffered a serious loss through the death of the beloved head of the family; after a few months they disappeared as they had come. Wavy lines, therefore, are also indicative of that ambivalence of hopes and fears which is caused by a grievous loss; or in a more lasting state of confusion, an ambivalence of reality and hallucination.*

---

* See Appendix, "Schizophrenia."

Theoretically, there may be as many directions of lines as there are writers. Even the same page may show lines of different types. Still, there is no reason to be bewildered or anxious. The main variations of the straight, regular line are listed below with their interpretations. And whatever experience offers in additional variations most probably can be interpreted by means of the imitative method. Indeed, he who adopts the imitative method cannot be permanently baffled by any of man's finest gestures.

DIRECTION OF LINES

Straight Lines:	Composure, methodicalness, orderliness, steadfastness, dullness
Irregular Changes in Direction:	Unsteady working habits; ambivalence of hopes and fears caused by grievous loss; dilemma between reality and hallucination
Ascending Lines:	Pushing and buoyant spirit, ambition, bellicosity, restlessness, optimism
Descending Lines:	Weak will, oversensitiveness, self-indulgence, melancholia, depression
Ascending Steps:	Overoptimism with little stamina; has to recall himself to reality
Descending Steps:	Writer fights against depressive mood and inner resistance to writing
Arched (Convex) Lines:	Ambition and self-confidence, but too little stamina; loses interest before aim is reached
Hollow (Concave) Lines:	Initial pessimism gives way to ambition and hard work until goal is reached

Chapter 5

THE SLANT

An Indicator of the Writer's Position Between Mother
Image and Father Image, Opposition and Assent,
Regression and Progress

The upper zone downstroke of any script forms two
supplementary angles with the line on which the script
stands. These angles may vary from word to word, and
even within the same word, but there are always these two
angles that are typical for a script. As a rule, one of them
is small, the other large. We determine the slant of a
script according to the smaller angle. Right slant exists
when the right-hand angle is the smaller, left slant when
the left-hand one is smaller; when both angles are approximately equal, we speak of an upright script.

Pulver is convinced that a person can change the slant
of his handwriting without too much effort, but only for as
long as this effort lasts. There are also fads in slant, he
continues, and he probably alludes here to the Continental
fad for left-slanted writing around 1900, then called the
English Hand.* "However," Pulver states, "to conclude
from these facts that the meaning of slant is psychologically
negligible would be going too far." For Saudek, on the
other hand, slant was mainly a matter of fashion. "We have
seen that the angle of writing is subject to fashion, that

---

* The term "English Hand" suggests that left-slanted writing was first
practiced on a large scale in England. At present America seems to have
more people who write left-slanted than any other country.

81

up to the seventeenth century upright writing was the fashion, that it then grew slanted, that this fashion prevailed for three generations, and that in our time the upright style is beginning to return."

Insofar as Saudek's contention seems to rest on old and ancient writings, my studies of these sources do not support him. Our present alphabet goes back to the Greek alphabet, which in turn was brought to Greece by seafaring Semitic tribes around 1500 B. C.* This Semitic alphabet was, of course, written from the right to the left, with the profiles of the characters turned to the left.

All early writings of which reproductions are easily accessible are upright, or mixed upright and left slant, or clearly left-slanted. No right slant can be seen. I mention the plainly left-slanted Umbrian Inscription (300 B. C.), the left-slanted Epitome of Livy (Egypt, 300 B. C.), and the famous Rosetta Stone with fifty-four lines of left-slanted Greek (200 B. C.)**

Early in the fifth century B. C., perhaps 1000 years after the alphabet (consisting of sixteen letters) had been brought to Greece, some Greeks (the Ionians) prepared themselves to change their writing from left-directed to right-directed, the way we write today. During the period of transition, they

* Thomas Astle, *The Origin and Progress of Handwriting* (London: The Author, 1784).
** Egyptian handwriting of 200 B.C. (and probably earlier) was also written from right to left and left-slanted.

wrote one line from left to right, the next from right to left, or vice versa. Thomas Astle gives this description of it: "The mode of writing called by the Greeks 'bustrophedon,' which is backwards and forwards, as the ox plows, is of very high antiquity. Of this writing there are two kinds; the most ancient commencing from the right to the left and the other from left to right." In a sample of the former type,* the first line begins at the right (*left-slanted*), the second at the left (*right-slanted*), the third at the right (*left-slanted*), and so on. In 565 B. C., according to Pliny, "all nations agreed to use the Ionic letters," by which he meant that the Greeks and the Romans at that time undertook to write from left to right.

However, only slowly, very slowly, was the new direction in writing generally accepted. Centuries after the Greeks and Romans had adopted it, the first writings of Germanic**

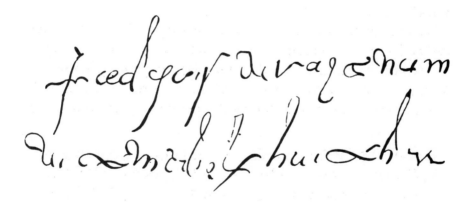

(Roman Running or Current Hand)

tribes were still carried out from right to left. But the new direction and right slant seemed to belong together. The

---

* Astle, *op. cit.*, p. 66, Tab. II.
** The writing of the Romans, and much later of the Germanic tribes, followed the same development, from left-directed, through a bustrophedon, to a right-directed script.

first real *handwriting* in Europe, the Roman Running or Current Hand (around 450 A. D.), with *d, h, l, f, p,* and *q* reaching beyond the rest of the letters, was clearly right-slanted. Therefore, one thousand years, if not more, were necessary to make Greeks and Romans convert their writing from mainly left-slanted to mainly right-slanted. How unstable this conversion was is perhaps best illustrated by the fact that the earliest printed Bibles (around 1450) show left-slanted letters.* And it is perhaps really only after 1700, probably for the most part through G. Shelley's *National Writing*** that the right slant becomes the generally taught slant in the English-speaking and -writing world.

At present we consider the right slant the normal slant. Indeed, it seems to follow from what has been said above that *whoever writes from left to right naturally uses the right slant.* The right slant is the slant taught in school, not only in the United States, but everywhere in the Western World, and most people maintain this slant in their after-school writing.

But some do not. Do they follow a fad? Are there any fads in writing now?

Authorities on penmanship know of none at the present time. Can those who write with left slant possibly give us a reason why? By all indications, left slant does not go well with a right-directed script, does not present any advantages; specifically, it does not facilitate the writing process. But if the left slant is not the result of a fashionable impulse or of some advantage in writing, if left-slanted writing is rather a vestige of ancient times, an atavism so to speak, then perhaps the writer's life history can give us some answer.

---

* In China, certain independent tribes still write from right to left, left-slanted. Hans Jansen, *Die Schrift* (Glückstadt: J. A. Augustin, 1935).
** London: 1709-14.

THE SLANT

The idea that the writer's life history may also be the history of his left-slanted writing is not purely conjectural. In the interpretation of handwriting, the left direction quite generally has been interpreted as the direction toward the past, the mother, and oneself. (Chapter 7, "Zones and Their Meaning," deals with the underlying principles.) If a writer chooses a left slant and maintains it in spite of its difficulties, then the story of his past, his childhood, and his relation to his mother, may tell us why.

To be sure, any attempts to explain left slant and slant in general through the "imitational" method, *i.e.,* the intuitive reliving of the movements in writing, have proved unsatisfactory. Klages, who is a major proponent of this method, has disclosed his failure. We may accept the fact that the right slant shows "inclination," the left slant (also called reversive), "disinclination." But this explanation is not sufficient.

To find the answer, scores of people with left-slanted writings have been interviewed, and seven (who were available for detailed study) were asked to give a short history of their childhood and particularly their relation to father and mother. Because left-slanted writing is seen much more often in women's than in men's handwriting, six of the seven subjects were female.

Case 1 Adeline, age 37, married, American

Seventh daughter in a family of eight. The father was a converted Jew who had become a Lutheran minister; the mother was of narrow-minded German peasant stock. During her early childhood the father completely withdrew himself from the children, leaving the mother as the focus of their attention. "Throughout childhood I was in greater fear of my father than of my mother (who often acted as go-between for children and father)." This girl embarked on an active academic career; she is adventurous. Since her father's death, when she was seventeen, she has dedicated

85

herself to the care of her mother, though she claims no conscious affection, but rather a growing estrangement.

Case 2   Barbara, age 54, twice divorced, American

Born after father's death, very attached to her mother. Deeply shocked when told that mother's husband was not her father. Twice divorced. Holds good professional position.

Case 3   Camilla, age 28, separated, American

After mother's death, father remained complete stranger to children because he (Chinese) could not speak English, the children could not speak Chinese. He was more feared than loved. The girl is very intelligent, independent, adventurous. Her marriage is not happy. She recalls that the father made some vaguely erotic advances when she was an adolescent, suggesting that she take her mother's place. She reacted to this thought with loathing. Has a good position, half literary, half commercial.

Case 4   Arthur, age 51, second marriage, German

Father died when Arthur, an only child, was four months old. Loves his mother dearly, "but would not permit her to interfere in his marriage." Married first an adventurous, almost criminal woman, then one of mother type. In this second marriage he shows all the dependent feminine traits which characterized his relationship to his own mother.

Case 5   Dagmar, age 23, divorced, Danish

Father divorced mother when the girl was 2. She professes to love mother dearly, rejects father, considers him as money source only. Very intelligent and independent, divorced her own husband after two years, with two children. Would like to study architecture and live as she pleases.

Case 6   Edith, age 40, married, American

Mother died when daughter four years old. Girl resented the strictness of her father, who was known as a domestic tyrant. She wanted to be an actress, to be free and live as she pleased. Superficially subscribing to father's precepts, she constantly flaunted his prohibitions behind his back. For a while she surreptitiously saved out of housekeeping money to take dramatics course. Dreamed of brothels where men would be kept. Dominated husband. Coquettish, calculating, bright, scheming.

Case 7   Faith, age 16, single, American

All questions on spelling and other student problems can be answered only by unusually well-read father; mother has very little schooling. Girl seems to feel that mother's position in house is threatened, that her rights are not sufficiently respected. Therefore she aggressively takes her mother's side in discussions. Is very intelligent and intellectually inclined, but does not have many friends.

Although these seven histories show similarities which might suggest a pattern according to which a left slant is developed, it has seemed advisable to look also into the childhood histories of certain well-known personalities whose handwriting shows a left slant*: George Bernard Shaw, William M. Thackeray, Maxim Gorki, Henry W. Longfellow, Henrik Ibsen, and William Booth.

Case 8   George Bernard Shaw

"George Shaw [the father] fell in love with Elizabeth Gurly. He was past forty, about twice her age. It was doubtful whether she loved him. . . . He assured her that he was a teetotaler. . . . During their honeymoon the youthful Mrs. Shaw . . . found a number of empty bottles in a cupboard. . . . By temperament she was well equipped for such a situation. There were no displays of affection in the family. Though not ill-treated . . . I hated the servants and I liked my mother. . . . Her almost complete neglect of me had the advantage that I could idolize her to the utmost pitch of my imagination and had no sordid or disillusioning contacts with her. It was a privilege to be taken for a walk or visit with her, or an excursion.' "
(Hesketh Pearson, *Bernard Shaw,* London: Collins, 1942)

Case 9   William M. Thackeray

His mother was only 19 at the time of his birth (1811), and was left a widow in 1816. "At his father's death

---

* Rudolf Geering, *Handbook of Facsimiles of Famous Personages* (Basle: 1925).

William was too young to be separated from his mother . . . remembering one of his parents only as a very tall man . . . he lavished the sum of his childish affections upon the lovely survivor. He adored her for her . . . tender love of himself . . . she created in the heart of an impressionable child an ideal of womanhood which was never supplanted." (Malcolm Elwin, *Thackeray.* London: Jonathan Cape, 1932) "Novelist Thackeray, 40, famed and lovesick ('My dearest Mammy') . . . falling in love with twenty women at a time." (*Time,* 1945)

Case 10   Henry W. Longfellow

About his mother: "With patient devotion Zilpha tended her growing family while she encouraged her modest, though capable husband toward wider horizons with her shrewd understanding. . . . Zilpha's husband had been taught . . . a calculating hardheadedness. She might have some difficulties in teaching Henry to understand his father." (Herbert S. Gorman, *A Victorian American, Henry W. Longfellow.* New York: George H. Doran Co., 1926) About his father: "He is intelligent, religious, a trifle strict, perhaps essentially didactic. . . . The mild-mannered, God-fearing lawyer who carefully bred his children to cultivate respect toward their seniors, to love duty . . ." About Longfellow: "His sympathies were broad and delicate, nay almost woman-like." (Hon. Charles F. Libby, "Unveiling the Statue of Longfellow," September 29, 1888)

Case 11   William Booth

(William Booth lost his father at thirteen.) "I had a good mother. I loved my mother. From infancy to manhood I lived in her. Home was not home to me without her. . . . When my father died I was so passionately attached to my mother that I can recollect, deeply though I felt his loss, my grief was all but forbidden by the thought that it was not my mother who had been taken from me." (Railton, Hodder & Stoughton, *The Authoritative Life of General William Booth.* New York: George H. Doran Co., 1912)

Case 12   Henrik Ibsen

"She was a quiet lovable woman, the soul of the household and everything to her husband and children. . . .[The father] his wit ever ready for combat . . . made him popular among his fellows, but caused him to be feared at the same time . . . he knew how to say bitter and unsparing things about people who in one way or another awakened his dislike." (Henrik Jager, *Henrik Ibsen.* Chicago: A. C. McClurg & Co., 1901) "Henrik had the sensitiveness of a withdrawn youth and suffered from the fact that he was the son of a degraded citizen." (Father went bankrupt.) (Gerhard Gran, *Henrik Ibsen und sein Werk.* Leipzig: F. A. Brockhaus, 1928) "He believed himself to have been, personally, much more mortified and humiliated in childhood by the change in the family status. Already, by all accounts he had begun to live a life of moral isolation." (Edmund Gosse, *Henrik Ibsen.* New York: Charles Scribner's Sons, 1917)

Case 13 Maxim Gorki

(The father died when Maxim was four.) "The mother had a way of saying short words that seemed to push people out of her path, to brush them aside and make them shrink. . . . Varvara dominated even her father. He had been forced to submit to his daughter's elopement with [Maxim's father], and later, to the indiscretion of her young widowhood. . . . Again mother won! This strong woman, who rose beautiful and independent above the drabness of shallow existence, eventually broke down. . . . The gloomiest pages in Gorki's autobiography are those where he records those days at his stepfather's. His young heart ached for his mother, the once beautiful, unusual, wonderful mother . . . meekly bearing abuse and mockery at the hands of her husband . . . his love for her grew in proportion to her misery, yet her coldness became ever more forbidding and kept him at a distance. [Concerning his later wife:] He lost his heart to this woman . . . despite her being ten years his senior. Concretely, she was to be a mother. . . ." (Alexander Kaun, *Maxim Gorki and His Russia.* New York: Jonathan Cape and Harrison Smith, 1931)

the evening with you
to see you and Lillian

In all these cases of left-slanted handwritings, selected only on the basis of their left slant, we see a child (the writer) faced with a disturbed balance in the parental equilibrium.*

Such a disturbance would exist if either of the parents achieved a dominant position in the house at the other parent's expense. But in nine of the above-quoted histories the mother has the dominant position in the child's life; only in four cases (3, 6, 10, 12) does the father seem to be the center of the child's attention, but in a negative sense. We must necessarily come to the conclusion that, whatever the stressed preference, in all cases there is a link to the mother, living or dead, as creating a disproportionate and decisive attraction.

But from here to the adoption of left-slanted handwriting a bridge must be built. The disturbed parental equilibrium must strike the child as odd and unnatural, and quite unlike the situation in the families of school comrades. *"I cannot remember a time when I was not longing to get outside the limited circle of filial duties. Neither can I now remember a time of tender feelings toward either of my parents although these may have existed when I was very young."*** The child must adjust to that disturbed equilibrium seemingly caused by a "dreadful" father. *"Throughout childhood and adolescence I was in greater fear of my father than of my mother."* Abandoned by or estranged from the father, the child must be deeply hurt and bitter. Whether he likes it or not, he takes refuge in the mother. *"Mother was both cushion and go-between."* But then the child can, it seems, either resign or fight back, fight against this father's and

---

* In Chapter 17, "The Mobile Axis," the reader will be shown that left-slantedness, while important, is not the only "solution" to such early dilemmas.

** This and the subsequent quotations are descriptions given by the subjects who were available for detailed study.

all men's rule, fight against and compete with them for
their privileges.

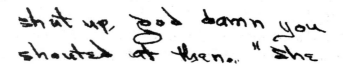

Such a step assumes a different meaning when taken by
a girl or a boy. For if a girl, by adopting the left slant, puts
herself in direct opposition to the majority of the other girls
and boys in her class she takes a provocative, bold and almost
masculine step. *"Throughout my high school and college days
I was accused by my female acquaintances and friends of
being 'aloof' and 'cold,' and they complained they could
not penetrate the 'stone wall' of my reserve."* At the same
time she demonstrates her failure to solve her conflicts
adequately (in a feminine way), and her resignation to a
world of taboos and inhibitions beyond which she cannot
and will not go But the boy who adopts the left slant, even
though he, too, acts in a revolutionary manner (or should I
rather say like a deserter?), actually relinquishes the role
in life for which he was destined in the natural course of
events: to follow the father and head a family. Instead,
we find that he prefers to be feminine or, sometimes, to
become a feminist. Therefore, to interpret the left slant,
graphology must offer various interpretations depending on
whether the left slant appears in a woman's or a man's
hand.

A woman with left-slanted handwriting, who has chosen
to oppose men's rule and to compete with them for their
prerogatives, can do so by following a calling or at least a
career, for instance, that of a university teacher. *"I insisted
on continuing my education beyond elementary school, a*

91

thing my six sisters, with one exception, had not done." Or that of a literary agent. "My ambition is to do as well as I can; I love my work as agent and want to be an agent;

Sorry to disappoint

it satisfies me completely." Another path is undermining and opposing the "natural" order, the family and its ruler, the father. "I soon learned to act in one way before my parents, and in a freer way when I was out of sight of father and/or mother." In any case, she is a "realist" and proud of it. "We are quite practical and realistic. . . . I am more inclined to accept the facts than to hope and dream of an unattainable ideal." She may also be said to be cold-blooded, sober,

Brahms First Symphony

egotistic, rarely quite sincere, but frequently filled with a strange joy of the forbidden. "The discrepancy between my actual behavior and what I thought to be the proper behavior really gave me a sense of quiet which was nearly always with me." But underneath this "quiet" her instinctual life is always burdened with an often veiled father fixation. "When I was 16 my father privately stated his preference for me. . . . I was very careful to keep the fact of my father's affectionate overtures from my mother." Of the six female cases I have quoted, two report "affectionate overtures" by the father or a suggestion that the girl "take her mother's place." The truth of the matter may be that at least these two subjects had an early start in the path to Amazonian libertinism and matriarchal promiscuousness, which seem to be connected with the left slant, the father merely reacting to what was unconsciously offered by the subjects. It is common knowledge that, among people who are closely associated with each other, one may give expression to what the other mutely and even unconsciously suggests. "*I had many short friendships with men, though there were two or three much longer ones. Throughout most of these friendships I felt that I would not care to marry the man.* For in spite of the awe in which I held my father I always felt that I should want to marry a man who was similar to him, especially in intellectual gifts.*" But all this only contributed to an undercurrent of isolation and frustration. "*I do not like to bring my childhood to mind, and rarely do I remember any happy moments. Those moments and times that stand out are nearly all filled with a certain fear, uneasiness or even active unhappiness.*"

A man with left-slanted hand, having renounced his

natural title to the father's prerogatives, can either turn against this father rule or prefer to forget and drift into the woman's realm. We therefore find the left slant in the handwriting of society's grimmest critics (Ibsen), satirists (Thackeray), satirists and socialists (Shaw), social reformers

---

* In the matriarchal society (when men seemed to have acted as tribal chiefs only, leaving the offspring and their problems to the community of women) it did not matter who the father of a child was. Of the Lycians, whom Bachofen-Echt cites as the foremost example of a matriarchal people, Herodotus (1, 173) reports: "They take the mother's and not the father's name. Ask a Lycian who he is, and he answers by giving his own name, that of his mother, and so on in the female line."

(William Booth), accusers (Gorki). But the feminist and feminine, the conciliatory attitude, is also taken by some who are true romantics (Longfellow), or who feel happier in an imitative attitude; they are the "home bodies" and the keepers of files and collections. (DeWitt B. Lucas, in his *Handwriting and Character*,* states: "Many statisticians and librarians are required to write vertical hand"—adding that the "vertical style or back hand is not natural.") It cannot astonish the reader that left-slanted handwriting is also preferred by sexual inverts, as well as sexually resigned or seemingly overvirile writers, in the latter case with the resulting libertinism and the undercurrent of remorse and frustration mentioned above. It has been clinically established that sexual inversion among males is linked to father protest and mother attachment in childhood.**

Not all children who have to adjust to a disturbed parental equilibrium adopt left-slanted handwriting. Being a manifestation of competitive opposition or ostensible resignation, those most likely to "turn back" are both the defiant and the meek—those who feel stronger in being different and those who have become resigned to it.

Before proceeding to the interpretation of the upright script, I should like to return to and deal with the problems of "veiled fixations" and "remorse and frustration" that seem to be closely connected with left-slantedness. It has been my experience that writers with a left-slanted hand profess a very tender feeling for their mothers. Shaw recorded the "advantage that I could idolize her to the utmost pitch,"

---

* DeWitt B. Lucas, *Handwriting and Character* (Philadelphia: David McKay Company, 1925).
** Terman and Miles studied 18 groups of 77 male inverts and found in each case a mother fixation of some degree; in 15 out of the 18 groups the father had either died during the boy's childhood or was the object of the boy's protest. Leonardo da Vinci (who, according to Freud, became homosexual through his erotic relations with his mother) "kept a diary; he made entries in his small hand, written from right to left. . . ." Sigmund Freud, *Leonardo da Vinci* (New York: Dodd, Mead & Co., 1932).

94

and William Booth stressed: "I loved my mother. From infancy to manhood I lived in her." In Case 7 a sixteen-year-old girl professes to be worried "that mother's position in the house is threatened, that her rights are not sufficiently respected." Therefore, "she aggressively takes her mother's side in discussions." A similar inclination toward the mother has been observed in most of the cases I have examined. Yet in at least one case the (female) writer, who also maintains a very close relation toward her mother, insists upon stating: *"I know now that my father was much more capable of understanding the human heart and mind than my mother."* Going even farther, she tells us: *"For in spite of the awe in which I held my father, I always felt I should marry a man who was similar to him."**

Do these "veiled fixations" contradict the interpretation of left slant? They do not. The words "left slant" and "right slant" are somewhat misleading. They take into consideration only that portion of our script that appears above the ground line. Actually, the same slantedness that the *t* of a script shows toward the left margin a *p* of the same script shows toward the right margin. In other words, to

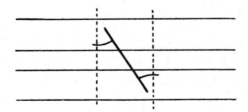

the same extent that a left-slanted script indicates a *conscious* inclination toward the mother, it betrays (when extended to

---

* To make sure that she never would be compelled to be partner to a normal traditional marriage, this subject married only in her late thirties a man in his late twenties, whom she easily surpassed in time spent in study and in the amount of formal education received.

the lower zone) an *unconscious* inclination toward the father. The missing links in this conclusion will be furnished in Chapter 7, "Zones and Their Meaning."

The same interpretation fits the natural or right slant, to which we shall turn in a moment. To the same extent that a right-slanted hand shows the *conscious* inclination to the father and his position, it betrays, in its *unconscious* part, an unconscious inclination toward the mother. Therefore, while a left-slanted *male writer* may be in opposition to his time, for instance, a champion of women's rights, he will rarely find true happiness and satisfaction in this position because it contradicts his unconscious desires. The right-slanted male writer, on the other hand, while a fighter for a man's world, will at the same time be prepared emotionally to make all concessions to the woman of his choice.

A *female writer* who "cultivates" a left-slanted script and therefore uneasily maintains a conscious and often proud and competitive opposition to the father rule, will nevertheless emotionally remain deeply bound to her father. The right-slanted female script indicates the woman who not only gladly recognizes man's prerogatives, but emotionally upholds a deep love for and traditional identification with her mother and her realm.

The left slant is now looked upon as "unnatural"; the right slant, the slant taught in school, is, so to speak, the official slant. The idea that the "official" position of the father (*pater familias*) is the basis of the "official" position of the right slant cannot be lightly dismissed. (It may be noted that the change in the slant and direction of our handwriting from left to right roughly paralleled the shift in Europe's social order from matriarchy to patriarchy.) It also can be assumed that as long as the school accepts the father as the head of the family, the right slant will remain official, and the left slant will be considered odd. But the

96

tolerance with which the left slant is being accepted in the schools suggests that tacitly the teachers accept the true status in many families.

The graphological interpretation of left-slanted handwriting has always been strongly negative. Even the early French and Italian graphologists, who interpreted handwriting intuitively only, never gave a positive interpretation to left-slanted script. The reason may be that, as far as I know, at no time in the history of writing (except ours) has there been recorded an attempt to write both from left to right and left-slanted. There were times, we know, when people wrote left-slanted, but then the hand moved from right to left; when people wrote from left to right, they did so with right slant. Definitely, left slant is incompatible with a movement of the hand toward the right; it is contradictory and, from the standpoint of penmanship, a monstrosity. And since writing is gesturing, how can we interpret otherwise than negatively a gesture that appears to express full agreement with the general trend, the common goal (writing movement from left to right), but actually covers up a less obvious gesture, one of disagreement, disapproval, opposition?

The *upright slant* will thus appear in the hand of children who make their way in life rather independently of either parent, with conscious emotional inclination neither toward the father (right) nor toward the mother (left). Wholly upright hands are not very common; but mixed hands, basically upright, with some letters slanted to the right, some to the left, are often seen. The writer of the following sample is nineteen years old. The marriage of his parents was very inharmonious, his father committing suicide when the boy was eight. At no time did the boy show a preference either for the highly educated and intellectual father or the domineering and self-centered mother. He is

97

very reserved, shy with girls, a very good scholar. There
are, to be sure, left- and right-slanted letters with all they

to see you in New York this Christmas to thank you in person. I have not heard definitely from the consul I am in touch with him and

imply. But the basic slant of his hand is upright; he has
been able to regain at least some independence from both
the morose father and the domineering mother.

The genuine upright hand (whose downstrokes maintain
an angle of 90° or almost 90° with the base line), like the
child's attempt to steer clear of that primary source of
human influence, father and mother, often shows a certain
artificiality and forced aloofness, and an uneasiness underneath a show of equanimity. (For a while a juggler can
balance a ball on the tip of his finger, but we do not expect
him to keep it up indefinitely.) In fact, I believe that a
perfect upright hand can be achieved only by a great show
of will power that few persons can maintain for any considerable length of time; if circumstances compel one to show,
for too long a period, supreme indifference and artificial
neutrality where one is not or ought not to be indifferent or
neutral, it is liable to result in neurotic disturbances.

More "human" and, as mentioned above, comparatively
more frequent is the upright hand with a good many left-
and right-slanted traits in between (or rather, a right slant

with a good many upright and left-slanted traits scattered in between). Such hands have been compared to battlefields,

climb up 4 flights at the above address? Around 8 o'clock*? We hope you will and shall expect you unless we hear from you

and, indeed, the writer has no easy life. Why? Upright, right-slanted, and left-slanted traits in one and the same script must betray the unresolved coexistence of both father's masculine and mother's feminine influence, persistent remembrances of the past and hopes for the future, thoughts of resignation and optimism, opposition and assent, selfishness (and introversion) and altruism (and extraversion). The explosive result cannot be pleasant either for the writer or for his associates.

But when, in extraordinarily gifted writers, through a supreme effort, these "ambivalent"* hands arrive at a temporary synthesis of their conflicting tendencies, the result is apt to be a creation. Beethoven's hand is best known for such "ambivalent" writing.

---

* "Ambivalence" is here used to characterize those personalities for whom conflict situations are unusually frequent, intense, and extended, and who typically show contradictory attitudes toward the same situation.

To be sure, ambivalence is not the only or the main source of creative ability. Out of 766 handwritings of statesmen, artists, scientists, and authors (in the second half of the

(Beethoven)

nineteenth century), 105 showed an upright, 189 a slightly right-slanted, and 472 a plainly right-slanted hand.* But there is perhaps a fundamental difference between creativeness in a person with an ambivalent hand and in a person with a harmoniously slanted hand. The revolutionary and sometimes disturbing or even shocking creation is more likely to originate in a battlefield hand such as Beethoven's. Every one of his manuscript pages attests to the fact that his stirring compositions were conceived out of chaos. On the

---

* That there are no instances of left slant can be attributed to the fact that this count was made in Germany around the 1870's, when the thought of turning against the father was considered sheer sacrilege; yet it was risked in Germany more frequently than in any other country.

other hand, the completion and perfection of something incomplete and imperfect is rather the task of the genius with the harmonious slant. Mozart's manuscript page is a pleasure to behold; his first draft was usually his last. He conceived his harmonies in harmony with himself and the world.

In an effort to keep calm and concentrate on the solution of a problem, writers with an habitually right-slanted hand often turn temporarily to an upright hand. They leave it as soon as the solution of the problem is well under way; they do not seem to feel right with that upright hand.

The *right slant* is the "official," the most frequent, and the most natural slant. The person in a hurry, the impatient person, and the active writer will always adopt the right slant. So will the excited and excitable and choleric; and the more excited and excitable they are, the more right-slanted will their hands be. To bend forward, to incline, also fits the person who wants to convince us of the right-eousness of his cause, and who, at the same time, is inclined to listen—the person of conviction and initiative, aggressive and pioneering, but also sympathetic and affectionate. The right slant is also preferred by the restless, uninhibited, and brutal. And is it not to be expected that the right slant would be maintained by those who wish to express assent and who, after all, believe this world to be quite acceptable?

The important question as to when an adjustment of slant, if any, is carried out has been answered by several writers on graphological subjects. Pulver says that left-slanted scripts appear not earlier than the third year of writing instruction and not later than the years of puberty, and "with girls more often than with boys."* Right slant

---

* Exceptions do occur, however. Thackeray, for instance, seems to have adopted a left slant in his thirties, after the loss of his wife. Can we not say that this change reflected his return to the past and his mother?

seems apt to become more upright with the years—growing disillusionment and diminishing virility, perhaps.*

From the foregoing brief discussion on slant it may appear that there is no end to its implications and allusions. And, indeed, slant is neither easy to define nor can its interpretation be limited to just so much and no more. From the very fact that slant can be detected or felt even in the most minute stroke, that the left-slanted stroke, for instance, (which in the upper and middle zones *recoils* from the right or father's side) in the lower zone, the zone of the instinctual and unconscious, *approaches* the right or father's side, it can be seen that its sway is basic, supreme, and inescapable, and that there is no end to its interpretation.

Let us take an example. Sometimes a handwriting will be dominantly right-slanted or upright, but the astute observer can detect a regularly occurring pattern of left-tending

strokes, particularly with the end strokes. These must generally be interpreted as left-slanted writing with the additional understanding that the father-protest is more deeply repressed in these cases.

Similar left-tending strokes in generally right-tending or upright hands may appear in the upper zone as t-strokes or in the middle zone, for instance, as left-slanted r's. Their very inharmonious suddenness is ominous: an unrepressed, clearly conscious and guiding protest amid what looks like peace and acceptance, characteristic of very difficult and unpredictable personalities (Hitler).

* William Preyer, *Zur Psychologie des Schreibens* (Leipzig: Leopold Voss, 1919).

In particular there are those writers who show a frequent left-slantedness, but only in the lower zone. They apparently maintain a consciously positive and co-operative social adjustment; yet underneath they withdraw from co-operation on their instinctual level. They feel basically inadequate or frustrated sexually and therefore turn back to the comforting mother-image.

It may seem contradictory that a generally left-slanted hand should be interpreted more positively than a single "sudden" left-tending stroke. But a writer with left-slanted hand, once he has adopted it, has arrived at a workable agreement with the world; the person with a sudden left-slantedness has not.

As for a definition of "slant," at the beginning of this chapter I called it "An indicator of the writer's relation . . ." and then proceeded to demonstrate my contention concerning the left slant. I started with the left slant because its nature has remained rather obscure while its oddness and provocative pose challenge the graphologist.

My probing into the nature of the left slant has yielded no really startling facts. Each feature I have brought to light could have been recognized through sufficiently imaginative interpretation of the facts established for the right slant. In short, that which holds true for the right slant applies to the left slant in reverse, with this reservation: the right slant is not odd, the left slant is not "natural."

But whether right or left, natural or odd, slant always indicates a stand *for* something and *against* something else. The upright slant seems to be able to evade the issue, to remain neutral. I am inclined to interpret this neutrality as basically artificial, unhealthy, escapist. Man, it appears, must take a stand for or against.

Of course, there is always a difference in degree. In the interpretation of the right slant, the stand *against* must be considered as secondary, not primary. Our pen, hastening from a base point·to carry out the upstroke of a right-slanted *l* chooses a right-tending direction, the direction toward "you," the future, progress, and father, and only incidentally turns its back to the past, the mother, oneself. A left-slanted stroke does exactly the opposite: it chooses an oppositional left-tending direction, away from "you," the future, progress, and the father, and only incidentally the direction toward the self, the past, the mother.

This is so at least as long as we consider slant an isolated feature. But loves and hatreds, for example, have strong emotional and instinctual components; they can be fully appraised only through simultaneous consideration of a handwriting's lower zone, where the emotional and instinctual life is projected. Indeed, no individual feature in a handwriting has more than suggestive analytical value; for a synthesis we must take into consideration its influence on other features and the influence of other features on it.

With slant now established as the indicator of the writer's position between father and mother, or more specifically, between male and female leadership, all interpretation of left and right slant must be made in the light of the writer's sex. The list of interpretations on the following pages is divided, first, on the basis of the direction of the slant, and second, according to whether the writer is male or female. The reader may then select the interpretations that fit the particular case. One interpretation will never suffice; many interpretations may be necessary to outline a personality picture.

A caution to bear in mind is that the *degree* of the slant, in either direction, has a bearing on the extent to which a given interpretation is applicable to the writer. For example, if, among the interpretations of right slant, "affectionate" is appropriate, the more pronounced the right slant is, the more affectionate the writer may be; the less pronounced the slant, the less affectionate the subject.

However, the interpretations of right-slanted writing listed at the end of this chapter are limited to angles of inclination between 55° and 85°. A script more upright than 85° can safely be characterized as upright. And a script more right-slanted than 55° may be said to belong to pathological persons. Their personality picture has become notorious the world over: the initial *H* of Hitler's (illegible) signature has an angle of inclination of 28°, the last letter is 14°, almost horizontal.

RIGHT SLANT
(55° - 85°)

Female Writer	Male Writer

Acceptance and furtherance of male leadership and traditional, father-led family

Female Writer	Male Writer
Agreeableness, sympathy, affection, heartiness, friendly advice, impressiveness, optimism, trust in future and in male action, sincerity, strong sympathies and antipathies	Initiative, optimism, spontaneity, strong sympathies and antipathies, drive for independence, ambition, radicalism, reformism, progressiveness, activity, aggressiveness, courage, idealism, pioneer spirit, defiance, impetuousness, energy, enterprise, adaptability, affection, humanitarianism, trust in future and action, advocacy of marriage in the prevailing sense, hero worship

Instinctual and emotional harmony with that acceptance

Female Writer	Male Writer
Attentiveness, receptivity, personableness, pliability, tractability, devotion, faith, humanitarianism, altruism, religiousness, advocacy of marriage in the prevailing sense, hero worship	He-mannishness, restlessness, lack of contemplativeness, adventurousness, lack of inhibition, insubordination, sensuality, libertinism

Generally:

Increasing Right Slant
at the end of words:

countryside

Writer's interest in a thing grows the more he studies it; inability to hide his true intentions: optimism overpowers his original reserve; hotheadedness; when excited, writer loses self-control; quick temper

Diminishing Right Slant
at the end of words:

Complete

Writer's interest in a thing diminishes the more he studies it; pessimism overcomes his original enthusiasm; skepticism is stronger than confidence; he backs out or asks for additional security just when everything seems settled; incurable pessimism

Upright Slant

(86°-90°)

Reasonableness, lack of sentimentality, sobriety, reserve, criticism, rationalization, concentration, objectivity, impartiality, judiciousness, neutrality, aloofness, temperateness, maturity, reliability, cool-headedness, poise, introspection, self-centeredness, self-criticism, inhibition, frugality, resignation, disillusionment, independence, reticence, retirement, passiveness, seclusion, inactivity, contemplation.

LEFT SLANT
(Over 90°)

Female Writer	Male Writer
Active or passive denial of male leadership through direct competition and guerrilla warfare against the traditional father-led family	

Independence, boldness, cold-bloodedness, forwardness, presumptuousness, cleverness, ambition, egotism, selfishness, "realism," masculine reasoning, pseudo-intellectuality; Amazon; promiscuousness, man-hating, cynicism, enjoyment of the forbidden, opposition to marriage in the prevailing sense, general negativism	Feminineness, sentimentality, tenderness, domesticity, garrulity; busybody; diligence, pettiness, pedantry, fussiness; homebody; zealousness, possessiveness, selfishness, eagerness to please, devotion to ladies; always disappointed and dissatisfied lover; promiscuousness, sexual inversion, escapism from marriage in the prevailing sense

Instinctual and emotional resistance to that denial

Coquettishness, possessiveness, egoism, insincerity, secretiveness, two-facedness, impenetrability, pessimism, disillusionment, bitterness, inhibitions, self-torment, fear of future and fervent hope for some sudden salvation	General negativism, opposition to existing ideals; fighter against the idea of a common goal; pseudo-individualism, polemicism, sarcasm, superciliousness, irony, satire, egotism, dissatisfaction, insincerity.

Middle Zone Left-slanted (upper zone and lower zone upright or right-slanted): *because*	Intellectually and emotionally drawn to fellow men, but has difficulty in bringing himself to be one of them; sacrifices himself for a family claim (his mother or sister)

108

Lower Zone Left-slanted (upper zone and middle zone upright or right-slanted):

Sexual inadequacy or resignation to an incomplete sexual life

patty

Increasing Left Slant (at the end of words in upright handwriting):

Pessimism overpowers initial interest in a thing

thought

Sporadic Left Traits (in upright or right-slanted handwriting):

Skepticism, distrust; victim of inner conflicts; (together with split letters) schizophrenic disposition

meeting

Left-Slanted End Strokes (in upright or right-slanted handwriting, with pressure):

Unresolved father-protest, obstinacy, stubbornness

mad

Chapter 6

PRESSURE

If Visible, a Measure of the Writer's Vitality
If Invisible, a Measure of the Writer's Persistence
and Precision

So obvious is the contrast between a dark and a pale script that even the impressionable layman is tempted to base on it some intuitive interpreting. The earliest scientific approaches to graphology, too, began with pressure.

In writing one has to press the ink-filled pen against the paper; simultaneously, the fingers must be pressed around the penholder. The pressure against the paper may be called *primary pressure,* the invisible pressure against the penholder, *secondary pressure,* the former indicating our display of strength, vigor, vitality, the second revealing the aims and the inner conviction behind that display. To illustrate the difference between these two pressures: Strength can lift a heavy stone and throw it a good distance; but only our grip on the stone (our secondary pressure) gives that throw direction, aim, sense.

Under heavy *primary pressure,* the pen traces a heavy, thick line over the paper; with slight pressure, the line remains light and fine; at any rate, the heavier the penstroke, the greater the resistance of the paper. As a rule, downstrokes are heavy, upstrokes light; curved lines are partly heavy and partly light. Primary pressure in a handwriting therefore can be quite accurately appraised through observ-

110

ing the contrast between the thinner upstrokes and the heavier downstrokes.* Their normal width relation is about 1:2.

With normal pens, where there is no contrast, there is no primary pressure (no matter how heavy the writing appears in general). Writers may use a stylo or a specially

constructed pen so cut that it automatically produces light and heavy strokes in order to show pressure in their handwriting regardless of the actual primary pressure exerted. These persons can be detected in their curved strokes where

up- and downstrokes seem to be connected like slightly twisted ribbon. Whether this type of pen or a stylo is used, the reverse side of the paper will always show the actual degree of primary pressure. *In examining writing, our fingers should glide over the furrows on the reverse side; we can feel primary pressure which the eye may not detect.*

---

* It has been said that writing is a kind of speech by means of graphic signs. If this is true, then a blind man's writing should be generally as devoid of stress as a deaf man's speech. The relation of writing to speaking is closer than generally assumed: the writing of the blind is devoid of pressure patterns; people with speech defects *cannot write fluently;* unpronounceable letter combinations *cannot be copied* with usual promptness; senseless but pronounceable letter combinations present no lasting difficulties.

From the standpoint of primary pressure, all writing is a fight between our will, vigor, strength, in short, our vitality, on the one hand, and the resistance of the paper (friction) on the other hand. Of this fight man is instinctively aware. Therefore, a script that shows much black impresses us as written by a man with much will power and vitality; pressure-less script seems to be the truthful mirror of a feminine, weak-willed or sickly person.

While this may sometimes be a correct conclusion, it is not always so. A barking sergeant may be a squabbler rather than a hero. Sickly people with little muscular strength can have iron wills and athletes weak ones. A cramp may contract our muscles as strongly as, or even more strongly than, our will. Therefore, even though we generally interpret pressure as *will power, vitality, fighting spirit,* the elements of *inhibition, heaviness,* and sometimes *frustration* inherent in pressure must not be overlooked. We experience this frustration whenever we try to produce more pressure than is adequate for us. The resistance of the paper mounts with our efforts, and sooner or later we are defeated. The result may be a heavy penstroke, but its unharmonious deformity testifies to our frustration rather than our strength. Our main task is to distinguish between pressure produced by will power ("genuine" pressure) and pressure betraying inhibition ("added, excessive" pressure).

There are at least three ways of establishing that distinction. The first test consists in "feeling" the traces genuine

until January 4th & he

pressure inevitably leaves in paper. But sometimes we have a photograph instead of the original script, or we are unable to examine the letter closely for other reasons. In such cases,

112

and always as a control measure, we employ as a second test method the means that permitted us, for instance, to evaluate margins: our sense of proportion. Genuine pressure fits a hand quite naturally and harmoniously; added pressure cries out, looks forced and even vulgar. The reason for this is that added pressure is bound to disturb a hand's equilibrium, rhythm.

[handwriting sample: "Finest Cigarette"]

The third test our eyes can carry out is the examination of the script for "weak spots." We know from experience that a chain is only as strong as its weakest link. In the following

[handwriting sample: "by you"]

sample the initial stroke of the *b* in "by" and the upstroke of the first *y* are quite light; by comparison the downstrokes of the two *y*'s look forced and disproportionately heavy; in fact the pen, stymied by the resistance of the paper, broke down. These small, fine lines tell us that they represent the true nature of this script (and its creator), and that the pressure shown is "added," excessive.

But why should a man wish to "demonstrate" more pressure in his script than he can produce naturally? We all know there are natural and affected demonstrations. Affected demonstrations (exhibitionism) have their meaning as well as natural ones. For instance, a sense of beauty, or vanity, or both may make a writer add extra pressure at some points

113

in his writing. As long as we recognize such "false" primary pressure as affected, it adds to our knowledge of the writer.

But not only vanity or a sense of beauty make us add extra pressure. Most sick or weak people have a desire at least to look healthy and strong; a bit of rouge may do the trick for their complexion; in writing it is pressure.

Kidnapped

The above sample comes from the hand of a man who, after a childhood spent in a chair and in the care of a loving mother, was able to acquire some strength; but he still remained basically weak. He has added "rouge," he shows off the prowess he has achieved, but the pressureless *i* and *a* in "kidnapped," as well as the obvious exaggeration, betray the true state of this subject's mind and vitality. It is important to recognize that such "camouflage" appears almost always in those parts of the script that need it; we see here that all prominent downstrokes (stable axis) are bolstered. In Chapter 15 I endeavor to show that in our handwriting movement pressure quite naturally falls on these downstrokes, the stable axis, and nowhere else. And inasmuch as such well-placed "overcompensation" presupposes a natural inner balance, or at least the desire for it or the attempt to regain it, we must give the subject credit for it.

Added, showy primary pressure is frequently seen in the hand of braggarts and criminals, particularly swindlers. Here the reason is not vanity alone. Tests have established the fact that most mature writers write automatically. They concentrate entirely or almost entirely on the contents of their message. Such automatism is quite alien to a swindler

114

(and to the aesthete). Not only the message, but its external form as well, is of importance to him. He is determined to make a favorable impression with his script; in fact, so favorable that the addressee's attention will, if possible, be more absorbed by the handwriting than by the (fraudulent) message. Pressure, he thinks quite rightly, is an excellent means to this end. But Freud has shown how a person's guilt may ooze from his every pore. In his zeal the swindler (and also the braggart) is bound to exaggerate the embellishment, and it becomes his Judas.

We may therefore repeat that pressure is indicative of will power, resoluteness, vitality; excessive pressure, on the other hand, may betray both vanity and a sense of beauty, but also inhibition, overcompensated weaknesses, and the excitability and obstinacy that often beset the person who feels compelled to play a role nature has not made him for.*

*uld be a pity for.
to have to read this
for information about
lter. However, think of*

Pressureless writing can be produced by "gliding" over the paper with the least possible loss of time and force. Consequently, lack of pressure can be seen in the hand of mobile, hasty, superficial, sickly, timid, as well as peaceable, sensitive, lofty, delicate, and feminine writers. It may also indicate a cultured person's unwillingness to boast of his physical prowess. The question as to when we interpret lack of pressure as an indication of superficiality or loftiness, or as gen-

---

* See chapters on "The Stable Axis" and "The Mobile Axis" for a further discussion of pressure.

erally negative, or positive, is answered, as was to be expected, by style evaluation.

The answer to another question is less obvious. If in one and the same script dark and light strokes mingle, is such a script to be interpreted as pressureless or as having pressure? The answer must be "both," and it is easy to understand that such intermingling is indicative of inner conflicts. Such writers may then be at one time delicate, at another resolute, now feminine, now masculine, now genial, now harsh, and always irritable.

The identification of primary pressure with the libido* is one of Pulver's contributions. If Pulver is right, *a man's hand* without pressure is exceptional. Its paleness, at any rate, does not go with our concept of manliness; but it goes well with "paleness of thought," with intellectuality (style value!). Since Palmer's penmanship seems to exclude primary pressure, any American taught along Palmer lines who has genuine primary pressure in the downstrokes of his script must be considered very virile, indeed.

However, it is only with due consideration of a hand's *secondary pressure* that we can arrive at any conclusive interpretation of primary pressure. Strong primary pressure, for instance, in the stable axis, together with evident secondary pressure, may indicate both a strongly disciplined will for self-preservation and the readiness to fight for one's ideals; without secondary pressure it is (as interpreted above) rather bellicosity and he-mannishness as well as a claim to leadership that borders on dictatorship.

Secondary pressure cannot be recognized easily. But some

---

* Noyes writes about libido: "Since Freud regarded the fundamental biological aim of all animal organisms, including man, to be procreation and the resulting perpetuation of the species, he assigned an important psychological role to libido, the term applied to the instinctive energy designed to insure such perpetuation." Arthur P. Noyes, *Modern Clinical Psychiatry* (Philadelphia: W. B. Saunders Co., 1939).

116

$$\underset{1}{A}\,\delta_{ik} + \underset{2}{A}\,\varkappa_i\,\varkappa_k + \underset{3}{A}\,(\varkappa_i\,\xi_{k_1}\,\varkappa_b$$

clues about secondary pressure can be drawn from the appearance of the writing: very small and neat characters, whether

Your woman's intuition probably told

heavy or light, particularly angles, suggest that secondary pressure was used. Also, the constant, regular change be-

National City Bank

tween heavy and light strokes cannot be carried out without a tightly gripped pen.

keine Bedingung.
Ungeordnetes und geschlossenes magnetisches Feld,

(Albert Einstein)

Many hardworking scientists and subtly persistent women show a very fine, light handwriting with carefully produced small letters. This may appear to indicate a lack of physical vigor, even feebleness. The concept of secondary pressure

117

suggests that though these people may seem to lack vitality, they have actually transferred their inner strength and persistence to their firm and careful handling of the pen—and most things they are concerned with.

Secondary pressure also has a negative interpretation. Not only the scientist is concentrated on his aims, but also the pedant. And does not "pettiness" imply just this close and really pitiless attention to trifles?

To recognize primary or secondary pressure in pencil-written scripts is difficult, often quite impossible. Therefore, I never accept pencil-written samples for analysis and interpretation. They may show us shape, size, symmetry, slant and simplification of a man's script, but how meaningful would these clues be without a reliable measure of the subject's pressure?

When I spoke above of pressure and its absence I always assumed a pressure pattern that appeared *harmoniously* in downstrokes of the writing. But sometimes the patterns are different.

Certain persons either cannot or will not follow the natural rhythm that is inherent in the distribution of pressure in handwriting. They displace, dislocate, conglomerate, and "coagulate" pressure into sometimes strange and threatening lumps. This phenomenon is most obvious in the handwriting of criminals with homicidal tendencies.

I had an opportunity to examine the handwritings of sixteen murderers. In all of them excessive primary pressure could be observed. But the pressure appeared not in patterns, that is, it did not recur in similar strokes, but in "eruptive" blotches, often of such irregular size and form that they seemed to be ink spots more than anything else. But these were not ordinary ink spots; they were "witnesses" of an eruptive and uncontrollable temperament that failed to manage its (contradictory) impulses.

118

The following script sample was written by a convicted murderer.*

There are many dark spots and heavy strokes in this script, but they are not arranged according to any reasonable, natural order. And indeed, they must be interpreted as indicative of an erratic and brutal temperament that does not shrink from anything.

Another murderer,

---

* Dr. Roda Wieser, *Der Rhythmus in der Verbrecherhandschrift* (Leipzig: J. A. Barth, 1933).

who butchered and robbed his victim, has in his script the same blotches, only more of them.

But the hired assassin

has not so much pressure in his hand, as arcades (even in the lower zone), heavy angles (See Chapter 11, "Connections of Letters"). And does not a certain stiff coldness radiate from that script: This is the "impressively" legible hand that betrays the wolf in sheep's clothing! (Chapter 12)

Yet, these writers not only have the destruction and abandonment of the natural rhythm of writing in common. Even more outspoken is the appearance of concealing strokes (Chapter 14) in the upper zone. On closer inspection the excessive pressure is not so much *in* the strokes as *between* them. Where two strokes usually form a loop, in these scripts they are brought so close to each other that they form a blotch, a small "ink lake"; they conceal each other, thereby indicating secretiveness, obscene imagery, brutal, murderous scheming, and, where those blotches appear in the lower zone, emotional blocks.

Pressure is one of those features of handwriting that are

not yet sufficiently explored. Kraepelin, the famous psychiatrist, built a balance to weigh the writer's pressure in writing, but the results, important as they were, were not conclusive. The graphologist, on the other hand, lacks the instruments and means to carry out systematic research. Kraepelin's tests ought to be continued on a much broader basis.

PEN, PRESSURE, AND THE WRITER

No satisfactory knowledge of handwriting in general, and pressure in particular, can be acquired without some knowledge of the instrument employed, the pen. As a matter of fact, the pen a person selects should be one of our first clues to his personality. In this chapter I have mentioned various pens and their effect on the appearance of the script. I want to add a few more words about the pen and the writer.

The selection of a pen is, I believe, completely dominated by the thought of its product: we buy the pen that produces the script we want, or allow, to be seen. Consequently, perhaps nowhere do we see such determined and unreserved disguising as in stationery stores. Since I feel certain that pressure in a script is deliberately produced and exhibited (or hidden), there can be little doubt as to the deliberateness of the selection of the pen.

Just as there are writers who add pressure because it

looks and feels good to them,* so there are writers who buy pens with *dull points* that show an over-all pressure without the exertion of any real pressure, primary or secondary.** They may do so because of a lack of material ambition and a lack of any desire or capacity to assert themselves, about which they are somewhat self-conscious. They are the warmhearted though inert, the contemplative and sensuous, but also the helpless, who (without "undue" eagerness) are prepared to conform to the majority of people, to simulate the vitally strong by means of a kind of easy mimicry. But the fact that they have a liking for the appearance of pressure (vivacity, health, strength, beauty) tells us that most probably they also have a sense of beauty, music, art, and the pleasures of life.

Other writers buy pens with *so fine a point* that ordinarily their script would show only very fine, light lines. Strong pressure, primary and secondary, is necessary to show vitality or force with such a pen. Bookkeepers buy such pens for professional reasons. But their daily use is typical of writers who *like the effort,* the working with all their senses and energy, whose pleasure mounts with the obstacles they have to overcome. The pen with a very fine point permits them to *enjoy writing with all their vitality* and still show only the script of the meek, the soft, the domesticated. Obviously, in both the aforementioned cases the script's first impression as to its pressure is and was meant to be deceptive. This circumstance merits detailed examination.

Those *who do not care* what pen they u ͻ may also prove to be people who cannot be deterred by unfavorable circum-

---

* If the principles of education and re-education through handwriting are sound, the use of pressureless models (Palmer) in the instruction of boys would tend to make them effeminate or retard their reaching maturity. In any case, such artificial pressurelessness implies a denial of natural emotional expression.

** I mean stylos, glass pens, or pens with an inflexible "life-time" nib.

stances; they are also not very fussy in their dress or in their choice of friends or in their food; it is easy to get along with them, for they fit. easily into any group or organization.

There are, on the other hand, people for whom the pen is an instrument of definite importance. I recently received the following letter: "This specimen of my handwriting is submitted for your analysis. In accordance with instructions I am using a pen to which I am accustomed. However, it is not a pen that I like, but because of war conditions I have been compelled to use it. My preference is for a pen with a finer and much more flexible point." The writer is an artist and an aesthete, a man whose senses are both his capital and the source of his greatest satisfaction.

In general, it may be assumed that the *duller* the pen point, the less secondary pressure is required and planned; the *finer* the point, the stronger is the need for secondary pressure—with all that it implies.

THE WRITER AND THE INK

Most people use an ink of dark blue color, which is at one end of the spectrum, whereas others prefer vividly colored inks—red, which is at the opposite end of the spectrum, or green. The latter are the same people who like vividly colored blouses, ties, and wallpaper, with one difference: while it is not unusual to wear red or green blouses or ties, it is unusual to use red or green ink. Unusually highly developed senses, which the users of blue ink lack, are ascribed to these persons.

The importance of the ink in graphology goes further still. Ink is a liquid. Most people can write with ink and yet produce a clean manuscript; others cannot.

123

The latter are probably not very clean either in their thoughts, actions, or bodies.

Some people's penstroke is clear, sharp, almost dry, with clean borders; we almost feel physically the cleanliness,

coldness, stiffness, and sobriety that emanate from those three words. That of others is much smoother, with soft borders as though written with a brush or a piece of chalk; this soft-bordered script is typical of people who live on

their senses, such as painters or art students.

But perhaps most remarkable is a particular tendency of the ink in the pens of very sensuous people to flow, as it were, more freely, and then to escape.

Graphology, while certain that sensuousness (as opposed to spirituality or dullness) is based on that tendency, tries to interpret it further by observing the amount of ink that escapes, whether or not it forms a disturbing or perhaps vulgar element in that person's script, and the direction, if any, in which the escaping ink flows.

It is on the basis of such concepts and the zone theory that a tendency of the ink to flow toward the lower zone is

interpreted as an indication of (a more or less disturbing or vulgar) oversexed temperament.

PRIMARY PRESSURE

Pressure Patterns (regular): Vitality, will power, resoluteness, masculinity, diligence, maturity, intelligence, health

Pressure Patterns (excessive): Heaviness, sternness, depressiveness, obstinacy, excitability, argumentativeness, exhibitionism, vanity, hot-bloodedness, inhibition

Pressure on Stable Axis: *With positive style value:* Initiative, uprightness, staunch adherence to principles, tenacity, authoritativeness, pride, self-reliance, magnanimity, persuasiveness, paternalism
With negative style value: Hemannishness, boastfulness, egotism, concupiscence, brutality

PRESSURE

Pressure on Stable Axis (excessive):

Overcompensated sexual insufficiency, sexual inhibition, overambition, impetuosity, egocentricity, irritability, vanity, cockiness, libertinism

Pressure on Mobile Axis (stable axis "clear"):

Sublimated libido, see Chapter 17 and Appendix "Schizophrenia"

Pressure on Mobile Axis (stable axis equally stressed):

Split of vitality, see Chapter 17 and Appendix "Schizophrenia"

Spotty Pressure (in blotches):

Emotional unbalance, eruptive temperament
In lower zone: oversexed

No Pressure (fine lines):

Expediency, mobility, alertness, adaptability, ability, optimism, superficiality, sensitiveness, delicacy of feeling, feminineness, impressionability, geniality, tolerance, peaceableness, timidity, vacillation, irritability, lack of substantiality, lack of inhibition
With high style value: spirituality, loftiness, idealism, modesty
With small, clean script: secondary pressure
With sizable script: lack of discipline, lawlessness

No Pressure (black lines):

Warmheartedness, sensuousness, indifference, vanity, love of art, love of music, contemplativeness; sybarite

SECONDARY PRESSURE

Concentration, precision, self-discipline, persistence, pedantry, egocentricity, pettiness, reserve, pride, firmness in one's conviction, creativeness

126

Chapter 7

ZONES AND THEIR MEANING

THE GRAPHOLOGIST'S COMPASS

I hope that by now it is fully accepted that every mature writer has his peculiar and particular handwriting.

If we recognize that every mature writer can produce without models or premeditation or hesitation, in fact, at a moment's notice, his own unique handwriting, and that each time it is essentially the same, not a slavish copy of what he has been taught in school, but an unmistakable variation, then we cannot but believe that his hand follows a definite "structure" within himself. Indeed, there are numerous psychologists who are convinced that man "portrays" himself with every stroke of his pen.

This "portrait," I believe, is more faithful than **any** artist's or camera's. Although always the same, yet **never** the same, it gives the writer's most minute and intimate view of his inner self which other attempts at portraying him cannot penetrate.

Handwriting is also a "likeness." Where, for example, in the graphic portrait is the writer's head, body, legs? Writing is as though a person puts himself down on paper, supine, so to speak, looking into his own face. The upper part of a given letter is his head; the lower part, his torso and legs.

This handwriting sample came from a man with a heart defect. In the upper part of this *l*, right upstroke, there is a small portion of the stroke lacking; where the "hole" is,

127

ℓ

there is the projection of the writer's weak heart;* his hand is assumed to have avoided the traumatic spot.

The sample that follows was written by a girl incapacitated through infantile paralysis. We see the two strokes of

I was so terribly sorry

the lower part of the letter *y* reduced and "frozen" into one and then "broken off" somewhat above the middle: her legs were paralyzed from the hips down. Such perfect cases are rare. In most cases we recognize infantile paralysis

New York, N.Y.

(or other lasting damage to a subject's legs) through disproportionately shortened lower projections. It is difficult here to explain why the same causes may produce different projections in different scripts. A minor disease of the foot (eczema) expressed itself in the subject's writing through

difficult jobs

* The same "small portion of the stroke lacking" has been observed in handwritings after a writer has consumed quantities of coffee or alcoholic beverages.

128

an unexpected pressure at the end of his lower zone projections; but it is noteworthy that out of three *f*'s only two show that pressure.

I therefore repeat that a person's (anatomic) body image, projected on his script before him, shows him with face "up," his left side to the right, his right side to the left.*

This is the subject's physical picture. How does his mental picture appear in his writing? The upper "third" of his script is located in the intellectual, the conscious, sphere; his script therefore shows in the upper zone what he thinks and how he thinks, what he strives for, whether or not he has imagination, his pride and his ethical ideal. The lower zone, on the other hand, harbors manifestations of things which are not even known to the writer himself. There we see what fills his unconscious, particularly the unconscious motives of his conscious activities and urges. In the middle zone, where these two spheres meet, the writer's daily routine is portrayed, his social behavior and relations, his preferences and what he rejects, in short, that part of his personality which is known even to his casual acquaintances.

But handwriting not only has an up and a down, it also has a left and a right. We start at the left and gradually proceed toward the right; consequently what remains on the left, what we have left behind, generally symbolizes our past (home) our infancy and childhood, and, because she was our home, our mother. But it also indicates what we turn our back on: obscure, cloudy recesses of time, the sinister and forbidden because it is opposed to what is generally considered right, upright, forthright, righteous, therefore socially valuable.

----

*It may be suggested that the crossing of the neurological pathways, typical in muscle-brain center correlations, is here also relevant. We know that the right, the usual writing hand, is controlled from the left side of the brain. Further research is necessary to establish the body images in left-hand writers, so much more frequent in the United States than in other countries.

The right, then, is the direction in which we all hasten, and which therefore is the common goal, the ideal humanity strives for, the right and proper thing to do. There, on the right, also is our good neighbor, and beyond, the future and future generations and eternity; therefore, the right side also stands for the fathers, our father, and, in a woman's script, for the husband and father of her children.

DARK PAST	THE CONSCIOUS: *Ethics,*	FUTURE
(Idolatry)	*Intellect, Imagination, Ideas*	(Monotheism)
(Promiscuity)		(Monogamy)
Materialism	*Script*	Spiritualism
The Temporal		The Eternal
Mother Image	THE UNCONSCIOUS: *Emotions,*	Father Image
Self (Egoism)		You (Common Goal)
Introversion	*Instinct, Intuition, Drives, Urges*	Extroversion

MIDDLE ZONE: *Daily Routine, Habits, Customs, Likes and Dislikes, Social Relations.*

But while the mental projection divides the "writing field" into three zones, slowly "merging" with one another, the body image must appear in every letter, tall or short, according to this letter's proportions. Whether it is a small *a*, or an *l* or *g* or *f*, whether the letter reaches through one, two, or three zones, the body image appears in every letter as a whole.*

---

* The entire subject of the body image in handwriting is still comparatively new and unsettled. I have only reluctantly come to the conviction stated above, especially through some thorough reading in British and German literature on graphology. In a few of my own cases, as the two cited, I had the opportunity to test my convictions.

I have seen an ulcer of the nose "diagnosed"* simultaneously at the top of the subject's capitals and of his small (minimum) letters; a seriously injured ankle seemed to appear at the lower end of the subject's *p*'s as well as of his small letters. (Defects or other trouble ought to be clearest in the zone where this would be projected in a letter that goes through all three zones.)

It should be pointed out that the size of the handwriting has nothing to do with the stature of the writer. A tall writer may have a minute script, a midget a tall one. For the size of a hand is wholly dependent on the writer's mental dimensions, his mood and ambition and self-confidence.

The zone doctrine was first formulated by Pulver in 1930, and it has never been successfully challenged. On the contrary, during the years it has been in existence, it has widened and clarified the field of action of graphology to a remarkable degree. It is clear that Pulver, in his three zones doctrine, adopts and adapts for graphology Freud's concepts of personality structure, the Id, the Ego, the Super-Ego.

As to right and left Pulver's interpretations rest on man's most basic ideas of himself, his body and his orientation on earth, A. K. Coomaraswamy,** the learned educator and eminent scholar, advised me to that effect. All languages express approval of all that is right, disapproval of what is left, left-handed. So did St. Augustine, Doctor of the Church, 354-430 A.D. Under the heading Night and Day,*** I found:

> "Any man who thinks that there is no happiness for man, save only in these temporal goods and delights, and in the affluence and abundance of this world, is a foolish and per-

---

* See the book by Graphysique (pseud.), *Some Effects on Handwriting of Employment, Environment, and Heredity,* with an introduction to the study of handwriting as showing the effects of accidents and diseases (London: L. Ansbacher & Son, 1921).
** Dr. Ananda K. Coomaraswamy, Museum of Fine Arts, Boston, Massachusetts.
*** Erich Przywara, *An Augustine Synthesis* (New York: Sheed & Ward, 1945).

verse man, who maketh his left hand his right. . . . Yet **any** just man might also enjoy the same prosperity, as did Job. But Job held it for his left hand, not for his right; for he had no right hand except his perpetual and eternal happiness with God. His left hand was therefore given up to be stricken, and his right sufficed for him. . . . "What is the left hand, temporal, mortal, bodily happiness, I do not desire thee to shun it, but I do not wish thee to think it is the right hand. . . . For what is in the right hand? . . . God, eternity, the years of God which fail not. . . . There is the right hand, there should be our desire. Let us use the left hand for the time, let us long for the right hand for eternity. . . . If thou doest what thou doest for the sake of human affairs and of this life alone, thy left hand alone worketh; but if thou doest work for life eternal, thy right hand alone worketh. But if thou hast earnest hope for eternal life, yet still the lusts of this temporal life creep upon thee, so that thou heedest this even when thou doest a good work, hoping thou mayest have some reward here, thy left hand mingleth with the works of thy right hand, and this God forbiddeth (Matt. iv, 3)."

"Right and left play, of course, an important part in all traditional philosophies," Dr. Coomaraswamy continued. "For right and left as male and female perhaps the most convenient reference would be: . . . ." and here he advised me to quote two passages from two of the Hindu scriptures. In *The Thirteen Principle Upanishads,* under "Maitri Upanishad," I found: "This person who is in the eye, Who has his place in the right eye—This one is Indra; this, his wife, Who has her place in the left eye." And in *The Sankhayana Aranyaka,* Adhyaya VII: "The earth is the symbol of the former, the heaven of the latter . . . . The wife is the symbol of the former, the husband of the latter . . . . The mother is the symbol of the former, the father of the latter."

Bearing the zone doctrine in mind, we shall not err in interpreting a curve or a stroke, whether it be in English or Chinese, in a modern or an antique hand, as long as we know the school models of which the handwriting before us is a variation.

II

AT SECOND SIGHT

Chapter 8

SYMMETRY

A Yardstick of the Writer's Inner Balance and Development

Symmetry is one of the features in handwriting which we examine to establish its style value. We do so because it gives us a measure of a person's inner balance. For if the

hand's *upper zone* is strongly developed, but not the middle and lower zones, we may conclude we are dealing with a person of intelligence and ambition whose emotional development remained infantile and who cannot carry out very well what he undertakes. Therefore, pride and arrogance and conceit may prick him as they offend others. Also, if *upper*

and middle zones are strongly developed, but not the lower zone, this is an indication that the subject lacks the material rootedness and concern which are inseparable from our idea of successful planning. And how deep would such a person's thinking be?

135

confirmed

If the *middle zone* is strongly developed, but neither the upper nor the lower zones, we have a person whose sentimental and irrational (feminine) sensitivity and concern for himself are likely to result in much emotional pain, for he lacks those consolations which a well-cultivated mind and a harmonious realism offer. And if the *lower zone* is more

for

strongly developed* than the upper and middle zones, this writer is too much concerned with material success and pleasures, and at the same time is too sober, ponderous and too slow in his thinking.

An underdeveloped *middle zone* between prominent upper and lower zones also disturbs the symmetry of a script.

Frankly

Writers with such handwritings are ambitious, intelligent

---

* I have encountered overdeveloped lower zones combined with heavy pressure and downward sloping lines in the script of persons who complained of depressed moods.

136

and can do successful planning, and their emotional life is mature, but their everyday life, the realization of their plans and hopes, are not what they ought to be; these writers are careless and oblivious of the impression they and their ways make upon others.

The saddest picture is perhaps that of a writer whose script seems to have everything but an *upper zone,* and who

therefore has neither imagination nor ideals, neither intellectual interests nor ambitions, no real pride, no ethics and, I dare to say, no brains.

There seems to be no such thing as a well-developed single zone. If one zone is clearly more strongly developed than the other two, it is usually overdeveloped. *Overdevelopment of one zone always occurs at the expense of one or both of the others.* The consequence of such one-sided excesses is that lack of inner balance which makes for deeply dissatisfied and hence unruly, revolutionary, and "explosive" humans. In the more extreme cases, they are the stuff of which anti-Semites, Negro and communist baiters, xenophobes, bullies, and other unbalanced foes* of democratic society are made.

Symmetry in handwriting is also threatened through excesses in pressure; the chapter on "Pressure" deals with these. And there are also the excessively narrow and excessively wide letters, treated in the chapter on "Size of Letters." Excesses in slant are treated in "Slant."

---

* In the Appendix ("Persecution Mania") I show that a paranoiac's script, in particular, is characterized by unbalanced development, for the most part, at the expense of the middle zone.

On the other hand, absolute symmetry exists only in theory. We accept a hand as symmetrical if the letters of each zone are more or less of the same height, width, and slant; if the distance between the letters is fairly even, and the proportions of the letters harmonious. This "more or less" standard is no concession to mediocrity nor an expression of laxity. Any better than "more or less" symmetry could be only of purely mechanical or artificial or neurotic origin. The proposition that neuroses are the punishment we suffer for the mechanization of life cannot be dismissed by graphology.

Fair symmetry, therefore, is satisfactory evidence of stability and inner self-control; more perfect symmetry would be less convincing. (Pulver is confident that the more mature the writer [or nation], the smaller is the difference in the development of the three zones.)

The writer of a symmetrical hand probably is not a very lively, spontaneous, or imaginative person. He is reliable, hospitable, helpful, industrious, judicious: the good citizen. With a not very high style value we may find him dull, even apathetic. At any rate, he will not enrich our lives. True, lack of inner balance which, in some individuals, is the cause of constant protests and asocial activities, in others plays a creative role. But only the dissatisfied *and* gifted will feel the urge to improve some things and create others.

That asymmetrical development may also be indicative of physical defects is now certain. A stunted lower zone, for instance, may be observed in the handwritings of people with leg or foot defects, such as club foot or paralysis.

138

SYMMETRY

Symmetry (generally):	Even temper, order, peaceableness, contemplativeness, serenity, indifference, rigidity, apathy, unresponsiveness, callousness
No Symmetry (generally):	Impressionability, sensitiveness, progressiveness, curiosity, alertness, irritability, moodiness, oversensitivity, excitability, unruliness, criticism, crankiness
Upper Zone, overdeveloped:	Enthusiasm, idealism, religiousness, pride; ambition, but lack of ability to realize it; eccentricity, lack of objectivity, unruliness, irritability, oversensitivity, egocentricity, conceit, zealousness
Upper Zone, neglected:	Irreligiousness, lack of intellectuality, lack of ideas, materialism
Middle Zone, overdeveloped:	Sentimentality, feminineness, overconcern with oneself, self-assurance, presumptuousness, conceit, (overcompensated inferiority complex)
Middle Zone, neglected:	Reserve, objectivity, philosophical outlook, frugality, unpretentiousness, modesty, masculinity, impracticality (inferiority complex)
Lower Zone, overdeveloped:	Heaviness, sentimentality, matter-of-factness, realism, athleticism, technical talent, exactness, conscientiousness, good observation, attention to details. sobriety, pedantry, slow thinking; with much pressure: passion, sensuousness; without pressure: materialism (money complex) (P)
Lower Zone, neglected:	Lack of realistic outlook, lack of a sense for materialistic necessities, sexual immaturity, sexual fear or trauma (damaged or incapacitated legs or feet)

139

SYMMETRY

Over-all Size of Script

Small script: Realism, concentration, sobriety, pedantry, devotion, modesty

Sizable script: Enthusiasm, exaltation, idealism, liberalism, spirit of enterprise, self-confidence, vaingloriousness

Chapter 9

LEGIBILITY

A Measure of the Writer's Sense of Purposefulness

Writing is a means of communicating with others. Its function as a means of keeping records for our own purposes is secondary. Even in the age of the typewriter the hand-written letter is still the preferred medium for personal communication. It is generally considered that a person's education is incomplete unless he has acquired an adequate penmanship. The necessity for a legible hand is therefore self-evident, and teachers try to impress this fact upon us. While we are taught the form of letters, we are admonished to write legibly.

After several years of instruction in penmanship the admonition to write legibly must be assumed to have become second nature with us. If a person can remember the form of letters, there does not appear to be any reason why he should forget the injunction to write legibly. In fact, in a normal person, the wish to write to someone and the wish to write legibly must be one and the same. Accordingly, if a person writes, but not legibly, we must assume that he does not want to. This is the consensus of most leading graphologists, and psychoanalysts would probably concur.* Certain mental defects are, of course, likely to nullify the most serious attempt to write legibly.** A normal mind produces a legible

---

* We refer to the psychoanalytic discussions of psychopathology in everyday life by Freud and others.
** See Appendix, "Schizophrenia."

hand—unless the particular mind's master chooses differently.

The fact of legibility in a handwriting and its degree are not so easy to establish. We read whole words at a time, some of us whole phrases. Consequently, one or even several illegible letters in a word will not prevent us from correctly guessing what the word is from the context. As experienced readers we really do not mind a not wholly legible hand. As graphologists we must be less lenient.

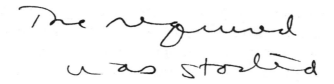

To establish the legibility of a handwriting, we must try to read it word by word. Only when a handwriting proves to be legible in a word-by-word examination can it be pronounced legible.

To interpret a hand graphologically, on the basis of its legibility, we must ask ourselves why a person may choose to write, yet at the same time write illegibly. *Lip service* is the phrase that comes first to our mind. To let the gesture stand for the act is the intent of one who writes but does so illegibly. Or he may consider himself so superior that reading his missive is the recipient's duty; *conceit* and *arrogance*, therefore, may also lead to illegible handwriting.

Or we may write the message though we would prefer to keep its contents to ourselves. In this case it may be *affectation of mysteriousness,* or *neurotic anxiety,* or *psychotic suspiciousness,* or perhaps even a *persecution complex* that blurs our hand. It was distrust that created cipher or code writing.

142

Paranoia or persecution mania, to be sure, does not make a handwriting wholly illegible. On the contrary, paranoiacs

often write meticulously legibly, as though trying their best not to arouse any suspicion. But there simultaneously appear certain *isolated illegible characters or words;* * they look like corrections, but the result is always almost complete illegibility. Paranoiacs seem to be feverishly bent on improving themselves and apprehensive over what might be misinterpreted and criticized by others, but it probably is part of their mental disorder not to succeed but rather to make things still worse.

A person with an illegible or neglected hand cannot be called either sincere or co-operative. For if he has nothing to hide, or really wants to be understood by his neighbor, why should he write illegibly? We must assume that he does not care whether or not we can read his letter. This is not the way of a considerate person. Indeed, *inconsiderateness, carelessness* (in clothing, too), *insincerity,* and even bad manners may be observed in people with barely legible hands. Very probably, they would also be unpunctual, disorderly, and indolent.

---

* See Appendix, "Persecution Mania."

143

There was a time when well-educated people, and especially intellectuals, thought it beneath them to write a legible

handwriting. Freud has, I think, interpreted the illegible hand of doctors, for instance, as part of their professional pride and secretiveness; they do not want the layman to understand their notes obviously reserved for other doctors or pharmacists. However, it is quite conceivable that some scientists or thinkers, *very much detached from the world,* forget that others may also wish to read their writings (Einstein obviously is not one of these; his handwriting is legible).

People with little training in penmanship do not write illegibly or carelessly. Their writing may look rather helpless, untrained, but it is often remarkably legible.

A person's illegible signature does not admit of any complimentary interpretation. For how much trust can be placed in a document if the signature that is to prove the signer's determination to carry out his promises cannot be deciphered? In a sense, *an illegible signature annuls* the document it pretends to put in force. (Only an anonymous letter or a ransom note go well with an illegible signature.) A special kind of illegible signature, the paraph, is used by people who think they are above the necessity of identify-

("Adolf" in Adolf Hitler's signature)

ing themselves by means of their signature. The best known case is Napoleon and the man with *Napoleonic aspirations.* If a man thinks of himself as one whom everybody must know and blindly obey, why should he bother to write his signature legibly? Indeed, a paraph will suffice.

If examination of the handwriting sample reveals that *here and there one letter stands for another* very plainly, for example, an *l* for a *b* or an *h* for a *k,* we know from experience that the sample originated with a liar, a swindler, or a cheat.*

Indistinct figures are made by *careless* people and people whose attitude in financial matters is not clear. But figures than *can be misread,* for example, a 5 for an 8, or a 1 for a 7, and so on, are associated with fraudulent intentions on the part of the writer.

Legibility, on the other hand, is characteristic of *sincere* individuals and of people who have a good capacity for *purposeful* work. Legible handwriting may also be associated with orators, teachers, and pedants; the style value will tell us whether the hand is that of a great teacher or merely a pedant's.

A very legible hand, of model penmanship, is desired by those who instinctively understand its implications and want to profit from our preferences: the *wolves in sheep's clothing* and the *confidence men.* (The head of the German Gestapo, Heinrich Himmler, had an "impressively" legible hand.) But the confidence man or swindler will certainly betray himself through ambiguous figures, "misplaced" letters, or other telltale signs such as "arcades."** To be sure, the legible hand is also the mark of merely *conventional* people.

---

* See Appendix, "Habitual Liar."
** See Chapter 11, "Connections of Letters."

LEGIBILITY

Illegible and Neglected
Handwriting:

Unworldliness, carelessness, individualism, unco-operativeness, inconsiderateness, bad manners, insincerity, unpunctuality, indolence; haughtiness, arrogance, impenetrability, suspicion, neurotic fear, distrust

Legible Handwriting:

Sincerity, purposefulness, co-operativeness (good speakers and teachers, pedants)

"Impressively" Legible:

Wolves in sheep's clothing; "confidence men"*

---

* See also the discussion of shark's tooth in the chapter on "Connection of Letters."

Chapter 10

SIZE OF LETTERS

The concept of handwriting as gesturing enables us immediately to understand why the size of a letter (gesture) is indicative of the writer's self-reliance, buoyancy, bearing, and largeness—the last word actually covering most of the interpretations in question: *big, extensive, liberal, pompous.* But the above interpretations are only generalities, contours. To make them yield details, we must define "size."

·Like any other design on paper, a letter may extend in four directions: up, down, to the right, and to the left. A "tall" letter has a mainly up-down dimension, a "wide" letter a left-right dimension. But a letter may be both tall and wide; and may it not be too tall in comparison to its width, too wide in comparison to its height?

The solution to these seemingly countless variations is provided by what we know about zones. To be classified as "tall" or "wide," a letter must reach beyond its "allotted"

zone into a neighboring zone. If, on the other hand, a letter is extremely small or narrow, it obviously fails to fill its "allotted" space, it shrinks from the neighboring zones.

Tall capitals, extending themselves beyond the propor-

tionately established height of the upper zone, are typical
of the person who "towers" above the rest of humanity,
of the one who would *like* to tower above the rest of us, and
of the one who has his head in the clouds. The farsighted
and the visionary, too, push higher and higher. So do the

proud and the religious, the magnanimous and the pre-
tenders, the independent and the haughty.

Beyond these interpretations, capitals also have a special
meaning as the first letters of a word, our name, for instance.
For initials, whether they are capitals or not, are the "face"

we present to the addressee, to the world. Tall initials are
characteristic of the person with the *impressive bearing,*
whose appearance (depending on the style value) commands
respect—or annoys us because of its presumptuousness.

Tall "minimum" letters,* "invading" the upper zone,
are generally demonstrations of the claim to more "lebens-

---

*A "minimum" letter is Palmer's term for those small letters which,
according to my scheme, occupy the middle zone only, such as *a, c, e,* etc.

raum," or more specifically, the *desire for greatness*. They also imply a certain overemphasis and overrating of the practical and sentimental aspects of life. Therefore, tall minimum letters (high middle zone) are one of the features in handwriting that betoken the female sex ("biological egoism" is the phrase Pulver has coined for it). For this

bes t

desire for greatness, without the proper tools or with no disposition to exert oneself, projected in the wrong place (the middle zone instead of the upper zone), together with the overemphasis on the sentimental, has a feminine aspect, in women and men. This interpretation is underlined by

afternoon

the fact that tall minimum letters crop up in the hands of writers who want to lift their drab daily work above the "pedestrian" level, and those who think their daily work ought to receive more recognition than it does.

We also find these tall small letters (high middle zone) in the hands of those who like good food, a well-kept cozy home, the assurance of "plenty"; of "regal" persons (mostly women), and of naïve or presumptuous claimants of this quality. And just as these claims and desires are fleeting and vain, so is the tallness of small letters: with impressive writers, they change from tall to small very quickly. A depressed mood (or depressing experience) first depresses

149

the letters of the middle zone; good news makes them soar.*

Both capitals and minimum letters may also extend themselves beyond their "allotted" zones by reaching into the lower zone. In such case, the writer's intention can only be to get hold of, to understand and utilize the instinctual

Sterling

and unconscious, which has its projection in our hand's lower third.

They have been observed in the hands of poets, painters,

Longfellow.

(Henry W. Longfellow)

musicians, and authors, whose themes are man's soul, his musical sense, his dreams, or his submerged traditions, including the mystic and the mysterious. Because most of these themes also force the writer (and his audience) to hark back to his and their remotest past, these extended letters of all sizes are always wide open toward the left, as

---

* I have had the opportunity to observe a case in which the middle zone in the script of a woman shrank to one-fourth its normal size after she had received news of the death of her beloved father.

(Martin Buber)

though they would try to capture the unconscious and un-
named contents of that lower zone; one cannot imagine a
poet's or musician's handwriting without these "ladles."

Their audience, also, is characterized, for the most part, by
letters that connect the lower with the middle zone; so are
people who employ psychology in their daily occupation:

psychologists, physicians, social workers, and all those interested in the practical application of psychological principles.

There are letters that naturally occupy both the middle
and the lower zones (such as g, j, p, q, y). If they reach into

(Washington Irving)

the upper zone, they are to be interpreted exactly like tall minimum letters. Their overextension into the lower zone, or simply a "long-legged" *f, g, j. p, q,* or *y,* is doubly significant. We are generally taught to keep our upper zone letters taller than our lower zone letters. The specimens of Palmer Method Penmanship show variable relations; sometimes the relation seems to be about 5:3. However, in many

hands we find *this relation reversed:* the upper zone, which is supposed to be taller, is shorter than the lower zone, which is supposed to be shorter: the lower zone is doubly strengthened at the expense of the upper. Interpretation must consider this double inversion, and cannot help concluding that it is indicative of a certain anti-intellectual and unintellectual outlook cultivated by crass realists, materialists, 100 per cent businessmen. These interpretations hold for the pressureless, overdeveloped lower zone.

But we also find inordinately extended *g*'s and so on *with pressure*. We may then assume that the writer is after more direct, tangible sense gratifications. (Athletes and dancers are among those whose hands show an extreme extension of the lower zone, with pressure.)

Small capitals are typical of the person who is modest and objective, who concentrates on facts, not on ideas; who

152

American

also does not care to or cannot look beyond his own "baili-wick." But he is what we call a good reliable worker, a realist, a collector of facts rather than an inventor.

provided

Small minimum letters show the concentrating, frugal, and masculine worker. Small and carefully executed mini-mum letters have been seen in the handwriting of first-rate research workers, teachers, scientists, and thinkers, who keep themselves under the strictest self-control so as to be able to accomplish what they undertake (Nietzsche, Einstein). However, it should be noted that inferiority feelings and temporary depressions also express themselves in small minimum letters (middle zone).

A letter may not only be tall or small or deep, but also wide or narrow; it may widen itself in a left-tending or right-tending direction, or shrink from these directions; it also may widen itself to a reasonable extent or at the expense of its neighbors.

To judge, for example, the width of a letter in an indi-vidual handwriting, we must know the penmanship models on which this handwriting is based. In Palmer's models such letters as *e, i, o, a,* and *s* are supposed to be taller than they are wide, the *m, n,* and *w* wider than they are tall. Only deviations from these norms can be considered "wide" or "too wide," "narrow" or "too narrow."

153

what

The wide letter, the letter that takes up more than its "allotted" space as it moves to the right, is typical of the spontaneous, broadminded, and "large" writer, who is sociable and sympathetic, eager to share with you and willing to let you share with him; he is "extroverted." But

and

if the letter is "too wide," if it seems to spread and unfold, as it were, at our expense, the writer is obtrusive, impudent, or simply an intruder.

The narrow letter, the letter that has surrendered part of its "allotted" space, is characteristic of the inhibited, un-

beneficial

easy, narrow-minded, economical writer, who is not sociable, who is neither prepared to share with you nor desirous of having you share with him; he is "introverted." But if a letter is "too narrow," then our subject is timid, seclusive, suspicious, and avaricious. A narrow initial letter of a word betrays particularly the socially timid.

We often see *narrow letters widely spaced, or wide letters closely following each other.* Obviously, this is a coincidence of two contradictory tendencies: narrow letters widely spaced reveal one whose sympathy and generosity are either simu-

154

Careful

lated or forced upon him by circumstances. Wide letters narrowly spaced betoken the liberal and sympathetic person

wart

who simulates the economical and concentrated worker either voluntarily or because of circumstances.

Another special case is *wide letters, right-slanted or left-slanted*. In the former there is an excess of extroversion, or boldness and lack of reserve; the latter constitutes the co-incidence of two contradictory tendencies, or, in the particu-

Very sincerely yours

lar instance, simulated width with all that it implies. This interpretation is based on the belief that certain traits en-hance, while others block each other. Width and right slant have the same tendency to the right, width and left slant contradict each other. So do tallness and narrowness,

Madison

width and smallness, tallness and lack of pressure, smallness and pressure, to mention just enough examples to give the reader a general feeling for compatibility and incompatibility in handwriting.

Sometimes we observe in a wide handwriting a *"sudden" narrowness,* or a *"sudden" width* in a narrow handwriting; in both cases we must assume that the sudden trait is the one to be interpreted, showing the true nature of the writer, camouflaged through self-imposed discipline or for the purpose of deception.

Wide handwriting is generally typical of the imaginative, the artistic, as well as the fantasy-filled and boastful writer. "Lean" handwriting, on the other hand, marks the reasonable, critical, sober, and also unimaginative, and therefore inartistic writer.

In the preceding discussion of an increase in width, we have assumed widening tendency to the right; but there are exceptions. On the basis of what we know about zones, a *left-tending increase* means the writer's desire to "include" the past and the mother. Such yearning, if conscious, appears in the upper and middle zones, if unconscious, in the lower zone.

But letters never stand like soldiers: one direction, one size. For the most part, they are a mixed crowd of short and tall, narrow and wide characters. Even the same letter will not always have the same shape and size; a person with imagination sometimes has two, or even more forms for it. As to size, only the very self-controlled person is able to maintain the same size throughout his script; the vivacious, moody, excitable, nervous, and hot-tempered express themselves in a variety of sizes.

In a class by themselves are the *capitals, initials,* and the *last letters* of words. We believe that man is in the habit of portraying himself in his handwriting. This portrait of man is most impressive in capitals and the first letter of a word. There the writer exhibits himself with gusto and, at least unconsciously, with the idea and hope of impressing us.

While I have stressed throughout this work the expressive importance of capitals, I wish to emphasize here the significance of the first and last letters of written words.

For the *first letter shows us the writer's "front,"* the way he looks at us and wants to be looked at, his intentions and also his pretensions. The *last letter betrays the decision* the writer has arrived at, his final standpoint, the result of his "labor."

Therefore, if we wish to determine the writer's bearing, his initiative and intelligence, we must examine his initials;

but whether or not and how he carries out his intentions, whether he is reliable and co-operative or arrogant, this is expressed in the size, legibility, and form of the last letter.

The letters between the first and the last letter, the body of the word, so to speak, portray the process of thinking that leads the writer from an intention to an accomplishment, a decision, an act. A clear, well-proportioned last letter indicates a clear and trustworthy decision; an illegible, neglected, or omitted last letter is a warning. A disproportionately tall last letter is characteristic of the person who not only has an opinion, but insists on it—because he has character, or because he is arrogant, opinionated.

Another important category is the *growing* and the *diminishing capital*. A capital, usually formed with evident pride and joy, and the most demonstrative character that dominates the handwriting, tells us more about the writer's intellectual aims (see discussion of tall capitals and small capitals) and the way he approaches them than the more modest (and

secretive) small letters. The growing capital, then, is an image of our *ambition,* and our envy of and our desire for

158

greatness; the diminishing capital denotes (condescending) *pride in intellectual achievement.*

The size of letters seems to belong to the features of a hand that can be analyzed at first sight, but this is not so. For only careful examination of a hand will show the "hidden" sizes.* A sizable handwriting that has, here and there, minute letters, a small hand that has, here and there, quite sizable characters (watch the middle zone!), do not at first sight show their true sizes. They readily exhibit the writer's pretensions, but his true "size" is hidden. We must therefore look twice before we can be sure what size of letters we have before us.

---

* See Appendix, "The Inharmonious Personality."

Size of Letters

GENERALLY

Wide Script: Imagination, warmth, artistic talent, sense of beauty, boastfulness, confusion, fantasy, insincerity

Lean Script: Reason, criticism, objectivity, coolness, aridity, harshness, sternness

UPPER ZONE

Tall Capitals: Intelligence, ambition, spirit of enterprise, farsightedness, independence, dignity, solemness, religiousness, unworldliness, magnanimity, pride, haughtiness, pretention, presumptuousness, megalomania, will to dominate; visionary, idealist, dreamer

Small Capitals: Dullness, sternness, docility, solidity, thoroughness, realism, materialism, provincialism, demonstrative modesty

Tall and Lean Capitals and Initials: Social timidity, professional jealousy, ambition without adequate imagination, sobriety, coolness, rigor

Tall and Wide Capitals and Initials: Imagination, broad-mindedness, artistic talent; muddleheaded, braggart

MIDDLE ZONE

Tall Minimum Letters: Desire for greatness, enthusiasm, hero worship, pretentiousness, eccentricity, hysteria, delusions of grandeur, fondness for food and comfort; female or feminine writer

160

Too Tall, Narrow Minimum Letters:	Overcompensated inferiority complex
Small Minimum Letters:	Gift for scientific work, objectivity, philosophical thinking, strict self-control, frugality, little concern for food and comfort, emotional independence, pedantry, feeling of inferiority, depression
Last Letter Taller Than Preceding Ones:	Readiness to defend own convictions, arrogance, lack of sensitivity to others
Last Letter Smaller Than Preceding Ones:	Tendency to yield, lack of backbone, human understanding
Last Letter Illegible, Carelessly Written, or Omitted:	Not always willing or able to finish task undertaken; mental reservations, indecision, opportunism; does not always keep word
Some Minimum Letters Reaching into Lower Zone:	Interest in practical application of psychology: psychologist, psychiatrist, author, poet, musician, social worker, pedagogue
Wide Minimum Letters:	Spontaneity, generosity, sociability, sympathy, vivacity, lack of affectation
Narrow Minimum Letters:	Modesty, economy, restraint, reserve, "introversion"
Too Wide Minimum Letters:	Superficiality, impatience, haste, negligence, lack of restraint
Too Narrow Minimum Letters:	Anxiety, distrust, timidity, calculation, egoism, inhibition
Sudden Narrow Letters in Wide Hand:	Width is only simulated, contrary interpretation applies
Sudden Wide Letters in Narrow Hand:	Narrowness is only simulated, contrary interpretation applies

LOWER ZONE

Capitals Reach into Lower Zone:	Intellectual interest in the unconscious, typical of: poets, authors, painters, mystics, musicians, great psychologists
Long-looped Wide Letters (with pressure):	Sensuality; natural man, student of nature, athlete, dancer, swimmer; fond of walking and dancing
Long-looped Wide Letters: (no pressure):	Realist, materialist, 100 per cent businessman, often anti-intellectual (money complex) (P)
Lower Zone Loops Open Themselves Toward Middle Zone:	Psychologist, psychiatrist, all those interested in man and his soul
Long and Wide Loops:	*Loop widened toward left (backward):* unconscious mother fixation; *loop widened toward right (forward):* unconscious father fixation

A FEW INCONSISTENT OCCURRENCES

Tall, Wide Letters, right-slanted, without pressure:	Lack of concentration, lack of reserve, prodigality, lack of thoroughness, impatience, lack of intellectual substance; pretender, schemer, dreamer, undisciplined and reckless person
Tall, Wide Letters, left-slanted, without pressure:	Simulated generosity, sociability, and sympathy; contrary interpretation applies
Small Letters, with pressure:	Inhibition, slowness, heaviness, excitability, explosiveness
Left Slant with heavy pressure:	Grave inhibitions

Chapter 11

CONNECTION OF LETTERS

THE WRITER'S ATTITUDE TOWARD CO-OPERATION WITH HIS FELLOW MEN

Writing is based on twenty-six letters which we assemble into words. The word "apple," for instance, is written by putting together an *a*, a *p*, another *p*, an *l*, and an *e*. This collecting of single, *unconnected* letters to form words was the original way of recording, and is still in use in oriental writing systems and in printing plants.

In the fourth century A. D. (if not earlier) man began to connect the letters comprising a word. This new way of writing was called "running" or "current." The purpose of connecting the letters was not to make them appear as a single word; spacing would have done this and still does in our printed records. But the connecting of letters facilitates the process of writing; to write fluently, spontaneously, we must join the letters.

Thinking also involves connecting. To think and act logically, we must and do connect our thoughts with one another. One of the great educational tasks is to teach us how to connect our thoughts. After people have reached maturity, we can distinguish between ways of thinking which they have been taught, and those that are more or less original. This "mixture" of traditional and individual thinking is often peculiar and always typical of a person and he is not likely to give it up overnight. Therefore, as soon as we know how a person connects his thoughts, as soon as we have a notion of his way of thinking, we know him pretty **well.** We can, with a good degree of accuracy, predict his attitudes and often also his actions. Particularly, we can predict his attitudes toward other people and the quality of his social behavior, for as we connect our letters and thoughts, so we connect ourselves with the people around us. We thereby follow both the advice and the admonitions of our educators, at home and in school, and our own idea of good neighborliness and co-operation.

For instance, American education insists on garlands. But a mature American's hand sometimes shows one or even two different "links," in addition to or without garlands. From this it is clear that a person uses the links he likes, irrespective of what is practical or has been taught him. Graphology, therefore, undertakes to interpret the writer's idea of co-operation on the basis of his letter connections.

There are three widely used links: the *garland*, the *arcade*, and the *angle*. In addition there are three less widely used links: the *thread*, the *s-link*, and the *shark's tooth*. Each of these will be dealt with here.

The *Garland*, which seems the "official" connective link in all countries that use the Latin alphabet, and in Russia, has the form either of a platter, or a cup, or a calix. It is the most practical, quick, easy, natural and agreeable way of connecting two letters—the shallower the garland, the quicker and easier the writing.

In tests* the writers of garlands gave the following descriptions of their feeling: "I feel free"; "It feels like playing, dancing, smoothly progressing"; "It's like meeting friends with happy faces on a beautiful day"; "Garlands are musical, light, lovely, like a pastorale"; "This may be the way to paint watercolors"; "I have a feeling that everything is good, beautiful, all burdens are being taken from me"; "It has a soothing quality." The subjects of these remarkable tests were habitual writers of arcades or angles as well as garlands. Conducted as recently as 1938, these tests quite generally confirmed graphological interpretations that are centuries old.

The garland, like every other letter connection, has the form of both a *movement* and a *gesture.* As a movement it seems to be practical for the rhythmical, mobile, hasty, and unstable writer. As a gesture it suggests, depending on whether it is shallow or deep, an offering or a receptacle. Hence, we are likely to see the garland in the script of the enthusiastic dancer and the traveler, the mobile and the elusive, the youthful, the playful, and the gullible, the peaceable and the easygoing, the practical businessman who wants progress without friction and the superficial "trouble shooter" who prefers the expedient solution of a problem to the more difficult but more thorough one; indeed, the garland is the preferred link not only of the practical person but also of the person who does not care one way or the other.

As a *platter* the garland is excellent to receive and offer freely or to demonstrate openly what one possesses. Seen this way, the garland writer is understood to be receptive to anything new; he is "open for suggestions." And he does

---

* Johannes Walther, *Die psychologische und charakterologische Bedeutung der handschriftlichen Bindungsarten* (München: Neue psychologische Studien, 1938). Bd. 11, 3.

necessary

not "shut himself away from the world"; his mind and house are always "open for inspection." He is no plotter, no hermit, but neither is he an abstract thinker; he is rather the progressive and outdoor type who hates being "fenced in." But his hospitality and open-mindedness have in them something demonstrative, exhibitionist, sometimes even something shallow and indiscriminate. Therefore, the garland also suggests a tendency toward being careless (conventional, thoughtless, unconcerned, indifferent, negligent, and reckless).

very well

Deeper, more *cuplike,* the garland indicates the kind-hearted and sympathetic, and the collector; it functions also like a garner to be filled with valuables or trifles; for these qualities the garland is supposed to be the preferred letter connection of female (feminine) writers. He who collects may devote himself to rarities or common stamps, and by the same token he may be basically conservative and picayune, even narrow-minded (the mobile qualities of the garland being given up in favor of sedateness, quiet, contemplativeness, and complacency).

Really deep, *calixlike* garlands seem better suited to a deeply rooted impressionability and sentimental conservatism than to dancing and quick progress.

But the platter or cup or calix necessarily have a *bottom*. We must therefore ask how deeply do those new ideas and suggestions sink into the writer's mind? Does he permit his unconscious to emerge, does he allow "the imponderables" to enter his consciousness? Obviously, the garland writer's world is the visible, tangible, measurable world; he shuns the mystical, the deep, the abstract. And because he avoids the "depths of life," we can understand why the garland writer remains young, naïve, or as some call it, "immature," all his life. One who habitually cuts himself off from his unconscious, who never draws upon his intuition, may not suffer but he can never experience life fully.

laughter

Certain letters, such as *a*'s, *u*'s, *d*'s, and *b*'s, have a garlandlike bottom. If this bottom has an unexpected and irregular opening, we should be on our guard against criminal tendencies in the writer. We have seen such writing "against the rules" in the hands of murderers and very dangerous swindlers. To them, this opening, where it is not expected or permitted, seems a proud symbol of their lawlessness; at the same time, they provide themselves with "direct access" to the lower zone, the zone of instinctual drives and the unconscious which, if there is no inner check, can be supposed to be "at the bottom" of many criminal activities. (Graphological ethics does not permit one to mention criminal tendencies unless there are in the script other indications of similar import.)

Warning: Pressureless (indicative of instability), the good-natured garland (mobility, superficiality), if coincident with right slant (restlessness) and sizable script (exaggerated self-confidence), or excessive width (lack of inhibition) betrays those undisciplined and indomitable persons who are capable even of crimes because of their lack of discipline, their restlessness and inability to foresee the consequences of their actions.

It may be noted in passing that the wide, shallow garland (platter) is a first cousin of the thread, which will be discussed below.

The *Arcade* is a platter or cup or calix turned upside down, a vault or arch. Therefore, the garland writer and the arcade writer are opposites. The following are some of the "confessions," elicited by the tests, as to the arcade writer's nature: "I feel like resisting"; "It is an unkind feeling, not as flexible as garlands"; "To me it is like a cramp"; "I cannot help thinking of a locomotive pushing before her heavy masses of snow"; "I feel stymied, like fighting against some resistance"; "To me it is like hide and seek, and like lying in wait for somebody, perhaps also like pride and haughtiness"; "I feel like disguising myself"; "Like a veil"; "A hide-out"; "Faithful to myself"; "Much more serious than garlands"; "Defense rather than attack";

168

"I could write garlands in my sleep, arcades only when very much awake."

Indeed, the "reversed cup or platter" has been interpreted most contradictorily: as a trap or a fortress, as a gesture of inner independence or haughty reserve, as a gesture of plotters or stalwart defenders, as indicative of the most trustworthy or plainly treacherous, of the deep or the inscrutable.

As a form of movement the arcade is slower than the garland, and it presupposes a writer who keeps his eyes open, has a good, perhaps even an artistic sense of proportion, who knows instinctively what to aim at and where to land. Further, as a gesture, the arcade seems to serve two evident purposes: to hide something or to protect it; to shut out light and strangers, or to retire and contemplate and search within oneself; to erect a structure or edifice, such as a cathedral or dome, or barricades for defense and a trap for the unsuspecting.

As a letter connection the arcade writer's way of thinking and acting (as may be seen from such almost inconsistent statements as, "lying in wait for somebody" and "faithful to myself") cannot be gauged by ordinary means. Closed above and wide open below, the arcade writer relies upon his instinct and intuition rather than reason. He may be a sinister plotter or an artist who goes his own way. For in itself the fact that a person tries to hide something does not mean anything. The liar hides the truth, the plotter his scheme, the assassin his dagger, but the conscientious official hides important documents that are entrusted to his care, and shy, inhibited people hide themselves because they fear to be hurt and imposed on. Or take the builder; his arcade (vault, arch) is no hide-out, but a symbol of his technical constructions. Zeppelin, the inventor of the dirigible, used arcades to connect letters, but was not known to have hidden anything reprehensible.

In the interpretation of the arcade the style evaluation becomes of prime importance. Through it, we need never have any doubt whether a script belongs to a plotter or to an architect, to a thief or a technical genius, to a confidence man or a persevering founder of great enterprises who develops his plans quietly and privately. The more arched the arcade,

the more prominent become its artistic qualities; the flatter it is, the more it reminds us of a lid to cover up something.

Flat arcades have been identified in the script of hypocrites and intriguers; they are very easily overlooked or mistaken for garlands—a serious error.

As for the *Angle,* the connective link, for instance, in German script, the tests brought forth the following statements: "To me the most unnatural and brutal gesture"; "You have to be well on your toes"; "Like steel girders";

"A feeling of safety and certainty"; "Of stability"; "A military, cool feeling"; "Capable of overcoming any resistance"; "I feel as though I have a task and must not fail"; "Attack and aggression"; "Hardy, curt, precise, like a saber." These are highly contradictory statements, and indeed, angle writers have to reconcile within themselves very contradictory tendencies.

Unlike the garland or arcade, the angle is not one but two movements, and the abrupt gestures that alone produce an angle are without grace, flexibility, or the spirit of reconciliation; rather, the angle reminds us of a "hard task in which we must not fail," and "attack and aggression" at least against the beauty and freedom of movement.

The movements that produce an angle are of necessity slow,* pedantic (thorough, clumsy, difficult, definitely unspontaneous). To illustrate, a garland or arcade *i* may be made with two movements; to write an angle *i* we need three movements: We start with an upward stroke and stop

abruptly; the next move is downward until another abrupt stop; then we move up again. The comparison with a military march or a precision watch is inescapable.

The resemblance to a military march brings "discipline" to mind. We therefore conceive of angle writers as people who are willing to submit themselves to a rigid discipline, and who are prepared to impose such a discipline on their environment. They are reliable, firm, steadfast, and imper-

---

* See Chapter 13, "Pace of Writing": "The angle writer, therefore, is always a hedger."

turbable, but they are also dull, heavy, brutal, not to be stopped.

"Hardy, curt, precise . . ." interprets the angle writer also as unyielding, uncompromising, intolerant, cold, pitilessly logical. Principles are more important to him than individual considerations, the method often more important than the result; his aim is reason, not humaneness, not practicality or feasibility.

As a letter connection the angle is circumstantial, a geometrical drawing or technical structure, rather than a connecting link. It reaches "heights" and "depths." An angle can rarely be "microscopic"; a certain minimum height is indispensable to produce an angle, whereas a garland and even an arcade may be "stretched and flattened" almost to a thread. We therefore conceive the angle writer as capable

wenn das aussergalaktische

(Albert Einstein)

of abstract thinking, technologic discoveries, philosophic interpretation, but also of sophistry and cunning. The angle writer cannot relax, unbend; he must be active to feel well; without the right occupation he becomes querulous. Small wonder that some angle writers are considered cranky, unconciliatory and even humorless, awkward, and restless.

The double move in two divergent directions, without which no angle can be produced, permits further interpretations. The garland has no connection with the lower zone; the arcade has no connection with the upper zone; but the angle has one connection with both the intellectual, spiritual zone, and another with the emotional, instinctual, and mystical zone. This means that the angle writer's position with

172

respect to these zones is ambiguous, two-faced, contradictory. Though uninterrupted access to upper and lower zones may indeed permit the angle writer insights not vouchsafed to other writers, though he may be an excellent psychologist and a writer of deepest understanding of the human mind and heart, by the same token, he may, yet, mix the evident with the mystical, the lofty with the materialistic; he may be both intellectual and emotional, concrete and obscure, open-minded and reactionary, plain and undefinable, ethical and barbarous, a benefactor and a fiend.*

Merely on the basis of their letter connections one would expect the angle writer to understand both the garland and arcade writers; but while he considers the arcade writer congenial, he may find the garland writer "soft" and generally "wanting." The arcade writer may be supposed to find the garland writer a pleasant counterpart and to have sympathy for the angle writer. The garland writer feels mysteriously attracted by the arcade belle, yet looks with awe on the angle writer, whom he cannot "figure out." However, the thread writer, whom we are going to meet in a moment, leads them all by the nose: the angle, the garland, and the arcade writers.

again Thank you so much for

Before I proceed to less widely used letter connections, I must mention that very few individuals can or do maintain one type of link throughout their writing. Many writers mix angles and garlands and, more rarely, arcades. This

---

* Graphologically, there is a clue to these cycles in the fact that angles open themselves simultaneously toward the intellectual and the instinctual zones, but in separate compartments.

complicates the task of interpretation, but also makes it more fruitful. For such writers carry within themselves the most irreconcilable character traits. They are the people of whom every acquaintance gives a different description. If the various links are not clearly and firmly executed, we have

man

writers who cannot make up their minds, who are procrastinating, uncertain, and vacillating between two contradictory points of view. *For a general rule of letter connections is that a positive interpretation is dependent on a clear and tight and firm execution of the letter connection.* Firm

man

execution is an indication of the writer's willingness to stand up for his social convictions—no doubt a positive attitude!

GARLANDS

The most practical, quick, easy, natural, and agreeable
letter connection

Generally:

Plainness, uncalculating nature, naturalness, amiability, easygoing nature, obligingness, tolerance, liberalism, indulgence, forbearance, hospitality, curiosity, tactlessness, gullibility, thoughtlessness, boastfulness, talkativeness, optimism, progressiveness, adaptability, pliability, flexibility, mobility, superficiality, hastiness, undecidedness, instability, inconstancy, carelessness, fickleness, youthfulness, peaceableness, laziness, indifference, indolence, playfulness, rhythm, musicality, sentimentality, sympathy, complacency

Deep Garlands (calices):

Depressiveness, tendency to take everything tragically, inability to free oneself from depressive thoughts, deep, feminine sympathy for the needy and helpless, contemplativeness, sedateness

Enclosing Garlands:

Mental reservations, unspontaneous and calculated "kindness," scheming, narrow-mindedness, "picayunishness"

Flat Garlands (platters):

Practiced businessman who wants to proceed without friction, "trouble shooter"; conventional amiability, obliging manners, mobility, elusiveness, boastfulness, recklessness, unconcern, inconsiderateness

Square Garlands:

Strict conventionality, rejection of instinctual drives, narrow-mindedness; "stuffed shirt"

175

Supported Garlands (with concealing strokes):	Emotional inhibitions; needs sympathy in emotional life, somebody to "pep him up" and encourage him to speak his mind
Superfluous Garlands (such as flourishes):	Calculated amiability in order to ingratiate himself with people
Garlandlike Lower parts of letters, open at the bottom:	Criminal tendencies. *Warning:* Watch also other indications, *i.e.,* ambiguous letters, arcades, irregular, overelaborate flourishes, irregular, spotty blotches

ARCADES

Impractical, unnatural, but most "artistic" letter connection

Generally:	Pensiveness, meditativeness, shyness, reserve, cautiousness, secretiveness, oversensitiveness, deepness, good manners, formalism, impenetrability, mysteriousness, circumspection; relies on instinct and intuition rather than reason; insincerity, distrust, pretension, mendacity, tendency to scheme and plot; technical constructor, founder, artist, individualist
High Arcades (calices reversed):	Inwardness, self-sufficiency, poise, pride, formalism, extreme reserve, profoundness, artistic gifts
Flat (creeping) Arcades (platters reversed):	Hypocrisy, skillful and unobtrusive scheming

ANGLES

The difficult, precise, impractical letter connection that cannot be carried out without self-discipline and persistence; therefore, in contradiction with the principles of penmanship of the garland writer

Generally:

Firmness, decisiveness, pretentiousness, punctiliousness, logic, preponderance of reason, cold-bloodedness, callousness, compulsiveness, intolerance, sophistry, strictness, sternness, pedantry, obdurateness, reliability, conscientiousness, obedience, persistence, aggressiveness, irresistibleness, slowness, thoroughness, orderliness; lack of humor, *weltschmerz* (world weariness), heaviness, dissatisfaction, crankiness, grumbling, cunning, unfathomableness; tendency toward romanticism and mysticism as a means of calming or resolving inner conflicts; contempt for easy life; generally showing sharp and irreconcilable contrasts in behavior and contradictions in feeling

Small, Quick, but Firm Angles:

Reliable and imperturbable worker

Toronto

Angles with Frequently Changing Slant:

Irritability, excitability, inner conflicts, suspicion

unusual

Angles with Heavy Pressure:

mem

Fighting spirit, vehemence, brutal opposition, heaviness, domineeringness; when vocationally misplaced, a querulous, restless person (manic-depressive)

Narrow, Small Angles:

Strong emotional inhibition, avarice.

The letter connections treated in the following paragraphs have, to the best of my knowledge, never been methodically examined. The interpretations offered here are the traditional interpretations established, for the most part, by early French graphologists. But in my experience they have proven their value, and it is quite conceivable that, as in the case of the garland, arcade, and angle, a methodical examination of thread, shark's tooth, and s-link would largely confirm these interpretations. I believe, therefore, that the reader should be acquainted with them.

The *Thread,* indefinite and indefinable in comparison with such clear letter connections as garlands, arcades, and angles, may, if written without pressure, be taken as the symbol of the hasty or muddleheaded writer; for if we do not care how it looks, no link is so easily, quickly, and carelessly executed as a thread.

Sober realists and pedants would not feel at ease with thread connections. Their lack of form, of "character," their suitability for "changing sides" easily, their lack of "face" and "backbone," seem to belong to one who receives his impressions and counsel from everywhere, who is open to everything and anything, who tries to "avoid the issues," and whose hysterical ambiguity and many-sidedness escape definition. At the same time we would like to believe such a writer to be broad-minded and talented (even brilliant), but exactly where can his accomplishments be seen? Quick, pressureless threads have been found in the handwriting of confidence men and of people who, if need be, can understand and sympathize with everybody: opportunists. Also in the hands of people who do not stand up for their convictions, who know how to turn almost everything to account, and who cannot be pinned down.

But there are threads that show pressure, and their interpretation cannot be based on hastiness and indefiniteness. Such a writer refuses to be chained to definite and traditional rules because he wants to be free to follow his talents, his instincts, and what he believes to be his destiny. Such threads with pressure are found in the writing of people who acknowledge no fetters, who have creative instincts, and who instinctively do the right thing—that is, right for themselves.

When such "lawlessness" turns toward instinctual spheres, when the thread points toward the lower zone, it

is interpreted as instinctual lawlessness. The thread with an upward slope characterizes persons with high, acute intel-

ligence, who have open eyes for all that happens around
180

them, and an excellent gift of integration. They also have a wide perspective; but they lack stamina, and will not put up a physical fight even where it is necessary.

A variation of the thread is the *S-link*. The s-link is neither impractical nor indefinite; its screwlike form suggests countless applications (interpretations), and is not without its aesthetic aspects. The s-link is therefore interpreted as the (occasional) tool of those who rely on their instinct and intuition to guide them; who have ambitious aims which they pursue instinctively and, so to speak, blindly, without much regard for bourgeois considerations. They are excellent negotiators adaptable to any circumstances. S-links occur in all three zones, and both at the beginning and end of words; the interpretation must, of course, consider zone and location.

(Henry W. Longfellow)

The *double s-link* is very rare. To be exact, it is not so much a letter connection as a way of shaping letters. Some graphologists claim to have seen it in Napoleon's handwriting, others remember it from the writing of impenetrable and highly diplomatic people of rather questionable character and income. The sample here reproduced was written by

181

Longfellow, and none of the above character descriptions apply to him. The solution is found in the style evaluation. In negative scripts the double s-link is compared to a snake, in positive ones it is associated with people who are unable or unwilling to take a stand and of whom it can be said, as Herbert S. Gorman* said of Longfellow: "Incapable of saying 'no' . . . he emanates an aura of benignity, sweetness . . . he unties, never cuts, string . . . keeps huge quantities of cartridge paper cut to exact size, upon which he indites his poems in that surprisingly plain, round (!) handwriting which is so evenly spaced."

The term, *Shark's Tooth,* is in itself an interpretation of the link to which it applies. It looks like an angle, but it is not an angle; or, rather, it looks like a covered stroke, but again it is not; it is a shark's tooth, and it can bite. Easily overlooked in handwriting, it is characteristic of people whose business it is to profit, broadly speaking, through other people's credulity. The business need not be illegal. I have seen shark's teeth in the writing of women who were able to outsmart everybody, particularly their friends and husbands. It takes naïveté to fall prey to a shark's tooth writer, and wherever a naïve person and a shark's tooth writer meet, the former is in for some quiet, systematic, and pitiless bloodletting.

As we have seen from the preceding discussion, connections of letters are, despite their smallness, very rich in meaning. Writers who watch and try to disguise every stroke

---

* Herbert S. Gorman, *A Victorian American, Henry Wadsworth Longfellow* (New York: George H. Doran Co., 1926).

182

in their upper and lower zones are likely to pay little attention to the middle zone and the connections of letters which, for the most part, are located there. Therefore, these links are "franker" and more "communicative" than capitals. But it sometimes takes several pages before we can distinguish a shark's tooth from an angle, or a thread from a quick and flat garland. To the serious student of graphology this is one more reason for asking for several pages of material for an analysis.

THREADS

The letter connection that is all movement and not writing at all. Therefore, nobody can beat the thread writer's mental speed, but his writing remains shapeless, unconventional, and largely ambiguous.

Generally:

Open above and below, left and right, the thread permits the writer to see everything and to receive impressions from everywhere; born statesmen and entrepreneurs, who are capable of dealing with any situation, are thread writers; also neurotics, who are unable to make a decision, and swindlers, whose business it is to remain elusive and to talk themselves into and out of anything

Primary Threads (with pressure):

Instinctual creativeness, capacity for doing the right thing

Secondary Threads (without pressure):

Turncoat; too many impressions fight each other in the writer's mind; neurotic incapability of making a decision; opportunist; "brilliant" talents; unprincipled, fashionably dressed swindler

183

Thread with Upward Slope: Strong impressionableness, remarkable intelligence, accurate observation, gift of integration, psychological talent; born statesman, entrepreneur

Thread with Downward Slope: Instinctual lawlessness

S-LINK

Intuition, creative instinct; ambitious aims are pursued unceasingly and almost instinctively without much ado or regard for moral considerations; impressionableness; adaptability, suppleness, agility

DOUBLE S-LINK

In positive scripts: Incapability of saying "no," benignity, "sweetness," humaneness

In negative scripts: Many-faceted personality, a seeming gift for art, elusiveness, lack of principle, diplomacy (if clearly executed), suppleness, adaptability, capacity for facing any situation

SHARK'S TOOTH

Cunning, craftiness, astuteness, slyness; confidence man

Chapter 12

SPACE BETWEEN LETTERS

THE EXTENT TO WHICH THE WRITER ACTUALLY RELIES UPON CO-OPERATION WITH HIS FELLOW MEN OR UPON HIS OWN INTUITION

We are taught that the word is the smallest unit of meaning. We are instructed to connect all the letters of a word. Later in life we deviate to varying degrees. Some of us may continue to connect all letters carefully as we were taught; or we may introduce our own individual methods of connection.

Since letter connections, particularly the garland, definitely facilitate the process of writing (just as friendly co-operation with our neighbors facilitates most of our activities), the question arises as to why some people would like to abandon the use of letter connections. These persons must feel ready to proceed without this normal connectedness; they apparently feel free to break up the simple, meaningful unity of the word. To the extent that they indulge in such willful breaks, they may be expressing their *readiness to stand alone,* to rely upon themselves—or their *incapacity to feel or act co-operatively.*

(W. H. Auden)

This discarding of a characteristic feature of handwriting

185

is inherent and, indeed, indispensable in certain occupations. An artist, creative writer, or inventor must, while at work, rely on himself; certain professionals, particularly artists, are expected to be fully, or at least in large part, the conscious creators of their products.

promisit amplим it flans

(Philip Melanchthon)

But not only the creative person cherishes independence. Any person may be loath to co-operate with others; he may be in more or less open revolt against the "fetters" with which society binds its members to one another. Rather than ask for help, he will bake his own bread, build his own house, to the best of his ability. He may be a genius, an individualist, a hermit, or an anti-social neurotic. To be sure, he must also be a person with a certain inner conviction, who has very personal and perhaps original ideas and would not, for the life of him, admit that he often feels very lonely.

Hillside Hosp
Bellevue L.I.

Sometimes his way of thinking may be criticized as desultory, his way of acting as without direction (erratic, selfish, hasty, or unorganized). He is rather contemptuous of logic (which he calls "sterile"), especially other people's; he relies on his intuition, the results of which he considers superior to those of logic; if a new solution to an old problem is needed, he is more likely than anyone else to find it.

If we want a practical and reasonable person, who always remains safely within the limits of the observable, we should insist on one who, if possible, drops no link between the letters.

The concept of the word as a unit of meaning, a microcosm, leads us, among other things, to wonder what meaning an i-dot may have. As a rule, the i-dot, although part of the word, is not connected with it, but "suspended" above it as the sun is above the earth. From the standpoint of penmanship, i-dots are inorganic and undesirable because their use disturbs and disorganizes the fluency of the writing movement. Some writers solve the problem by omitting the i-dots from their script. They cannot be commended, however, for this solution. As in the case of the omitted t-bar (Chapter 17), we can, if need be, dispense with the i-dots, but in both cases the reading of a script is rendered difficult.

However, in the script of a few very intelligent, always discriminating, and sometimes creative thinkers we find a solution of the i-dot problem that is quite impressive: there the i-dots are no longer problems, they are included in the writing movement. This solution is satisfactory from both

the standpoint of penmanship and graphology. For what can better characterize the creative mind and the useful genius than his ability to dispose of a problem by making it part and parcel of our conscious world?

For most people, heaven and earth, convictions and practical life, intellect and emotions, are incompatible and kept apart; they think (or profess to think) one way and act an-

other. A few are able to unite these two "worlds." They
live as they think, they act according to their beliefs; for
them heaven and earth are one indivisible whole. We are
therefore not astonished to find the connected i-dot, for
instance, in the script of integral and comprehensive thinkers,
often of world stature, such as the historian and economist
Sismondi; of great physicists, such as Torricelli and Einstein;
of poets and moralists, such as Eichendorff and Lessing; and
of great discoverers, such as Pasteur.

If we look more closely, we see three distinct ways of
connecting the i-dots with the word: The connecting link

liefern, weil der

(Albert Einstein)

may start with the *preceding* letter and end with the i-dot;
or it may start with the i-dot and end with the *following*
letter.

simplified

Or it may connect the i-dot *both ways,* from the preceding letter to the i-dot to the following letter.

closer

We call a thinker, who approaches a problem (i-dot), so
to speak, with an opinion intuitively conceived and formed
188

in the abstract, a theorist, a philosopher, or a dogmatist; **to** him who "draws" conclusions from a given case or experience (i-dot) we attribute the gift of integration; and to the person who connects his i-dots on both sides we attribute **both an intuitive and philosophical, and a logical and integral** way of thinking. (Since these two ways of thinking cannot always be reconciled with each other, we must ascribe to the latter writer a certain intellectual inconsistency, and a tendency to get stuck in an argument or problem.)

In order that the reader may fully understand the connected i-dot, I must add that I have not yet seen a script in which all the i-dots are connected with the body of the word; there are always some connected and some separate. My impression is that those writers who solve the i-dot problem by including the dot in their writing movement, do so only when and where it is reasonable. For instance, in the following word, both i-dots are included.

In the word "distribute" only the first i-dot is included, the second remains unconnected. If we try to imitate this

script, we shall find that only in the first case is the inclusion of the i-dots unquestionably practical because the letters *s* and *n* that follow the *i*'s are as high as the *i*'s. But in the second sample, the pen has to jump from the second *i* to a *b*; in such a case the writer can dot the *i* just as well. The connected i-dot, therefore, seems to be the badge of the highly intelligent, discriminating, and inventive, though perhaps sometimes compulsive, writer.

Much less interpretation can be offered by graphology in the case of missing i-dots. A script without a sufficient number of i-dots is difficult to read. For instance, the following words,

I'd point it out to friends,

written by a student of psychology, cannot be read easily. At least equally difficult to read are the following two lines from a message written by Bruno Hauptmann:

Mr Lindbergh only wasting time with his search

The question now arises what these two subjects have in common. Of Hauptmann we know that he was convicted of a murder which he never confessed; his script looks like that of a schizophrenic. The first sample also impresses me as seriously disturbed. Remembering that the well-placed i-dot belongs to the intellectual and ethical zone, can we assume that persons who leave out their i-dots lack well-grounded ethical ideals? Or would the absence of i-dots be indicative rather of a disturbance in the writer's intellectual mechanism? I am not yet prepared to go beyond these guesses.

Noon

Palmer encourages the use of elaborate extra garland strokes or links even after the last letter of a word. Since these strokes do not always facilitate the writing, I believe they should be dropped; they are redundant. But in the script of a writer who has not, with good sense, simplified and shortened them, even a redundant link is meaningful. Its meaning is treated in Chapter 18, "The Circular Stroke." Here I am interested only in those who have dropped these links completely.

To omit such an end stroke takes a special effort, to be sure, for nobody can bring his pen to a dead stop without determination and self-discipline. I therefore concede such a writer a *strong will*—but only in minor tasks (obstinacy) —as well as a lack of sympathy and a definite unwilling-ness to make concessions to sentimentality (utilitarianism).

Sometimes all letters of a word are well connected

except the first or the last. In the first case we see the writer pause before he undertakes anything; he is cautious. In the second, he starts pondering after he has undertaken all but the last step; he is given to reconsidering what has appeared settled.

When I speak here of unconnected letters, I assume that the word nevertheless *looks* connected. Yet this is not always the case. Sometimes words fall apart. The implication here

may be that a rather low intelligence or outright imbecility (or insanity) is at work. Such falling apart may sometimes

also be seen within the single letter. Particularly in the letters *a, d, b,* and *k* this phenomenon is observable; if it appears in "decayed or deteriorated" hands, it is part of the graphological picture of a schizophrenic writer. In the normal hand, it may be indicative of writers who are inclined to erratic, irrational acts (schizoid).

According to Klages, words with well-connected letters betray the male (masculine), with poorly connected letters, the female (feminine), writer. He has reported that among 100 well-educated men, 80 connect their letters, 10 separate them for the most part, and 10 follow no set pattern; among 100 women, the proportion was 50 to 50. I should like to refine the interpretation of these data by pointing out that more women than men have intuition.

SPACE BETWEEN LETTERS

All Letters Connected:	Logical and systematic thinking; co-operativeness, reasonableness, realism, unimaginativeness, inconsiderateness, lack of initiative, lack of intuitive thinking or acting
Some Letters Unconnected:	Inventiveness, initiative: "idea man," critical observer and examiner, individualist; self-reliance, artistic and intuitive thinking and acting, feeling of loneliness
Most Letters Unconnected:	Discursiveness, egotism, egocentricity, inconsistency, moodiness, restlessness, selfishness, avarice, shyness, unsociability; desultory and utopian thinking
Lack of End Strokes:	Shyness, self-discipline, compulsiveness, self-sufficiency, selfishness, obstinacy
First Letter Stands Apart:	Cautiousness, procrastination
Last Letter Stands Apart:	Vacillator, starts considering when everything seems settled, postpones signing of concluded contracts; ambivalence, hesitancy

I-dot Connected with First Part of Word:	Intuition; abstract, deductive thinker, theoretical worker, sometimes tending toward fanaticism
I-dot Connected with Latter Part of Word:	Gift of integration; inductive thinker
I-dot Connected with Both Parts of Word:	Intuitive, deductive, and philosophical as well as integral thinker; tending toward intellectual inconsistency
Even the Words Connected:	Stickler for principles, pedant; compulsive defense against anxiety

Chapter 13

PACE OF WRITING

A Yardstick of the Writer's Spontaneity

"Even an office manager," writes Saudek (concerning "The Relative Speed of the Act of Writing"),* "who takes no interest in psychology is in duty bound to know, if he considers the handwriting of an applicant purely from the standpoint of its suitability for business purposes, whether its beauty and legibility are produced at the expense of rapidity, or whether the applicant is able to produce so beautiful and legible a script rapidly. . . ." He continues: "But the psychological critic of a handwriting must ascertain by analysis the degree of rapidity with which the script is produced, because this is the basic hypothesis for the psychological comprehension of the handwriting, and because the value of every single feature of the handwriting varies with the speed of production."

We value a spontaneous act more highly than a reluctant one, because we value spontaneity as an indication of sincerity and genuineness, and despise hesitancy because it seems rather to be concealed willingness. The question, therefore, whether a sample of writing was produced spontaneously or hesitantly is of graphological significance.

Saudek quotes Freeman** to the effect that nobody main-

---

* Robert Saudek, *Experiments with Handwriting* (London: G. Allen & Unwin. Ltd.. 1928).
** Frank N. Freeman, *The Handwriting Movement* (Chicago: The University of Chicago Press, 1918).

195

tains one pace throughout one document, and that curves, for example, are more fluently written than straight lines or angles, or broken lines. Nevertheless, he stressed, there is an average over-all pace in every written sample, and this pace can be established.

There are some peculiarities regarding the pace of writing which we must know in order to draw correct conclusions. For instance, Saudek (Freeman) found that tall letters, such as *f*, are always more quickly written than minimum (small) letters, such as *i*; therefore, *a small script is always more reluctantly performed than a sizable one.* The rounded letters are produced "without pause," angular formations never without "stopping for a fraction of a second before the transition from one direction to the other." *The angle writer*, therefore, *is always a hedger.* The same holds true of a handwriting with many broken lines, or with many

my brown shoes?

changes in direction, particularly left-tending strokes (in a writing movement which, as ours, is mainly right-tending). "No one is capable of making a dot when writing at a high rate of speed, but will instead produce . . . a comma or accent." By the same token, a spontaneous writer will not place the dots exactly over the *i*'s. On the other hand, only spontaneity can produce a straight line, a slowly executed straight line being necessarily broken. Moreover, *spontaneity will always slant its writing to the right; upright or left-slanted writing is never performed spontaneously.*

Likewise unspontaneously executed is the so-called *light hand*, written without pressure (for example, that of Palmer's Business Writing), *as well as a continuously heavy* *hand;* these two styles are more tiring to the writer than one in which light and heavy strokes alternate naturally.* In short, the handwriting with naturally alternating pace and pressure** is more easily performed and consequently suggests more spontaneity.

These findings have been of distinct significance in making possible a more accurate evaluation of the general facts of pace. I believe, however, that they do not cover the whole problem. It is interesting to note, for instance, that some graphologists have been able to draw remarkable interpretative conclusions from those changes of pace that always occur within the sample, convinced that we instinctively hedge when writing a word we would rather not write, and hasten the pace when our emotions are aroused. Therefore, while it is important to know the general pace of a sample, it is advisable not to neglect the pace of writing in individual words, particularly key words, but to scrutinize it for the clues it may offer.

This idea needs explanation. Not all the words of a letter are of the same importance. And those which are important are not equally so to everyone. In the sentence: "All the evidence tends to suggest that he went home alone and remained alone at least until after the first visit of the postman next morning, for he had come downstairs barefoot and in his wrinkled pajamas, and was reading a letter out of the morning mail when he was shot," the reader receives all the information he needs to understand and enjoy the paragraph from one word, "alone," and that is why Alexander Woollcott repeated it; for, as a good writer, he enjoyed his story as a reader would. To both the average reader and the

---

* In pressureless writing the hand is suspended above the paper, a tiresome position for the writer; to write heavy strokes continuously requires too much direct application of muscular strength.

** As taught in all Western countries with the exception of the United States.

writer the key word here is "alone." To the murderer who might have written this passage, the key word would be "shot," and to his defense lawyer it would be "evidence," whereas if the laundryman had written this story in his leisure time, the words "wrinkled pajamas" would have special emotional value.

Hence, the key word in a written document, which the writer singles out for special speed or hesitancy, is characteristic of his true relation and particularly his immediate aims in relation to what that key word stands for.

Such changes of pace are detected either through a change in slant or the position on the page which the writer gives to such key word. An increase in right-slantedness is indicative of a (perhaps unadmitted) warm feeling, and a lifting up into a higher zone is characteristic of hope, joy, and elation; a slower, joyless pace can be recognized through a decrease of right-slantedness and a dropping of the word.

*

In one case, an application for employment, I found that the name of the former employer had been almost imperceptibly dropped below the line more or less as in the above sample. Upon questioning, the applicant admitted that she had left her previous position after a series of disagreements with her former employer.

The attention we give both to the pace of the words and the over-all pace, is implied, I believe, in Saudek's own finding that no one maintains one pace throughout one docu-

---

* In this signature the Christian name is well placed, the family name markedly dropped; the interpretation suggests itself.

ment. People vary in their mastery of the mechanics of writing. The slow writer may actually pause frequently between words in order to search within and open up fully his feelings and sentiments for communication; he will still be spontaneous even though slow.

True, we each have a personal pace of writing that may characterize the entire letter. But since it depends on at least three independent factors, namely, our mastery of the mechanics of writing, our vivaciousness, and our method of work, it seems advisable not only to take advantage of Saudek's important findings, but also to study the pace of writing single words, especially key words.

Quite generally, smoothly fluent writing (rather than hurried writing) is accepted as indicative of the writer's *spontaneity,* sincerity, self-confidence, and garrulity, as well as his manual skill and adequate *schooling.* Reluctant writing is the expression of *self-control,* cautiousness, lack of self-confidence, and insincerity, combined with a certain clumsiness and probably *lack of adequate schooling.* We hasten because we are impatient to reach our goal, or because we are temperamental, perhaps restless, impulsive, and easily irritated. We take our time because we are slow thinkers, perhaps considerate, contemplative, imperturbable, passive, procrastinating, or indolent.

When a person writes more quickly than his customary personal pace, his writing becomes careless, illegible. When a skilled and deft writer purposely holds back, the result looks stiff and pedantic. No forgery or disguised script can be executed well, fluently; the "perfect penmanship" of a "wolf in sheep's clothing" is the result of very slow writing. But a person who can write quickly in a legible script is trustworthy and a competent worker.

In short, a clear knowledge of the writer's general and

specific pace furnishes us with a variety of human character traits that are essential to any character analysis.

Spontaneous Writing has:	Unspontaneous Writing has:
Growing left margin	Steady or diminishing left margin
Wavy right margin	Steady or growing right margin
Slant increasingly right-tending	Same slant throughout sample or even increasingly upright or left-slanted script
Extended finals (end strokes)	No finals
Rounded letters and letter connections	Angular letters and letter connections
Comma-shaped, inexactly placed i-dots	Exactly placed i-dots
Connected letters	Isolated (not connected) letters
Wide, sizable writing	Narrow, small writing
Straight lines	Broken "straight" lines
Heavier strokes alternating with light strokes	Constant over-all pressure, light or heavy
Right-tending direction of strokes	Right-tending direction counteracted and interrupted by left-tending strokes

PACE OF WRITING

Spontaneous Writing:	Temperament, mobility, impulsiveness, spontaneity, quick thinking, agility, ambition, industry, activity, impatience, busyness, vivacity, restlessness, hastiness, superficiality, irritability, instability, aimlessness, distractibility, precipitateness
Unspontaneous Writing:	Inflexibility, caution, considerateness, contemplativeness, sluggishness, temperament, passiveness, slow thinking, coolheadedness, indecision, irresolution, weak will, indolence, slowness; hedger, schemer, plotter (NOTE: A study of the handwritings of criminals gave evidence that 70 per cent habitually write slowly.)

Chapter 14

CONCEALING AND COUNTERSTROKES

Concealing Strokes

Inhibition (Reserve, Self-discipline) or Insincerity or Both

It is characteristic of the concealing stroke that it is not seen at first glance. The unsuspecting reader is very likely to overlook it. Suppose we make a pen stroke, and then another that conceals it; in such a case, the least we must admit is that we have taken time out of a continuous process (writing), for without arresting the writing movement, we could never have placed the second stroke directly or almost directly on top of the first (see letters *u, l, e,* and *d*). And then we must admit that the second stroke conceals or covers the first.

pulled — pulling

So, as was to be expected, there are two permissible interpretations of the concealing stroke: either the writer is beset by an anxiety to hold back, to retard the movement forward toward his "neighbor," to avoid facing the facts, the future; or he wants to hide something. Indeed, inhibition and insincerity are the basic meanings of concealing strokes, and it is difficult to state where the one leaves off and the other begins. There is probably no insincerity that is not caused by some inhibition, and no inhibition without some insincerity to help the writer rationalize and justify it.

But inhibitions are not born in us: they are usually forced on us, at least early in our development. *"When I was five or six, I became aware that guests who came to our house admired my sisters but not me; in the street people would stop us to compliment our mother on the looks of her daughters, but they did not mean me; I soon understood that I was ugly."* Such a sad experience as this in childhood can make or "break" a sensitive child. If the child is broken and resigned to lasting feelings of defeat and valuelessness, we find the middle zone depressed to almost nothing.

If he is intelligent, flexible, and ambitious, he takes up the gauntlet and fights back—he overcompensates his lack of self-esteem.

The purpose of overcompensation is to convince everyone, including the subject himself, that he is not resigned, not broken. With the feeling of defeat still lurking within him, neither he nor, it seems to him, anybody else, believes in his victory. Fearing that his performance may fall short of his expectations, he exaggerates it. In writing, he is not satisfied with a normal middle zone; the subject quoted above had to double its height!

On the basis of this line of reasoning throughout graphology, any exaggeration in a script, be it in pressure, size,

*slant, or other features, is looked upon as a gesture toward
compensation or overcompensation of some deficiency.*

The normal meaning of this exaggerated height—an almost queenly self-esteem—is contradicted by the heaviness
and narrowness of the script and the concealing strokes—
the well-known signs of inhibition. Of the six downstrokes
in this word "and," all but two are concealing strokes. How,
then, is this writer's personality to be interpreted? Underneath a deceptive veneer of self-assurance, reserve and com-
posure, lies an anxious, uncertain, fainthearted fugitive from
reality. That she is not satisfied with this situation is most
emphatically and pathetically expressed in the way she
writes her name.

(Mimi)

Slowly yet carelessly written, quite illegible, and of
almost gigantic height, this signature seems to say: "I am
not what I seem to be; don't try to decipher me. . . ."

Since I am dealing here with handwriting, I can speak
only of such human gestures as come to the fore after the
child has been taught writing. This writer told me something about her anxieties in school and her fear of her classmates' criticism: "*I was a good student, and in due time I
recognized that my ambition and intelligence outweighed
my ugliness. But this did not make me much happier. Would
I ever find a boy friend, a husband?*"

Unfortunately, our system of education offers little
assistance to such early heroes. At best, the child is driven
to the conviction that all her failures go back to herself, to
her unattractive exterior. "*I soon came to the point where*

203

I could prove to myself that whenever I failed, it was because I was so much uglier than my sisters and friends." But when she begins to guess, to know that men like her because of her intelligence and wit, that she can have a "steady" who loves her dearly and admires her spirit, she also experiences a tendency in her handwriting to let the middle zone shrink, to loosen up her cramped style, (narrowness and concealing strokes) and the pressure exerted. But because she is intelligent, she knows that one "steady" will not help her beauty, that her "ailment" cannot be healed by external successes. What seemed to be a solution and was meant to resemble a victory for her, remains an unresolved feeling of defeat. Therefore, when, during a courtship that ended with marriage, she again feels her handwriting shrink in height and loosen up, she does not feel comfortable about it, she does not welcome it. *"I had recently the impression that my writing had become smaller and wider; but I did not think that a wider handwriting would fit me, I did not feel well with it."* She has "reconciled" herself to that defense mechanism, and what to others would seem like an unbearable "armor," is to her a well-tried protection which she must keep.

The socially timid, too, feel the need to "bolster" their bearing with a concealing stroke, this time the first letter of the word, of course, particularly in the signature.

Other varieties of concealing strokes may be interpreted by observing the zone in which they appear, or the type of stroke so utilized, whether the garland, the arcade, or the angle. The habitual liar and the crafty embezzler employ the

concealing stroke with their arcades, and the shrewd and sly use it with their angles. But because the concealing stroke can and does hide something weak or bad, we cannot interpret it without considering the general status of the script, the value of the style. (See Chapter 1)

The interpretation of concealing strokes must also be undertaken from a different angle. Of inhibitions I have said earlier that they are not born with us, that they are usually forced on us, at least in our development. Indeed, one aim of our education is to make us work, live, and move about with a certain restraint, reserve. This teaching need not, and is not meant to, cripple us emotionally for a lifetime; its aim is to prevent a status of chaos and licentiousness in socie-

ty. In the middle zone of the above sample virtually no concealing stroke can be seen. The writer, a divorced woman of about thirty, is remarkably frank, even forward, very friendly, good-natured, undisguised; when first talking to her we feel that she hides nothing or little, that we can accept and trust her sociability.

But this first impression is deceptive. For sooner or later we are disappointed to learn that this subject rarely keeps her word, is never punctual, does not maintain a home or follow a calling, and altogether has rather free moral standards. The otherwise so desirable status of freedom from inhibitions (concealing strokes) has here been distorted and at last burst through the simultaneous excessive width and

205

lack of pressure in the script: "mobility, lack of restraint, vacillation, superficiality, lack of substantiality"; and the result of such "unholy" coincidence has then been tinged with the well-known spirit that left slant betrays. There is no script value in this writing to allow for a more positive interpretation.

In the written text of which the above sample is a part this subject unhesitatingly stated: *"My one and most vivid recollection of my early family life is the conservative religious and rigid adherence to what is right—right from a purely adult imposed standard. My father taught it and my mother saw that it was practiced. God forbid that I impose such a standard of self-decorum in my own house and with my own family! It did not help me morally (as they firmly believed). As a matter of fact, it made me a rebel—and I've been rebellious ever since."*

COUNTERSTROKES

THE MANIFESTATION OF AMORALITY

If someone extended his hand to you and, when you reached to shake it, he then gave you a body blow, you would more than resent it. A blow given when a sign of friendship is expected must be called foul. And if a master of penmanship were asked to make an "illustration" for such a foul mentality, he could offer no better sign than that which is called the counterstroke.

The counterstroke is not primarily a stroke; the stress is on the "counter" quality, the contrariness. Therefore,

the "counterstroke" may sometimes be an opening where a continuous line is expected, or an arcade where a garland

ought to be, or simply a left-tending stroke instead of a right-tending stroke, a downstroke where an upstroke is correct.

The counterstroke is interpreted as a sign of amorality, the "sphere outside the sphere in which moral distinctions or judgments apply," active resistance to the accepted, the normal, the legal. Consequently, the counterstroke is encountered not only in the hands of mere braggarts and bluffers, but also in the hands of corrupters, seducers, thieves, forgers, felons, embezzlers, and potential murderers. I want to add quickly that probably more social harm can be done through a false accusation than through the release of a guilty criminal. It is therefore advisable not to base an accusation on any one sign of moral corruption.

By the same token, I disagree with the principle of searching for a "similar" handwriting where a ransom note or other handwriting sample has been found at the scene of a crime. Not similarity of handwriting but criminality ought to be the touchstone. Among those who have been taught one system of penmanship there are a number of "similar" handwritings. The person sought is a criminal; therefore, the handwriting must be a criminal's; and much as the culprit may try to disguise his hand, he can never disguise certain features that may mark him as a guilty outcast—or as mentally diseased.

The forger of a handwriting is quite certain that two handwritings are generally accepted as identical in origin if their most obvious features resemble each other. He will spare no trouble to imitate them. He will make them more obvious and dominant for two good reasons: to draw the attention more particularly to these points and to draw it away from the small letters that he is too lazy or not skilled enough to imitate. In a ransom note, the writer proceeds in the same way: all he changes are the most obvious features. His right slant he changes into a left slant, his fluent penmanship is disguised into a clumsy script, out of garlands he may make angles. But since he cannot resist making counterstrokes, the disguised handwriting, too, is that of a criminal! Despite this fact, forgers rather easily pass the scrutiny of bank cashiers. Always in a hurry, the bank cashier is likely to look for obvious similarities in the signature of the check presented and the specimen deposited with the bank; and he finds what he is looking for.

To this may be added the fact that many criminals are mentally diseased. Upon study, Hauptmann's and William Heirens' writing, for instance, is clearly seen to be that of schizoids (see Appendix, "Schizophrenia"). On examining handwriting samples in twenty-four cases of murder or attempted murder, I found that five of the criminals were schizoid, two giving additional indications of a persecution mania. Six handwritings were marked with the features of persons likely to commit sex crimes. And four showed a certain lack of inner balance (see Chapter 8, "Symmetry") together with that immaturity and discontent which is so characteristic of the person who can be talked, bribed, or cajoled into murder—the assassin.

Nine handwritings out of the twenty-four showed the principal feature of criminal tendency: counterstrokes together with arcades. That is why I disagree with the superficial principle of searching for a "similar" handwriting when a criminal is sought. Similarity proves little, criminality is the touchstone!

CONCEALING STROKES

In the first letter of the word:	(Middle zone) timidity; (in capitals) frustrated ambition
In upper zone, generally:	Secretiveness about plans and ideas
In middle zone, Generally:	Emotional delusions, exaggerated or compulsive taciturnity
In garlands:	Constraint, shyness, emotional inhibitions
In arcades:	Shrewd restraint or sly lying and hypocrisy
In angles:	Cant, shrewdness; confidence man
In threads:	Refusal to take a stand or be pinned down; many-sidedness, deception.
In lower zone, generally:	Secretiveness about facts in writer's instinctual life

209

COUNTERSTROKES

[signature: J. W. McDonald]

Fingerprint Classification

22	0	21	**W**	000	7
	I	20	**W**	00I	

In general: In the first letter of a word it is interpreted as signify-
ing: boastfulness, bluff, pomposity; together with indication
of sensuality: a seducer. Most alarming are counterstrokes *within*
words because there they are most easily overlooked.

SOME TYPICAL COUNTERSTROKES

Left-tending strokes or curves that
should be right-tending

[handwritten: Island,]

Downstrokes that should be upstrokes

[handwritten signature]

Openings at the bottom of letters    Arcades instead of garlands

[handwritten: inside]   *[handwritten: well]*

III

AT THIRD SIGHT

INTRODUCTORY REMARKS

In the following chapters I shall continue to systematize graphology by looking at it in whole aspects. This is always worth while because it permits us to arrive at basic concepts which make our interpretations independent of mere accidental features or details of the individual script.

For instance, in these samples a rather heavy left-right stroke is observed at the top of the *N* in "New York." The same stroke, slightly right-slanted, appears in the t-bar in "what," with one difference, the zone. The heavy left-right stroke appears again in the *Y* of "York," but there it has a distinct right slant and is located in the lower zone. Therefore, with pressure and direction much the same, these three strokes may be interpreted merely by taking into consideration their location in different zones and the difference in slant. If the common elements of all handwriting strokes could be clarified, graphology would be greatly simplified.

How many different strokes are there in handwriting? That, of course, would be the next question. For, if I could systematize the direction and form of all strokes in handwriting, it would be another step toward simplifying graphology. The letters of the Latin alphabet are composed of four fundamental strokes, the vertical, the diagonal, the horizontal, and the circular with all its segments. Once we knew how to interpret them, we would be virtually capable of interpreting penstrokes in any script based on the Latin alphabet. The following chapters are therefore devoted to the interpretation of these four strokes.

Chapter 15

THE STABLE AXIS

In the interpretation of handwriting all strokes of the
pen are potentially of equal importance; there is no thorough analysis that does not attempt to consider all elements
the sample offers. However, a person's handwriting contains
one penstroke that carries more weight than others.

For the legibility of our script, the downstroke in our
writing, which I call the stable axis, is of prime importance.
If all the downstrokes in a word are erased, it becomes

almost illegible; yet without the upstrokes and letter connections its legibility is almost undiminished. Seen from the standpoint of penmanship, therefore, the downstrokes alone give the script structure and continuity.

This fact, I assume, is known to the intelligent writer, whether or not he has made the above analysis for himself. At least, he acts as though he knew it. For, ordinarily, a writer deliberately puts force in the downstrokes, and from so doing he derives, I believe, a certain amount of pleasure. (I have seen writers return pens or pencils because they did not permit a show of sufficient pressure; the Palmer system, by insisting on a penmanship without pressure, not only tires the pupil quickly, but, it now seems, takes out of writing some of the pleasure that naturally is experienced in it.)

It could be argued that a penstroke that is produced deliberately and with evident pleasure cannot be taken as a reliable basis for character interpretation; too many essential characteristics, we have learned, are hidden and, probably with an appropriate motive, expressed with the least pressure possible. On the other hand, character analysis cannot afford to neglect a feature that attracts so much of the writer's attention. A stroke of the pen that bears, so to speak, the responsibility for the very legibility of writing and, therefore, its meaning, is meaningful, even crucial.

Small wonder, therefore, that the downstroke has always

attracted the attention of graphologists. Some call it a phallic symbol, some the "writer's backbone." I find that

216

most female (feminine) writers keep the downstroke about as light as the rest of their writing; most male (masculine) writers show pressure in just such downstrokes. Actually, when I speak of a feminine script, I mean one without or

Alfred   *Ruth*

almost without pressure, whereas a masculine hand seems to be one that has pressure, particularly in the stable axis.

To clarify my concept of the stable axis and add as much as possible to the graphological knowledge of the reader, I interviewed a writer whose *excessive* display of pressure in the downstrokes attracted my attention. Of course, I was aware that excessive pressure, as any excess in handwriting, covered an insufficiency—but which? To obtain the answer to this question would mean to recognize the meaning of the stable axis. I felt that an intelligent man, particularly

I am the third child

one with excessive pressure in the stable axis, should be able to tell me something about its meaning, just as a weak and fearful man often knows more about the meaning of physical strength than a lumberjack, and a hungry man more about food than a satisfied one.

The subject, thirty-four years old, is a writer, well educated, married for the second time. I first ascertained that he actually used two handwritings, one with excessive pressure and the other pressureless. Would this pressureless script be characteristic, so to speak, of the "old self," the original personality of the writer? *"I am the third child, the second son of the family. Beginning life particularly weak, timid,*

So now I deposit

*sickly and oversensitive . . ."** Yes, the pressureless script mirrors the writer's original personality. In our search for the meaning of the stable axis, it might be fruitful to follow for a while the development of this handicapped boy as presented by himself.

The early inadequacy mentioned by the subject may lead either to a lasting state of dependence upon others, or contrariwise, to a desire to overcompensate it. The latter course, I have come to believe, is indicative of, and natural for, an intelligent and ambitious child. *"I learned to read before I was four years old, and from my first printed page I went on to devour books."*

That a child in bad health should depend on his mother was quite natural. That at the same time the boy began to glorify her is indicative of his helplessness and imagination. *"The heroines and heroes of my dreams and books were real, and only my mother could rival them in my imagination-*

You

realities." Unfortunately, a mother fixation seems to have been unavoidable. (See "pointed" loop in sample, and con-

---

* This and the following quotations are from letters in my possession.

218

sult Chapter 18, "The Circular Stroke.") It was equally probable that sooner or later the father would become aware of the boy's preference for his mother; some fathers react violently to such discoveries. *"But at the age of nine I was torn from both mother and father by a great act of mental and physical cruelty. My father supplied the brute force; my mother disappointed me by not being an Elaine of Astolat or a Cordelia."* As one of the results, the boy adopted the sign

and

of "father protest" in his script. Fortunately, he did not choose a left-slanted handwriting, but he could not, it seems, altogether avoid left-slanted strokes in his hand.

According to this subject, his father's "act of cruelty" furnished him with the impulse to take up the fight against his own inadequacies. *"No longer could I evade the world outside my library chair—the battle beyond my mother's arms."* As a result of this fight, he became an athlete and a man of unusual physical strength. Indeed, pronounced pressure in his script, as indicative of pronounced vitality, would have furnished us with much the same information. But what we see is excessive, not pronounced, pressure. What is the insufficiency in question and why is it covered up by excessive pressure just in his script's stable axis?

The subject speaks of his "frail body" and his "many illnesses." *"Dreams and troubles from 10 to 14. Then resignation. Then my first marriage. A complete flop from the start. Then huge animal pleasure. But only for MYSELF.* No thought of her. And disgust . . ."* This is an outcome that probably was to be expected. The second, pressureless script, is indicative of lack of vitality; it is also, we remember, a feminine script.

---

* The capitals are the subject's.

This marriage, after six days, ended in complete separation *"because my wife was no Catherine de Medici or Beatrice or sonnet-writing Mrs. Robert Browning."*

For the purposes of graphology this subject's case history can now be summarized as follows: Born weak and timid, the subject would have liked to stay at home with his mother and "devour books." His father tore him from mother and books and forced him to fight his weakness and timidity. The boy succeeded beyond his own expectations. He became a man of extraordinary strength and a crack athlete. At least, that probably is the way the father saw it. The son characterized his father's methods of education as "a great act of mental and physical cruelty." Why? Is he not proud of his muscles and athletic prowess?

He is and he is not. His weakness is not a muscular one. It is his sexual insufficiency, and this has not been overcome. The "flop" was not accidental. Similar experiences happened to him repeatedly. *"Always hungry. But always disappointed by women. After first, there were four or five. But what disgust!"*

In his second marriage he is much more cautious, much less ambitious sexually. His wife is to him *"a human being who answers as many of my demands and needs as are necessary to keep me a husband."* He does not say what she may expect from him. Such egocentricity is, we shall see, characteristic of persons with excessive pressure in the stable axis.

That excessive pressure in the stable axis indicates sexual inhibition and insufficiency permits the conclusion that adequate pressure would indicate virility. Or perhaps "libido" is a better word. Noyes, in his *Modern Clinical Psychiatry,** gives us a definition of "libido": "The intrinsic characteristic of life is the ability to adjust and to transform physical

---

* Philadelphia: W. B. Saunders Co., 1939.

energy into special dynamic manifestations. This driving vital force continues to operate under the most adverse conditions. We have all seen shrubs in a fissured rock, not only continuing to live under conditions that would seem to preclude life, but even in response to a vital urge, continuing to grow and reproduce. There is, however, another—and for psychiatry the most important—aspect of biological energy, that of psychic energy containing the driving forces basic to human nature . . . Freud calls such an energy concept libido, giving a sexual definition to it, as he believes that psychic energy is a matter of transformation of energy inherent in the sex instinct."

Undoubtedly, this definition fits perfectly our subject's fight for life. In spite of his weaknesses he showed a considerable amount of vital force; he was able to adjust himself to adverse conditions and to amass psychic energy. We can speak of "libido" instead of "vitality." The stable axis can, at least in this subject's history, be called the stage of the writer's libido.

To be sure, not only did his original weakness remain with him, but also his more enjoyable original qualities: love for books and literary and intellectual work. *"I hate the things I must do with my mind and body, yet I do those odious things well. My mind and hopes versus my blood and flesh . . . may I soon be free . . . I want to write sonnets."* To sonnets, intellectual work, the pressureless script fits perfectly.

My hand is stiff & sore

The meaning of the stable axis, however, goes further. When a writer decides to protest against and oppose the

221

rules of our human society (the father's), the slant of his stable axis manifests his decision and demonstration. And when he is old and tired, its frailty and trembling seem to appeal for help.

Pressure in the entire length of the axis is comparatively rare in handwriting. Most writers stress the axis only in an

l, or *y* or *g.* Very rare, at any rate, is a script of good style value with evident pressure the full length of the down-stroke.

The one interpretative word for stress in the stable axis that always fits is "egocentricity," with strength of character on the intellectual level (upper zone only) and irrational obstinacy and blind virility on the instinctual level (lower zone only). Another term is "life-preserving instinct," still another, "complete personality," again for one who stresses the whole axis. His positive personality description appears to me as follows:

Able to conceive ideas, or at least to take the initiative, he also has the will and the capacity to carry out what he

222

undertakes; the strong and full-length stable axis is a good illustration of this. No doubt he is headstrong, too, and that frequently makes him a difficult person to deal with. He is of upright character, though somewhat stiff and inflexible, and a reliable and thorough worker—so long as his personal interests go with the task at hand. No appeal to his "magnanimity" will ever fail, for he wants to be the protector of the weak. But once his personal interest is extinguished, he breaks away as easily and impetuously as he conceived, or joined in, the undertaking. For better or for worse, he is made of one piece, wholly with or against you. Therefore, as a person of convictions, he is willing to fight for his beliefs, and his most unshakable belief is his belief in himself. In fact, he may be called an egoist of the first water. By the same token, he is Don Juan, Julius Caesar, and King Solomon in one, and no matter how old he is, his mind remains young and bold. Since he has convictions, he can convince others. Since he has the strength to carry out his ideas, he also has the power to eliminate resisting forces. He is a man, a leader, a "father ideal."

The negative description of a writer who stresses the whole stable axis runs somewhat as follows:

To him the concept of egocentricity assumes a more primitive and negative hue. He is the "he-man" in the negative sense of the word. Under any pretext he will seize the reins and drive any undertaking with which he is connected in the direction his boundless pride and selfishness point. He cannot be appeased because he is unwilling to listen. Besides, he wants his decisions to be looked upon as laws. Therefore, where he has passed through once, no one can dwell. He is often brutal and inconsiderate, and this becomes particularly apparent as soon as his interest in a matter or a person ends. For then he assumes the right to crush it or him. Indeed, his relation to his fellow men is one of complete disregard; he recognizes neither the rights nor cherished traditions of others. He takes a person when he needs him, and drops him when he has served his purpose. These jungle principles also determine his relations to the other sex. All his thinking and doing are exclusively directed toward self-preservation. He is a "he-man," a "mis-leader," a "father terror."

This negative personality portrait, together with that of the writer with the positive full-length accent on the stable axis, bears some resemblance to what may be called the masculine character. Certain graphologists, perhaps with this thought in mind, have taken the stable axis as the masculine symbol. I am inclined to concur.

I have mentioned that the stable axis, through its slantedness or frailty, mirrors the writer's protest or his weakness and sensitivity. It does still more. Sometimes the downstrokes are arched (particularly in such letters as *H, T, h, t,* and *f*) .

The interpretation assumes that these arcs, when they open toward the right, do so under "pressure" from the right (future), and when they open toward the left, do so to ward

off those invigorating forces. I am speaking here of the writers who "face" the future hopefully and in good fighting trim, and of the others who do not wish to "face" it at all.

In the interpretation of "limited" downstrokes, such as in

224

g's and *y*'s, our sense of proportion is of decisive importance. Disproportionately short, these downstrokes are suggestive of early sexual trauma resulting in an infantile emotionality.

Particularly when coquettishly ornate they betray a playful (feminine) pretense of maturity.

Even though my experience is too limited for certainty, I believe it is necessary to mention here that shrunken lower projections have also been indicative of writers with deformed or incapacitated feet. (The *p* in "Hopkins," which looks like a golf club, was written by a man with a club foot.)

A disproportionately long downstroke in the lower zone, on the other hand, betrays a desire for sexual satisfaction and an inversely proportionate capacity for finding it. Such elongated, heavy, yet "trembling" downstrokes have been seen in the hands of senile writers, whose thoughts would not leave the instinctual zone.

The well-proportioned and stressed downstroke in the lower zone is suggestive of stressed sexual desire and the determination to find satisfaction. But because of its location in the lower zone, this stroke has also been identified with

a certain assertiveness and obstinacy that is all the more difficult to dispel because its background is purely emotional. The same stroke, left-slanted (in a right-slanted script), would then betray either opposition to or resignation (frustration) with respect to sexual intercourse. These downstrokes, heavy and left-slanted, were quite characteristic of soldiers' letters, particularly those from the less "hospitable" Pacific fronts.

And the stable axis completely devoid of any stress and pressure, in the presence of pressure in left-right strokes, has been found in the handwriting of men with "heavy lapses of potency."

From the foregoing facts and considerations the conclusion seems indeed permissible that, whatever its name, the stable axis is a most important penstroke in a person's script. Without the strokes of the stable axis the script would be illegible, the personality indefinable. With all strokes erased but those of the stable axis, we still could not only read the script but interpret the personality of the subject to a considerable degree. Provided we are told of its length and its place in relation to the three zones, the strength, shape, and slantedness of this one stroke furnish us with many very valuable clues. The stable axis, therefore, is not only the backbone of a person's script, it is also the backbone of his character picture.

Moreover, the stable axis is the stage of a person's libido. Pressure in the stable axis gives us a means of determining the amount of libido invested there. Excessive pressure warns us of serious sexual inhibitions and of an overcompensated libidinal deficiency, while in some cases lack of pressure betrays an accomplished sublimation, as Chapter 17 will demonstrate.

That the stable axis is the masculine symbol in handwriting appears confirmed in my experience. For whenever I found stress in the stable axis of a script, I assumed the subject to be male or masculine, and when the stable axis was free of stress, I took it for granted that a female or feminine person had written the sample, and I have never been wrong in this respect. It is true, of course, the "masculine" and "feminine" have to be defined anew in each case.

Chapter 16

THE DIAGONAL STROKE
ITS LOCUS AND DIFFUSION
Libido in Transition, Pro and Con

One of the primary interpretations of the diagonal stroke
is furnished by what is known of slant in general: The right-
slanted stroke expresses overt assertion of inner convictions
(through conflict and co-operation); the left-slanted, on the
contrary, inner denial of constituted authorities (through
competitive guerilla warfare). This interpretation will not
always suffice. It will not, since slant is so basic and general
a concept, and since diagonal strokes may begin in any of
the three zones, and may or may not extend to other zones.
We must, therefore, develop and refine the concept of slant
to comprise such elements as the varying locus, diffusion,
and pressure.

While the vertical stroke is always a downstroke, the
diagonal stroke may be an upstroke as well as a downstroke.
This fact furnishes us with a number of new clues, for it is
obvious that, in handwriting, downstrokes and upstrokes
have different meanings. To some readers, particularly those
who are here for the first time concerning themselves with
graphology, such a distinction between "similar" strokes
may seem to be trifling. However, even they must admit that
the sameness of the final appearance never excludes a wide
difference in origin, process, and purpose.

The difference I am speaking of comes from a difference
in origin and purpose or aim. The upstroke aims at going

228

from a lower zone to a higher one; the downstroke, from a higher to a lower. For instance, this diagonal upstroke has

been found to appear in the script of argumentative writers. Part of this meaning lies in the stroke's slantedness. But since it comes from the emotional realm and heads into the conscious, it must be assumed that the writer wishes, as it were, to "air" a problem of emotional origin. It is this origin which has earned the writer the reputation of being argumentative. For, in general, we do not censure "the overt assertion of convictions" even though this may occur through "conflict." We tend to be stubborn, excited, unwilling to listen, when our emotions are deeply involved. Starting from the lower zone, the right-slanted upstroke, therefore, is always indicative of (a rather irrational) argumentativeness.

On the other hand, a similar stroke in a similar zone at the same angle of slant, but executed as a downstroke,

would not imply argumentativeness. At least this is the contention of most leading graphologists. Why not? Because the path from the conscious (middle zone) to the unconscious (lower zone) is also the path from articulation to muteness.

This concept of the diffusion of strokes as they go from one zone to the other is important and of great assistance in the endeavors to interpret handwriting because it adds to slant and pressure a new interpretative element. There are only two diagonal strokes. With slantedness and pressure at our service we can do much useful work; but with the help of "transition" or diffusion, we can do even more.

For example, the "argumentative" upstroke may be met in many forms and even disguises. Where slant and pressure have given what they can, "locus and diffusion" help out, and also the place within the word. In this sample, this

stroke may be seen just behind the first letter of the word—lying in wait, so to speak; this writer will not start the argument, but he is well prepared to meet a challenge. And in this "wing" the stroke is disguised as part of a *g*; placed

wholly in the lower zone and at the end of the word, this upstroke may be indicative of a certain bellicosity which, however, is kept down by a sense of propriety—if the standard proportions of the word are to be trusted.

On the basis of an end-adjustment, in transit from the lower to the middle zone, this writer may also be called argumentative, for even though he may be willing to post-

230

pone the argument, when it comes, he will not be able to keep it free from purely emotional influences—at least that is what the origin of this stroke in the lower zone would indicate.

Of course, just as it may start in the lower zone, this stroke may also start in the middle zone and continue its way into the upper. It is the businessman's upstroke, and its

purpose is not an irrational argument for emotional reasons, but the "overt assertion" of intentions (rather than contentions) to further matters, not to "complicate" them. (There may seem to be pressure in this latter upstroke. However, on close scrutiny it may be seen that all strokes in this sample have the same pressure, and it must therefore be assumed that it was written by means of a "stylo" which shows only uniform pressure, or actually no pressure.)

The same upstroke may also appear as the t-bar or *T*

$$\mathcal{T}$$

stroke. But here, completely located in the intellectual zone, the meaning of "argumentative" must be changed to "pretentious." For an argument that is carried on for purely intellectual reasons is most probably motivated by the writer's pedantic ambitions and pretensions.

Quite generally, upstrokes have no pressure, downstrokes often do. Pressure in any stroke implies the exertion of physical strength (libido) and sometimes the retarding (inhibition) that inevitably results from pressure and the paper's resistance to it. Therefore, pressure in an upstroke is unusual,* whereas it is quite natural in a downstroke, which moves from the conscious to the unconscious and instinctual zone.

The left-slanted stroke, as has been shown, is the symbol of open or hidden opposition. In the lower zone, this opposition refers to the instinctual and has been treated in Chapter 15, "The Stable Axis." But we also know the left-slanted

downstroke from certain t-bars. It is the t-bar of the intellectual (simplified writing), who may have a preference for taking the opposition standpoint in a discussion because it gives him a chance to impress people with his intelligence and wit. And even though such a discussion does not leave the strictly intellectual sphere, it can be carried on in a headstrong and unreasonable manner.

The same t-bar, written without pressure (stylo), can only be the symbol of this writer's quiet opposition; and in the upper zone, again without pressure (stylo), but in a feminine script, it is associated with the somewhat haughty

---

* See also Chapter 17, "The Mobile Axis" (the discussion of pressure in the mobile axis).

disapproval and demonstrative opposition of the "old maid."
Unfortunately, I am unable to show the same downstroke
written with pressure. It is considered as indicative of a
rather defiant ideological opposition and, as such, it has recently been found in the script of the leader of a political
group who assassinated a famous statesman in the seventeenth century.*

The *occasional* left-slanted stroke may also be observed
in the middle zone—either with pressure or without, which-
ever is consistent with the writer's style—of writers who are
torn between co-operation and opposition, trust and distrust,
"yes" and "no." Scattered among right-slanted strokes, they

give the script a nervous and uncertain look, and the writers
are nervous, uncertain, and sensitive. On the other hand, it
is the uncertain, sensitive citizen who is willing to try
something new and change his mind if and when sufficiently
impressed with another person's opinions and suggestions.
Probably not much real progress and deliberate co-operation
can be achieved without such temporary "uncertainty" and
its resultant mobility.

Only when this nervousness and uncertainty appear in
a "decayed" hand such as this do we have before us the script
of the neurotic and unstable writer who cannot make up his

---

* Wallenstein, Duke of Friedland (1583-1634).

mind because too many aspects present themselves to his too impressionable intellect.

Where the middle zone "melts" into the lower zone, there is often seen the projection of those half-conscious problems which, in my opinion, the writer hopes and wishes to be able to drop into the vast reservoir of his unconscious. The best-known is the left-slanted, heavy symbol of the unresolved father protest.

Combing scripts for diagonal strokes leads to the conclusion that there is hardly a script without some of them, just as there is scarcely a person so rigid or primitive that he does not either disapprove (or oppose) or compromise (or assert) in his expressions of libidinal energy. And because I have reserved the right to be frankly evaluative, I question the values of a human being without any doubts or compromises. For only those who sometimes question provide humanity with lasting answers.

Chapter 17

THE MOBILE AXIS

(The Horizontal Stroke)

OUR ATTITUDES TOWARD THE FUTURE AND OUR FELLOW MEN—
LIBIDO OUTWARD BOUND

The gesture with which we draw a horizontal straight line would, if fully carried out, find us with our outstretched hand lifted almost to shoulder height, our index finger pointing toward the horizon. This pose is familiar to us from monuments to victorious generals and explorers. Consequently, graphology assumes that the horizontal line in a script is an indication of the writer's *plans for the future* and with regard to his *fellow men*—provided the horizontal

interests

line has been written with a right-tending movement. The same horizontal line, written in a left-tending movement, must necessarily reflect the writer's *regression toward his past* and his previous life experience.

Mary

The right-tending, horizontal stroke can, therefore, be found in almost everyone's script, for there is scarcely a person who does not have some plans with respect to his

235

future and his fellow men. The left-tending, more or less horizontal stroke is most typical of the poet, musician, historian, and, of course, the egoist. There are at least two means of distinguishing between these two groups: style value and zone. Not that the poet could not be selfish; on the contrary, he is the prototype of egocentricity (self-involvement, retrospection, introspection) at least in his intellectual work. But his horizontal stroke as well as his whole script has an intellectual and often aesthetic aspect, whereas

(Washington Irving)

the egoist's horizontal stroke would most probably originate in the middle, the "practical" zone, and remain there. I have

therefore thought it advisable to deal with the horizontal stroke, which I call the "mobile axis," according to zones.

THE MOBILE AXIS IN THE UPPER ZONE

In the upper zone there are two prominent horizontal strokes: the t-bar and the stroke that covers the capital *T*, the t-stroke. According to Palmer, the t-bar is practically as long as the stem, or to be exact, about one quarter of an inch for the stem, three sixteenths for the bar. They cross each other at a height of three-sixteenths of an inch above the ground line. The capital *T* is just as high as the *t*, but

236

ttttt

the stroke covers the capital T at a height of five-sixteenths of an inch above the ground line—I do not know why. I also do not know why the T-stroke should have a fancy

T

S-curve form instead of the horizontal stroke. A sketchy check of 100 scripts (50 women's, 50 men's) showed that 96 per cent of the writers covered their capital T's with a more or less simple horizontal stroke; they had unlearned what they had been taught in their penmanship lessons.

A writer's mobile axis may be higher or lower, longer or shorter, than Palmer's; or it may be missing altogether. Also, it may be pressureless like Palmer's, or show pressure and other peculiarities which will be discussed.

Always on the intellectual level, short t-bars appear in the script of timorous people who have little confidence in their own ideas and therefore do not plan very far ahead. By the same token the short t-bar is indicative of the sober and matter-of-fact.

These excessively long and fine t-bars reveal the dreamer and the schemer. Planning too far ahead, he dreams of successes he is rarely able to realize. Lacking common sense as well as a sense of proportion, he sometimes is a danger

237

to those who have both. How are these excessively long
t-bars and T-strokes produced? In most cases this may be

[handwritten word]

the procedure: The writer first finishes the word, then he
adds the t-bar; but instead of lifting his pen at its end,
he lets it drag on; the result is a pen trace on paper which
is called excessively long. May we not therefore assume a
certain laziness? And an unwillingness and even an inability
to stop one's pondering when it is time to do so? At any
rate, the question whether or not the writer can fully utilize
his unbridled imagination depends on other features of the
script: its middle zone, its pressure.

[handwritten words]

For the case of the writer who replaces the horizontal
t-bar or T-stroke with a garland or arcade or (if he has not
been taught it in school) with an S-link, the interpretation
can be found in Chapter 11, "Connection of Letters," apply-
ing only to the intellectual level.

[handwritten word]

Whereas I sometimes see a *t* without its bar, I have never
seen a capital *T* without its stroke. With respect to this, it
may be said that a capital *T* without its stroke would be quite
"faceless," and that a *t* without a bar may still be legible.
On these observations I base my interpretation of the missing
238

t-bars: They are indicative of a very discriminating intelligence that will not tolerate a waste of time or imagination or strength, that disdains all scheming and dreaming to get down to "brass tacks" sooner. By the same token, such a writer, feeling beyond and above the limitations that tradition and bourgeois convention force upon us, will be and prefers to be an individualist, an original and unconventional thinker, rather than a follower or a team worker— provided he is at all creative and a thinker (style value!). Sometimes it is possible to see only the negative side of missing t-bars. In such case, the subject is a writer who

(to)

drifts from day to day, without definite plans, or one who, like the guerrilla fighter, may come to rely on impulsive decisions (often anti-social), in short, an opportunist or an adventurer. And since such a writer evidently has no predilection for leading his fellow men, the missing t-bar is also identified with one who shuns responsibilities.

The Mobile Axis in the Middle Zone

The mobile axis in the middle—the practical zone—if right-tending, is a useful letter connection; if left-tending, it is the plainest gesture of selfishness. As a letter connection it is treated in Chapter 11. I shall deal with it here in its other aspects, particularly the final stroke at the end of a word.

We cannot stop our pen exactly when and where we want to, unless we make a special effort. Therefore, most

239

systems of penmanship teach or permit a final, an end stroke. If clearly "mechanized," they do not tell anything positive

West 91 Street

about the writer's personality. However, in the process of maturing, many writers invent finals of their own or modify the traditional finals; these inventions and modifications are, of course, of graphological significance.

A widespread tendency among writers is toward shortening or dropping these finals. No doubt finals are of no importance in the real task of writing; they are "senseless"; but they are sometimes convenient. Consequently, wherever in a writer's mind the power of reasoning and the sense of utility are stronger than that of being "like everybody else," the final is dropped.

putting

Such a writer is usually recognized as a person of practical as well as utilitarian intelligence, also as an unsentimental or rather emotionally inhibited individual. (It should be remembered that most finals belong to the uppermost layers of the lower zone.) And on the basis of a final as an end link, an "outstretched hand," it is assumed that such a writer would not be a mixer, or joiner, or truly obliging. All

member

these characteristics take on a clearly egoistic tinge when the final is not dropped but turned back contrary to the writing motion and against the natural tendency toward co-operation with one's fellow men.

But sometimes the final is turned back and, at the same time, lifted up into the intellectual zone. To interpret this

As per

final, I must first state that I have seen it mostly in rather primitive scripts. I know the special care many writers take with finals. But why should a person, who is able and about to express himself in intelligible writing, spend time and space and effort on elaborate and unintelligible symbolic finals? I believe he does this because he does not care or dare to tell their meaning; because these elaborate finals are projections of the writer's pent-up yearnings, hopes, dreams, and secret demands. These flaring-up, left-tending finals, therefore, impress me as betraying the sentimentally immature and ill-equipped writer's hopes for and claims to an intellectuality and, possibly, a "spiritual calling," which he feels but rarely admits openly.

A somewhat similar situation is pictured in this script,

to

but here the writer has, as it were, reconsidered his "selfish," introspective tendencies and so ends the word with a straight final—on an almost intellectual, or better, impersonal level. (The higher style value of this "narrow" script supports this interpretation.) It may also be assumed that here true intellectual and selfish inclinations are in steady conflict with more practical and altruistic ones.

Sometimes the end link is turned downward, in the form of an arcade. As a final of a word that shows only (flat) garlands, such an arcade can be interpreted only negatively; particularly the contradiction between what is shown (in the word) and what is half "dreamily" admitted (in the end adjustment) is disturbing. A comparable gesture that occurs to me is that of the criminal in the dock who crosses his fingers while taking the oath.

And when the "good-natured" garland is turned inward, then this "hand" has been "stretched out," not to bid "Good morning," but to receive something: A neat symbol of selfishness.

Palmer teaches middle zone, horizontal strokes in G, J, and S. They are neither an improvement of these letters, nor do they facilitate the writing process. Since they are useless by all standards, the majority of mature writers have discarded them.*

The final case is that of the "endless" end stroke which

---

* A check of 100 handwritings (50 male, 50 female writers) as to their fidelity to these horizontal strokes showed that 68 per cent of the men and 52 per cent of the women had dropped them; 4 per cent of the female writers had introduced them in their capital *T* where it had not been taught them.

implies as much discomfort for the writer as it disfigures his handwriting. He cannot free himself from thoughts that

have been taking hold of him. A little argument in the office may keep him brooding and worrying until he falls asleep at night.

The Mobile Axis in the Lower Zone

There are only two kinds of horizontal strokes in the lower zone: one with, the other without, pressure.

We underline a word to draw the reader's special attention to it. The horizontal stroke underlining the writer's name is interpreted as the writer's unconscious desire for

greatness, importance, fame, immortality. The same pressureless stroke, but short and not below the writer's name, is indicative of the writer's unconscious desire to dominate. It is the prerogative of feminine (female) writers, both the "domestic tyrant" and the crank. Close scrutiny may reveal that these are sisters under the skin. However, in

243

writing, the nagger's stroke may be written without pressure, whereas the people who write "letters to the editor" under-

myself any life deagu

line certain words or phrases in these letters with all the pressure they can exert. I shall give this aspect of the mobile axis special attention.

please

Underlined words and phrases in personal letters are not often seen. Normally, if need be, the writer will phrase his sentences so that the stress quite naturally falls on a certain word; to underline it would seem to be an improper over-emphasis that offends first his, then the addressee's, taste. In fact, the habit of underlining words or phrases has always been associated with people who insist on their own opinions, whether or not they thereby offend anyone, and who are not only prepared but willing to fight anyone who is so imprudent as to contradict them. Such an irrational (and sometimes pathological) attitude is indicative of the choleric or irascible (or paranoiac) writer to whom almost every word (and the thought it stands for) is emotionally stressed and fraught with repressed and suppressed meanings, so that every doubt, even the mildest, or any counterproposal arouses in him all the resistance and emotional opposition he is able to muster.

Pressure in the Mobile Axis

A Feminine Symbol

Normally, the strokes of the mobile axis are pressure-less. In fact, their thinness (or at least their fine-pointed-ness) is accepted as an indication of the writer's cultured taste and intellectuality. We admire the fine t-bars in Long-fellow's and Washington Irving's rather heavy script.

Pressure and the projection of our plans in the intellectual zone obviously do not go well together. Mere reasonableness, too, would suggest leaving the mobile axis pressure-less. In Chapter 15, I attempted to demonstrate that down-strokes, by reason of their importance for the legibility of our handwriting (as well as certain psychological implications), deserve and receive the writer's special attention; he gives them accent, pressure. Such "discrimination" seems agreeable to everyone. So I was all the more baffled when I

245

first met writers who did their utmost to keep the stable axis light and "clean," while at the same time putting heavy pressure on the mobile axis. When I showed such a script to a colleague of mine, he sighed: "Ah, those fussy women!" Pulver refers to this phenomenon as a case of a "displaced libido."

I can understand the "fussiness." If the procedure of intelligent writing tends to concentrate all pressure on the stable axis, insistence on pressure in the mobile axis seems to betray an inability or unwillingness to see the real issues, to face facts, to be reasonable, self-critical, or simply intelligent—if my definition of intelligence as the faculty of distinguishing the important from the unimportant holds true; all of which can, perhaps, be summarized in the word "fussiness."

But the concept of a displaced libido is less obvious. I therefore tried to meet and interview a few writers who habitually neglect the stable axis. They are not too rare, and all of them seemed eager to tell and to explain.*

I expected to find them very unstable and aggressive (pressure directed against their fellow men), but I could not figure out why they should have chosen such an impractical way of writing, or such a philosophy of life. Above all, I wanted to know whether, if the concept of displaced libido is appropriate and correct, some knowledge of the writer's past would again facilitate the graphologist's task of interpreting these finest gestures of man.

Case 14 Alma, age 42, single, European
> Youngest daughter in a family of four. Father, a very devout Jewish businessman; mother, of haughty, antireligious, intellectual family. Father felt and was made to feel inferior because he could not meet mother's educa-

---

* The statements of the subjects quoted in the following pages of this chapter were not checked as to their veracity.

tional standards. Mother complained that she had to live outside the circle of her equals. Father sickly; mother energetically took over his business. Alma recalls a feeling of great pity for both her parents. She was determined to lead a quite different life, without quite knowing what kind of life. Also recalls pitying older married friends who soon after their marriage looked worried and unfree. "Sex" was for her an object of contempt. She wanted to develop her intellectual capacities, never look like those "downtrodden housewives"; the average marriageable man seemed to her rather comic. But she did want to have children very badly. Impresses one as well educated, though spottily, extremely curious, aggressive though helpless, never quite sincere, dissatisfied and aimless, "always" in a new job, and in trouble.

Case 15 Bernice, age 21, single, American
"My father was a temperamental though shy musician in his thirty-ninth year, my mother, a woman of torrid temper, was in her twenty-seventh year, when I was born. They were married a year and eight months (I was eight months old) when they parted, my mother taking the initiative, since it was her father's home in which they had been living. In retrospect, I can remember my looking longingly at another father showing affection to his daughter. I would come back to my mother, who at various times such as this, would take me in her arms and fondle me, saying that her love would make up for both father and mother. Since my mother's death I have been trying to assert myself. I seek for a man who has strong character, one endowed with a warm heart, one who can return all the kindness, understanding, and consideration which I know I can give him. So far I haven't found this person, and I don't think I ever will. My actual ambitions are to read and become informed about peoples, lands, and old cultures. Since graduation from high school I have studied in my spare time: voice, ballet, painting, costume design, Spanish, philosophy, religions, cultures."

Case 16 Claudia, age 42, divorced, European
"I was an only child, conceived accidentally, as far as I know. My mother was a typical intellectual woman, a successful writer before her marriage, with a best seller to her credit. After my birth, she re-entered college and turned to the study of history of art; she took her degree when I

247

was six years old. My father was a lawyer by profession. He was very intelligent, but rather helpless in practical matters; he could write poetry and mother made him study history of art, and he too took a degree in it. Mother loved father but in a jealous and possessive way. Once he asked me for help against mother. That was my proudest day. I too had many literary successes, but I am also a very good cook, hostess, storyteller; men love talking with me. I have two degrees, one in anthropology, and one in sociology. I was terribly ambitious. Now, as to men: I have hardly any difficulty getting them. The difficulty comes in holding them; here my success ends as a rule. My marriage lasted not quite three years. Thinking back, I was a neglected child. When I was sick, mother would spend days and nights at my bed. But she would not buy me any new clothes, I had to wear her old ones. My successes were taken for granted, my failures were deeply resented. All smiles and kisses I got as a child came from an old cook of ours. I was psychoanalyzed."

Case 17 Doris, age 40, married, American
Only daughter in a family of two children and mother. Father committed suicide when the girl was one year old. Mother, left without means, was a singer and reared her children as best she could. The girl seems to be extremely talented: a singer, pianist, piano teacher, physical culture teacher, percussion player in a symphony orchestra, expert dressmaker, first-rate homemaker and cook. She impresses one as uncertain of herself, but always eager to help, restless, melancholy, admittedly an habitual liar. Her husband complains about her coldness. Her greatest pleasure seems to be to serve, particularly to have her house full of guests and to satisfy all their wishes.

Case 18 Ernest, age 40, married, American
He is a successful lawyer who holds a degree in literature. He loved his mother dearly, but was very much afraid of his father, who would, for instance, make him repeat his "Good morning," until he broke down and cried, because the boy had speech difficulties. His married life is very unhappy; he is suffering under his wife's domineering ways and her physical strength, which he cannot hope to match. He has frequent lapses of potency. His wife has accused him of having homosexual relations.

To the extent that five cases can indicate a pattern, it may be said that the peculiar accent on the mobile axis seems to be preferred by not too robust writers who began life under particularly unwholesome circumstances. The mother appears to be the actively domineering or aggressive head of the family; the father remains relatively weak and ineffectual, though perhaps a man of intellectual stature; or he may be hated, or dead, or absent.

The child feels neglected or overpowered by the mother, depending on whether her love is lacking or overwhelming. The child never really feels secure, is always either slighted or fondled, emotionally starved or smothered; in one word, confused. [Claudia: *"All I remember from my childhood are anxieties, gloom, loneliness; but, then, I reread my parents' tender and happy letters (which I still treasure), and I don't know what to think."*]

A similar pattern has been discussed in the chapter on "Slant." There I listed two alternative reactions to such a situation: active, competitive opposition or guerrilla warfare, the open or the secret rebel. Here we have, it seems to me, two additional alternatives, perhaps somewhat more complicated: the *fugitive* and the *malcontent.*

Unfortunately, these additional alternatives are not at all satisfying. Left slant, whether an expression of opposition or meekness, offers the unfortunate children a workable solution. Pressure in the mobile axis at the expense of a weakened stable axis is, I believe, too great a risk, too small a consolation. Claudia and Bernice eagerly and aggressively follow that way and arrive nowhere, as we shall see. Alma, who tries to split her "vitality," her pressure, between the stable and the mobile axis may be still worse off. Noyes, under the heading "Schizophrenia," writes:

"It is now recognized that there is a continuous transition in behavior between the methods of dealing with sexual and other instinctive urges, with persistent childhood attitudes and fantasies and with social cravings and requirements on the part of persons whom we meet daily and the caricatures of these methods manifested by the schizophrenic. One will therefore seek to formulate the clinical picture of schizophrenia in terms of the familiar problems. . . . Only through a careful analysis of the personality and its evolution . . . are the causes of the psychosis to be found, its manifestations understood and its psychological connections discovered and formulated."

We shall see how both the fugitive and the malcontent develop schizoid personalities, Claudia and Bernice almost anxiously, Alma rather sadly, reluctantly.

They are intelligent and sensitive observers, these "neglected children," and they start early to ponder whether what claims to be a home and a parent really is their home and their parent. Claudia: *"My care was chiefly left to a nurse, so that in due course I began to doubt whether I was really my parents' child or that of some beggar, to whom I feared being sent back some day."* The decision of the three girls seems to have been negative; these homes were not theirs. How, then, can they escape daily confusion and humiliation? How restore their offended pride, satisfy their natural desire for a father's love? Two ways seem to suggest themselves: The (symbolic) flight from home to external success, later to return as the admired victor; or the strike, the infantile malcontent refusal to co-operate in the least, to satisfy even the basic parental expectations. The school offers the first stage for these early undertakings, and we shall see that the experiences gained there may set patterns for individual adult lives.

Claudia's flight to success got under way quickly—*"I always was a very successful student, a striver, never had any trouble holding first or second place"*—whereas Alma, the

malcontent, whose method is non-co-operation, was soon recognized as the most stupid child in school—to the perfect
consternation of her parents. *"I was supposed to be so stupid
that my teacher told me and the class that I was a disgrace
to my parents."*

Did these first attempts at self-assertion yield any results? Did they repair the fatal, parental dilemma about the
children, change their parents' attitude toward their offspring? Claudia: *"My father was disappointed that I was not a
a boy; this took the form of constantly minimizing my intellectual achievements which objectively were very good. Needless
to say that it started a vicious circle—I strove still harder,
hoped to shine brighter, and father maintained the role of
the disappointed."* Alma, too, was not willing to call off her
passive resistance of the malcontent. Too bright permanently
to enjoy the sad reputation of a stupid scholar, she changed
her tactics. *"When I was nine I suddenly became a very good
scholar. But I still was a disgrace to my parents' name, for I
would simply run wild in school; when I lacked a mischievous
idea, I proudly took upon myself my friends' pranks, and I
was duly punished."*

Claudia, out for fame, would have loved to have beautiful
dresses (she calls herself "quality-conscious"), but could
not get them from her mother. *"Mother would not buy me
any new clothes, I had to wear her old ones."* Alma, on the
other hand, an attractive girl, but deeply malcontent, would
refuse to take dresses seriously. *"I would put up with anything, even old garments; would never make any fuss about
dresses like my sisters. The black dress mother bought me to
wear to father's funeral was the dress I liked best."* She per-
sists in playing the unassuming, taciturn one when with her
family. *"At home I was modest, quiet, even unwilling to reveal my most cherished wishes, because I believed that I
ought to be treated kindly and considerately without my ask-*

ing for it." She would never invite friends to visit her at home; home was to her nothing to be proud of. The parents were all the more shocked, therefore, when time and time again the school report revealed Alma as incorrigibly naughty.

When Claudia went to college, she told me she continued her series of successes. *"In college I also was always first or second, and while I did study for my exams, I never had any difficulties, and it was easy and demanded no effort for me to shine."* Alma, who maintained a good high school record, also deserved a college education. Her parents suggested it to her; she refused. *"Of all my sisters, I am the only one who did not go to college. I simply refused to go. Now I am sorry I did not."* Whether stupid or a good scholar, Alma persisted in remaining on strike, in being a malcontent.

She even extended her aggressive "passive" resistance to the sisters. *"I would not speak to any of my sisters but one, and they would tell me that I actually was no member of the family but had been found somewhere, dirty and stupid."*

Claudia married early. *"I married in order to get out of my home. He was a good-looking, promising scientist."* The father had died, and the idea of living with the mother did not appeal to her. *"I knew when I married him that it would probably not last. But the idea of living with my mother, after father's death, was unbearable."* For reasons which will become apparent soon, she could not make this marriage a success. *"My marriage lasted not quite three years. It broke apart, because we were entirely incompatible sexually."* Incompatibility was only one of several reasons, however; later she will tell us another, and whatever she asserts cannot any longer convincingly present this marriage as a marriage; it was another flight.

Alma did not even consider marriage; she remained malcontent. And here for the first time it is clearly evident that

252

her inner dissatisfaction must present itself to the outside world as a mixture of envy, disputatiousness, queerness, even ill nature, and an unwillingness or inability to see and admit the true issues. *"First I loved to ridicule my sisters' beaux. Men seemed to me both comic and a menace, definitely morally corrupt. Later I mistreated my own boy friends. When, at 17, I received my first serious proposal, I was very depressed."* Why was she depressed? Was it the man or the idea of marrying? *"There was nothing wrong with the man, I suppose. But marriage was to me something lofty, a spiritual union, and men did not seem to care for that."* Such insistence on "loftiness" and "spiritual union" may be the indirect admission that she feels unable to be a woman; this would also explain her depression. (The unwholesome example of marriage her parents had paraded before her must also be borne in mind.)

Bernice, too, cherished the same yearning for loftiness. *"In all the friendships I have had with men, younger and older, I have found that sex has halted our friendship. I do prefer an older man, without a doubt. In such, I believe, can be found a greater capacity for understanding."* Most emphatically, sex is ruled out; Bernice will not even give vent to her feelings. *"After some period of time, he will make amorous advances. As a rule, I will not be interested. However, at times I feel I should be more tender to a man, in a clean way. This he interprets as a sex impulse of mine. When an occasion such as this arises, he is usually more than happy to take the greatest advantage of this opening. I, on the other hand, no matter how much I care for this party, will not give vent to my feelings."* She is, of course, aware of this man's hurt pride, and, obligingly, tries to bridge the gulf. *"Trying to be polite, I will do my utmost not to show that I am not interested in his advances, by acting coy. This the man interprets as 'teasing.' This I most certainly do not want*

253

to do. So after a nice friendship, the thing ends, always the same." And after this happened several times, her friends, boys and girls, considered her not only queer, but superficial, haughty, aggressive, and selfish. And she became depressed, unable to understand herself and the world.

Here, too, the refusal to meet sex otherwise than "in a clean way" may be indicative of an unconscious desire not to repeat the parents' grave mistakes, at any rate, not to have a child such as she was. The same refusal, slightly disguised, was found in the cases of Claudia and Alma. It would therefore be only logical for them also to "clean up" the stable axis, the stage of the writer's libido. No doubt, this would be the appropriate manifestation of a "clean" life. But what could these writers do with the surplus of libido they are endowed with? They could, for instance, displace it into the mobile axis. And what would be the personality of one who has put all the pressure he is capable of into "his plans and attitude toward the future and his fellow men"?

Terrace Furniture

The fact that American advertising—as suggested by this ad and the countless number like it, particularly in fashion magazines—finds most effective a type of script which indicates a "displaced libido" might offer a provacative field for speculation. Bernice: *"My intellectual ambition are to read and become more informed about peoples, lands, and old cultures. I also read and endeavor to meditate on things, abstruse to the average person, but to me, necessary and potent."* The words "abstruse" and "to me" betray that Bernice cannot suppress a feeling that she is quite different from "average" people, and that they might criticize her doings as abstruse.

This is only the bare outline of Bernice's quest for happiness. *"I wish to be able to speak in some other languages besides my own native tongue. I have never felt that I made the most of myself. I have been endowed with many talents, that I am certain of, but as the old saying goes, I am a 'Jack of all trades and master of none.'"*

It is typical of writers with most of their pressure in the mobile axis that they can neither conceive of their own nor, for that matter, of any limitations, nor can they stop "making the best of themselves." Bernice: *"I have a consuming desire to make the most of one of these talents, not to be recognized for it, professionally, shall I say, but at least to know myself that I am good."* Now she has stated her aim: ". . . that I know that I am good." Not wisdom or professional success, only self-confidence and belief in herself are her goals. Disappointed in her hopes, first as a child, then as a woman, she fervently desires that one of her "talents" may let her "know that I am good" (overcompensation).

With Claudia, twenty years Bernice's senior and starting with every educational advantage, the same tendencies persist, only on a somewhat higher intellectual level. *"It was easy for me to shine at the college. Later, whenever I wrote a piece, I sold it immediately. Now, with two degrees secured, I think of studying for a third. That's why I hardly have any time to see friends; yes, I am terribly busy."* Actually, success is not enough for her. It must be a succession of successes, not as an end, but as a means that keeps her ego alive, one

255

that goes on indefinitely, like a treadmill. That is why my graphologist friend spoke of "fussiness."

In spite of everything, the eternally natural feminine aspirations will not remain entirely submerged. Only Claudia, the more mature of the two fugitives, has become more skeptical. "*Now as to men, this is the average situation and always has been: I have hardly any difficulty getting them. The difficulty comes in holding them—here my success ends as a rule.*" And young Bernice, though still trying very hard, is not really hopeful. "*When I think of marriage, I do not think of being shackled to someone for life, as a great deal of people think of marriage, but two people harmoniously together and yet apart. I seek for a man who has strong character, one endowed with a warm heart. . . . So far I haven't found this person, and I don't think I ever will. It seems that what I ask is more difficult to find than rubies.*" This is a pretty pessimistic statement for a girl of twenty-one. Yet it also is a very truthful one. For in view of her special attitudes and sexual inadequacies, what are her chances of getting married and enjoying married life? That she does not relax her endeavors must be taken as further proof of her inability to think reasonably, objectively, in short, intelligently.

There is, of course, also the openly tragic side to this picture. For, without self-criticism and common sense, but full of yearning, both the fugitive and the malcontent are ready victims of every kind of deception. Alma: "*When I was twenty I met at a dance a man at least twice my age. His conversation was fascinating. Soon he had found a way to see me alone. And at our first secret meeting he made a declaration of love that was so faithful a copy of what I had seen in the theater that I thought all my dreams had come true. To make a long story short, . . . after one year of bliss-ful hours, mutual friends told me that they had seen him*

256

with other girls of my age. The sad truth was that I actually was only one of many. I had trusted him completely. I felt crushed. But as he was a 'heel,' so was he only the first in a number I seem to have been destined to meet. Yet I cannot live without men."

This last statement should give us pause. It is quite different from Claudia's and Bernice's remarks about sex. What these two seem to hope for is the love of their fathers of which they have been deprived. And because they have been so cruelly deprived of something so precious, tender and soothing as well as "invigorating," they respond either with a sex life that is "incompatible" or must be "clean." They also seem to suffer for the rest of their lives from a desire to escape into "delusions of grandeur." Alma no longer insists on a "clean" life. Therefore, before we proceed, I would like to have the reader re-examine these three scripts.

Claudia's handwriting shows heavy pressure in the mobile axis, but there is sometimes some pressure in the stable axis,

cannot be any doubt

too. Particularly the middle zone of her script has a fairly normal pressure pattern.

Bernice puts all her pressure in the mobile axis while otherwise maintaining the pressureless script that Palmer teaches; her t-stroke and the finals are very evident. She is a

lecture on

doctor's secretary, but dislikes "that kind of work" and is

257

not aware of the fact that she cannot satisfy her employer's expectations.

Alma's script, however, is very different. There is, of course, pressure in the mobile axis (t-strokes, finals), but since there is always pressure in the stable axis also, it is

Let me tell you that

possible to speak here of "split pressure," that is, the equal or almost equal distribution of pressure in both axes. In addition, Alma's handwriting is very disturbed, unruly, undisciplined. The lines are very unstable.

Let us now review these three cases. We find that Claudia's and Bernice's stories are almost identical; Alma's parallels them only to a certain extent. Her childhood with a weak father and a domineering mother was unhappy, but her sisters found it bearable, it seems. She hates men but "cannot live without them." She is intelligent but capable of playing the stupid pupil for a number of years. In short, Claudia and Bernice are true fugitives; Alma, whom I call the malcontent, actually is two-faced or split in her attitude toward her environment. Musical, well-read, and still attractive, she continues to "mock" men, yet yields to them; she offends people, then longs for their friendship. She seems bound to arrive at a point where she is not worthy of more lasting love and kindness; if really misunderstood, mistreated, and exploited, she almost accepts this punishment as her due, today just as she did when a child in school.

In only this aspect are all three alike, that they are loath to suffer anything that smacks of parental authority. Claudia:

"My husband tried to dominate me, and I couldn't take it."
Bernice: *"I am not living with my family because I do not wish to be subjugated by their will. Even now that I am away from them, they still wish to lead my life for me. This I will not permit."* Alma: *"With colleagues as well as superiors I feel very uncomfortable; I am unable to be just like them, and all my efforts to be popular fail. Frankly, I cannot take competition or orders."*

I shall now go on to further interpretations, which seem to emerge naturally from a graphological evaluation of pressure in the mobile axis, as illustrated by the foregoing case histories.

As the discussion has covered a large number of possible personality traits, doubt may arise as to whether it is permissible in each case to go all out in every interpretation. One heavy stroke in the direction of the mobile axis, and a few dozen interpretations are applicable. Can this be? Quite generally, handwriting is a microcosm, a little world. Man, six feet tall, makes gestures as small as one-sixteenth of an inch. Since these gestures are discernible, even in such a reduction, they cannot but be greatly simplified portraits or truly microcosmic epitomes of that greater world which is man. In analyzing handwritings, the interpretation must fit the stature of the subject, not that of his finest gestures.

To this it must be added that gestures which extend mainly in one of the two axial directions, the up-down and the left-right directions, deserve special attention. This is why I have called them the stable and mobile axes. It seems to me that in the main it is upon these two axes that man's personality rests.

Clearly deducible from the five case histories, I feel, is a strong desire on the part of the fugitive writers to know and understand, to widen their horizons (else I would not have been able to collect such enlightening information about the

259

subjects), but unless they are unusually intelligent and talented, their (usually female or feminine subjects) "thirst for wisdom" manifests itself as restlessness and curiosity. At the same time they show a pathetic inability to judge objectively either themselves or the world about them. For all their studies and quests are aimed at winning recognition and self-confidence, not at deepening their outlook, or, as Bernice says, ". . . not to be recognized for it professionally . . ."* As a consequence, our *fugitives* in quest of an object in life are often obliging and hospitable and seemingly filled with a craving for knowledge, but mainly self-complacent, boastful, chatty, vain, and basically sterile. In company, they are sometimes accused of being aggressive or too loud (they speak only of themselves), but since they lack pressure in the stable axis, they rightly feel unjustly accused. Hurt in their pride, they ponder about the true meaning of life and their part in it; their conclusions depress them still more, but they rarely recognize that what they lack to be content and less aggressive is true self-confidence, a bit of inner stability, or, graphologically speaking, some pressure in the stable axis.

The *malcontent,* for the most part, is in the same boat, but her conclusion is to go on a total strike. Thinking little of herself, she is frugal and even not unwilling to stay at the bottom of the social ladder, if need be. But underneath that mask of contempt of everything and everybody she is often full of a sad envy and powerless hatred. Since her strike does not ease her inner pressure, her temperament is

---

* "When we find in the portrait of a person one single impulse very forcibly developed, as curiosity in the case of Leonardo, we look for the explanation in a special constitution. . . . We consider it probable that this very forcible impulse was already active in the earliest childhood of the person, and that its supreme sway was fixed by infantile impressions; and we further assume that originally it drew upon sexual motive powers for its reinforcement so that it later can take the place of a part of the sexual life. Such a person would then, e.g., investigate with that passionate devotion which another would give to his love, and he could investigate instead of loving." Freud, *Leonardo da Vinci* (New York: Dodd, Mead & Co., 1932).

aggressive and explosive.* She also is shy and especially reluctant to call on friends. If they come to her home, she is overhospitable; to visit them would make her look like a beggar, she thinks. For she is both terribly haughty and easily hurt. Neither she nor the fugitives are prepared to take orders or to listen to advice. By the same token they consider marriage a yoke that cannot be tolerated; therefore, (remembering their youth) sex is either taboo or a source of disappointment.

To summarize the cases of Alma, Bernice, and Claudia, I present here samples of their most recent handwritings.

Bernice: Her handwriting is light; most of the pressure she has at her disposal is in the mobile axis. I suggest calling this a

"clean split." If the "draining" of the script in favor of pressure in the mobile axis is continued to the extent that the script looks "brittle, glassy," then we have the script illustrated in the Appendix ("Schizophrenia") and a case of delusions of grandeur. Clean split, therefore, may sometimes be interpreted as indicating a disposition to delusions of grandeur.**

Alma: Her handwriting shows approximately equal pressure in the strokes of both axes. I suggest calling this "split pressure." If split pressure coincides with decayed and split letter forms and meandering lines, we have, I believe,

---

* Alma told me that she attacked one of those "heels" (see p. 257) with a hammer and was arrested.
** With regard to clean split and left slant, I have been able to observe the following: A (fatherless) girl who, at the age of fourteen, wrote left-slanted, showed at the age of twenty-five a clean split in her upright script.

the handwriting of a schizophrenic (Appendix, "Schizophrenia"). The most recent sample of Alma's script exhibits a dropping of the last letter into the lower zone
and meandering lines, but the letter forms cannot be called
decayed.

Claudia: Her handwriting sometimes shows a clean split, sometimes split pressure. She was psychoanalyzed. Her friends

parents

complain to an increasing degree that she dominates every
party she is invited to because in her presence no one else
can speak. She can manage her everyday life, and works
hard.

But the graphological picture of those who put their
"vital capital" into the mobile axis is not yet complete. Seen
from a different angle, the transfer of pressure from the
downstroke to the *upper zone* mobile axis may be conceived
of as proof of an accomplished sublimation, "the unconscious
process by which libido or the energy inherent in instinctive
drives is transformed and directed to socially useful goals,"
as Noyes has formulated it.

Freud gave much thought to sublimation and the artist,
and I must therefore mention that, in my search for a greater
number of, and more interesting, scripts with indications of
clean split, I found this phenomenon in the handwritings of
the painter Rubens, the writers William Wordsworth, Robert
Southey, Cervantes, Romain Rolland, Bernard Shaw, W. H.
Auden, also Fridtjof Nansen, and the composers, Franz
Schubert, Verdi, Richard Wagner, and Tchaikovsky. Here
is what Freud thought of it:

"The artist . . . is one who is urged on by instinctual needs
which are too glamorous; he longs to attain honor, power,
riches, fame, and the love of women; but he lacks the means

of achieving these gratifications. So like any other with an
unsatisfied longing, he turns away from reality and transfers
all his interest, and all his libido too, onto the creation of

his wishes in the life of phantasy. . . .A true artist under-
stands how to elaborate his daydreams, so that they lose that
personal note which grates upon strange ears and become enjoyable to others. . . . When he can do all this, he opens out
to others the way back to the comfort and consolation of their

own unconscious sources of pleasure, and so reaps their
gratitude and admiration; then he has won—through his
phantasy—what before he could only win in phantasy:
honor, power, and the love of women."*

Unfortunately, what may be true of certain artists is

not true of Claudia and Bernice. "But to those who are not
artists the gratification that can be drawn from the springs of
phantasy is very limited; their inexorable repressions prevent

---

* Freud, *A General Introduction to Psychoanalysis* (Garden City: Garden
City Publishing Co., Inc., 1943).

enjoyment of all but the meagre daydreams which can become conscious."*

But clean split needs some further elucidation. Why cannot Claudia and Bernice love? Why cannot Tchaikovsky,** as is well known, consummate his marriage in spite of Freud's formula? Is there any relation between these facts and the fact that Bernice has no pressure at her disposal except the

little we see in her t-strokes, or that Tchaikovsky's script (split pressure) is interrupted by upper zone left-right strokes of evident force?

It seems to me that those whom nature has endowed only sparingly with libido are under the necessity of choosing where and how to invest it; either in their own "household" or outside, fully or partly; either aggressively (pressure in middle and lower zone mobile axis strokes) or in intellectu-

alized form (pressure in upper zone mobile axis strokes)..

In order to explain this thought further, I remind the reader of Chapter 15 and the subject I dealt with there, a sickly tot of only four years who was an avid reader of poetry and Shakespeare's dramas. At the age of nine, he tells, he was separated from his mother and books by his father,

---

* *Ibid.*

** The prevailing opinion that Tchaikovsky was homosexual is not supported by any known facts about his life; however, it is quite possible that an impotent man should strike his friends as feminine.

and he became an athlete. Some ten years later his first marriage was, to quote him, a "flop." After a divorce, he embarked upon a successful literary career. For his second wife he chose "a human being who answers as many of my demands and needs as are necessary to keep me a husband," so that he could be married after a fashion and nevertheless pursue his literary ambitions. When he has to work temporarily with his hands, he complains that he wants to write sonnets. Time and time again this subject has to choose between physical prowess and intellectual creativeness. He cannot both play tennis and write poetry, love and write stories.

Tchaikovsky, too, a frail, "excitable and morbidly sensitive"* child and man, could, it seems, be a great though pathological composer, but not a family man or lover at the same time. This, there is reason to believe, was known to him. When, in 1868, the French singer Artot took a more than friendly interest in him, he "responded shyly to her advances. We find him, even in the first flush of happiness, speculating as to what might become of his own career. . . ."* The year 1876 was a year of grave disappointments to the composer; everywhere his compositions were rejected; "things could not go on much longer." Can we not infer that serious doubts as to whether he really was a great composer assailed him then? The fact is that at the peak of his depression, in the summer of 1877, Tchaikovsky married. "The marriage turned out miserably."* A few weeks later he was divorced. "Broken in health and spirits he fled from Moscow. . . ."* But later his "love" for Frau von Meck (whom he never met) did not prevent him from "devoting himself exclusively to composition,"* from becoming a composer whom millions still admire.

---

* Grove's *Dictionary of Music and Musicians* (New York: Macmillan, 1935).

Clean split and split pressure, it now seems to me, are indications that the writer, probably because of lack of sufficient libido (power of resistance) in the face of overpowering "hostile" forces in his early childhood, chose to escape by fully or partly sublimating his libido.

The question of the graphological interpretation of clean split and split pressure, whether positive (artist) or negative (Bernice) is, of course, answered by other features of the script, particularly its style value: Bernice's script is still Palmer's. The above artists' scripts are most individualized.

In the interpretation of split pressure, too, it is the sum of all features of the script that determine the personality picture. Alma's script shows indications of a schizoid personality even if we refrain from interpreting her script's split pressure. Therefore, it cannot astonish one that split pressure can also occur in the handwriting of persons whose sanity nobody would doubt. In these cases the desire for self-sacrifice in order to find recognition may be in the foreground.

This fact becomes obvious in a case I have been able to observe over a period of almost twenty years. The girl was born with a heart defect. Consequently she could not take part in her brothers' and friends' plays and pleasures. We may assume that she found her childhood a chain of disappointments and sacrifices, that she thought she was not good for anything. . .

what

When she married she provoked general sympathy because she evidently sacrificed herself for her selfish husband's pleasure and gain. Whoever asked for a favor was received by her with open arms. When during the Second World War she was separated from husband and parents, she joined the underground and became an admired hero. She

Theaters

so persistently tried to sacrifice herself for the common cause that she had to be saved from herself. Today, at the age of forty-five, and sick, tired, discouraged, her script's split pressure seems to me to have changed to clean split.

Chapter 18

THE CIRCULAR STROKE
The Return of the Libido and Its Degrees
A Mother Symbol

The natural gesture of the tired hand that must continue to write is the circular stroke clockwise. This stroke expresses the most relaxed movement, and it generally permits the arm to retire toward the body. The most common type of counterclockwise circular stroke in writing, the garland, is only a segment of the complete circular stroke. The full circular stroke, the circle, is best exemplified by the *o*. Here I shall deal with the circular strokes not discussed in previous chapters.

To the geometrist, the circle is "the simplest and most useful plain curve." Indeed, to separate and "appropriate" any part of a whole (sheet of paper), we simply draw a circle around it. A natural reaction to the tiny space circumscribed by a circle or *o* is that of private possession, as though it were the writer's hedged-in property where he can do as he pleases, because nobody else can look in or enter.

The meaning of the circular movement, and especially of the circle, in graphology, therefore, may be twofold: conservative, that is, keeping what we have, and appropriative, like a hiding place or den; in both cases the writer's libidinal energy may be conceived as returning unto itself. Both these meanings, it is now seen, imply a certain "selfishness" on the part of the writer. This implication is supported by the fact that no complete circle can be drawn in writing without

268

the movement backward, against the direction of the writing movement—thus temporarily withdrawing from the flow and current of our forward communication, and making a gesture to retire to our private self. Such a return into one-self and self-preoccupation are most characteristic of the poet or artist who never could make us understand ourselves and others except by searching into his own world of feeling.

This left-tending movement is less complete in open circles (discussed later); it is most pronounced in firmly closed circles, either "fortified" or "double-walled," and particularly in external circles. The retention, in our style, of circles taught us in school would, then, have a merely conservative meaning, whereas writers who "fortify" these copy-book circles either by a "seal" or a "double wall" or invent new circles, may be supposed to do so to hide themselves or their most treasured thoughts or emotions for egocentric reasons.

The commonest circles in our penmanship are *a* and *o* (and the corresponding parts in the letters *b, d, g,* and *q*). We have been taught to keep them closed, but some of us overdo it, as we have seen, and others leave these circles wide open as though they had never been taught otherwise.

Quarter of Vacations

arrange

Of course, all these writers represent only different degrees of open-mindedness and openness; there are those who thirst for knowledge, and those who are merely curious; those whom we call frank, and those who are tactless; but none of them can be called selfish.

A few overdo the openness, too. To entrust such a writer

Cum.

with a delicate secret may be disastrous, for he probably is not able even to hide his own; and since the opening exposes the lower zone, this may suggest a quality of indelicacy, possibly the exhibitionism of a libertine.

Would   *Supposed*

Here I touch on a problem of openness that confronts us daily. Some people are frank, but not toward us; they speak their minds, but we learn of it last. Both the *o*'s and the *d*'s in these samples are open, but they are not open toward us (right margin). The question "What prevents a person from being 'open' to the 'right' people?" is not difficult to answer: **He is either a hypocrite or an intriguer, or so inhibited that he cannot bring himself to speak freely.** In order to decide whether he is one or the other, we must first determine the style value and then see whether there are additional signs of inhibition in the hand (such as smallness of the script or concealing strokes in the middle zone).

Intellectual curiosity or, as it is commonly called, thirst for knowledge, may produce openings at the very top of a

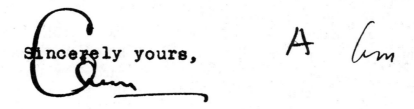

capital, in accordance with the theory of zones, whereas the

creative person's attempt to search his self must make him move the opening to the left, or to the bottom when he tries to draw upon his primary instincts.

"Sealed" and "fortified" circular letters, on the other hand, belong to conservative, taciturn, secretive, and inhibited people, as well as to the possessive and the haughty. And because these circles can be fortified so well, some writers actually use theirs as "forts" or "safes," "forts" by the neurotics, "safes" by liars and schemers.

Here it is well to keep in mind that the "treasures" hidden within a circle are actually drawn before the circle: First the writer draws the symbol of what is dear to him, then he draws his circle around it. We can thus truly speak here of something hidden within the letter which is then fortified. These "filled" and "fortified" circles, therefore, have always been attributed to insincere, even deceiving, and at the same time neurotic writers.

I have spoken above of symbols "of what is dear to him." In writing, the hidden "treasures" are always represented by symbols, which may be interpreted. Sometimes, they are quite elaborate and understandable to everyone. To be sure, this writing within writing represents gestures which are performed unconsciously. In both the following cases the subjects knew nothing of the "betrayal" their script committed while they remained mute.

The following word was written by an eighteen-year-old girl who was obsessed with the desire to have a baby. With-

out drawing too much on the imagination, the shape of the symbol can be recognized as that of an embryo. This girl feels so powerless to plan and hope for a normal fulfillment of this desire that she has conceived this infantile substitute satisfaction. Innocent as such playful writing may appear,

272

her indulgence in this mechanism is characteristic of her indirect and unstraightforward handling of her normal responsibilities, and she is generally considered dishonest and deceitful, as our graphological clue might have suggested from the beginning.

That a similar obsession may take hold of a man becomes evident in the following word, "world," written by a man of thirty-six (not at all acquainted with the preceding subject) who, prematurely impotent, has an unquenchable desire to father more and more babies.

Here, too, both circular strokes, the *o* and the o-like part of the *d,* hide embryos. (This writer is also notoriously unreliable, and yet so easily upset by his private preoccupations and anxieties that he cannot carry out even his own schemes. Note how disturbed each letter is, particularly the *d,* as a result of the burden of secrets in his two circles.)

The deciphering of such symbols is important for psychologists and psychiatrists. Certain graphologists, particularly the internationally known Schermann, have concentrated on this aspect of graphology.

Sometimes in the "imposed" copybook models, the circles interest us, not so much because they are open or sealed or filled, but because they are inflated or deflated, and in this process have become more or less deformed. In the chapter on "Size of Letters," it was seen that deflated letters were indicative of the inhibited, sober, narrow-minded, and timid, and inflated letters of the liberal, imaginative, and sociable. For example, this is Palmer's copybook *A,*

but this writer has deflated it to

without adding anything: a conventional, unimaginative businessman; while I believe the writer of this initial *o*

suffers from social timidity. Deflation may progress to the point where the two strokes meet each other. We then speak

of concealing strokes

which are treated in Chapter 14.

Inflation, on the other hand, is an opportunity the hand of the imaginative (or sometimes merely fanciful) writer never will miss: widening his circles, "grasping and accepting" a new era, so to speak, comparable to the pretensions of his intellectual horizon and the broadness of his imagina-

tion. The handwritten *P* covers much more territory than Palmer's, and the same holds true of the *b.* (Both letters are from the hand of a professional journalist and author; the inflation is therefore in the upper zone.)
274

Most inflated letters may be interpreted according to the zone in which they stand. In the upper zone the inflated letter indicates intellectual imagination, in the middle zone it bespeaks the writer's self-confidence.

The height of the two *t*'s being approximately the same, the writer (female) has inflated and widened her *o*; she also has widened the connecting link between the *t* and the *o*; and she has split the *t*. She is receptive and aware of her values, with a pet idea hidden within the purposely split *t*.

In the lower zone are the circular gestures that betray our unconscious drives and urges. As is always the case with pressure, they speak for our instinctual, sexual anxieties and hopes; without pressure, for our (unconscious) preoccupation with a person's deep, instinctual, yet somewhat socialized, needs for security, financial and otherwise. The former is exemplified by the signature; the latter by the *f*.

Pulver described these highly inflated lower loops as "money bags," originating in a "money complex." The crass disproportion between this hand's upper (intellectual) zone and the inflated lower zone loop seems to confirm Pulver's view.

Sometimes, inflated letters give a hint as to their meaning because they are "deformed" and the deformation "points" in certain directions. The most frequent case in the lower

275

zone is the unconscious mother fixation. It is, of course, no accident that three out of the four samples of mother fixation are taken from left-slanted handwritings; left slant and mother fixation go together, as I suggested in Chapter 5.

Returning to the complete circular stroke, it may be recalled that one meaning of the circle is that of defense. Neurotic writers sometimes use the circle to "protect" themselves against the "outside forces" that cause their neurotic fears and anxieties, and in such cases they draw a circle or

circles around their name. Experience shows that these "magic circles" not only protect their deep neurotic fearfulness, but may also contain anti-social impulses, which lurk within the hidden recesses.

Sometimes, though rarely, the circular gesture is not a circle, but a spiral. While the circle around a word may be interpreted as a neurotic attempt on the part of the writer to hide himself, the spiral movement has always been interpreted as the epitome of egocentricity, from stark emotional selfishness to pathological narcissism (note the lower zone in the samples).

276

Menninger* describes the narcissus complex as follows: "Most tragic of all, the love fixation may be upon the individual himself, so that he loves himself too much to spare any love to anyone else. . . . This concentration of libido upon self is normal at certain stages in the psychosexual evolution. It is the *persistence* . . . into adult life that deserves to be called fixation and regarded as pathological."

---

* Karl A. Menninger, *The Human Mind* (New York: Alfred A. Knopf, 1945).

Chapter 19

SIMPLIFICATION

A Yardstick of the Writer's Intellectual Maturity,
Culture, Imagination, Creativeness, and Taste

That simplified handwriting (not merely the simple school-copy of the immature) should be a proof of the writer's creativeness and intellectual maturity is not self-evident. Gifted graphologists, such as Magda Olyanova,* believe that "simple capitals" show "simple taste" in addition to "mental development, independence, idealism, and concise thinking." But to my mind, this interpretation is not adequate. "Simple taste" may too easily be associated with simple-mindedness, with which "mental development" obviously conflicts. Besides, what does "simple taste" mean? May not a preference for the simple betray the cautiousness of the man who has no confidence in his taste as well as the utter refinement of the fastidious?

I shall endeavor to demonstrate that simplification is an intellectual achievement of the first order, which requires persons of first-class intellect. This is not necessarily true of mechanical simplification. The streamlining of an automobile fender, for instance, may take a great deal of paper and a capable man's entire attention for a week, a month, a year. But we scarcely arrive at a simplified handwriting before at least thirty years of studying, meditating, and writing; and humanity's intellectual "simplifications" take centuries.

---

* Magda Olyanova, *What Does Your Handwriting Reveal?* (New York: Grosset & Dunlap, 1929).

278

This comparison is in keeping with what we know of physical and intellectual exhaustion. A man who, without previous experience, tries to unload a heavy truck may feel so exhausted afterwards that the only means of really renewing his old self is a good night's sleep. Intellectual exhaustion may leave a person a nervous wreck, an invalid for months, or for the rest of his life.

As for human, intellectual simplification—so simple and plausible a statement as, "All men are created equal," was probably several thousand years in the making. Mythologies, such as that of the Babylonians, with a principal god and lesser deities, encouraged and supported the idea that there must be princes and paupers on earth. Moses presented the one and only God upon whom all men were equally dependent. Were they not also created equal? Many centuries later Christianity proclaimed the equality of men *before God.* "Ye are all one in Jesus Christ." It took several more centuries and at least a score of deep and courageous thinkers, such as Shaftesbury and Rousseau, to establish and assert that equality may have been humanity's original condition.

It may therefore be assumed that several thousand years of constant and often perilous intellectual struggle by man-

kind's foremost minds were necessary in order to break down the vast and mystic Mosaic concept of a Supreme Being and Christianity's dogma that all men are equal before God to the simple and plausible democratic belief that "All men are created equal." And even then it took as mature, imaginative, and learned a man as Thomas Jefferson to incorporate this belief into a Declaration of Independence.

In the twentieth century, good and fluent penmanship is one of the significant goals of the education of all civilized nations. We are not only taught, but drilled, to copy certain models. Hundreds of hours are given to this drill. Any deviation, if it occurs, is frowned on, not only in elementary school, but much later—for instance, in some offices. Today, no religious creed is taught with equal earnestness, zeal, and bigotry.

Yet certain individuals, some of them comparable in intellectual stature to Shaftesbury, Rousseau, and Jefferson, after several decades of writing, adapt and adopt for their private use short cuts, simplified letters, and letter combinations. Why? To the pupil in the first grade, writing is an aim; to the vain and naïve, an object of pride; to the mature intellectual, a means and a tool. The pupil's hope and ambition is the perfect imitation of copybook models; he paints rather than writes a sizable script, as faithful and legible as possible: copybook-faithful, sizable handwriting is therefore one of the signs of mental immaturity and of the self-complacency of the "good scholar."

Our very best

After the pupil has overcome his first shortcomings, after he has written, often for hours on end, through two or three decades, he masters this tool. In his new "authority" he does one of two things. He reduces his handwriting to a mere cipher or code, intelligible perhaps only to himself,

oblivious or neglectful of writing's own qualities as a means of communicating with our fellow men—which we take as an indication of the writer's seclusiveness, asocial, neurotic inhibitions, and inconsiderateness. Or he simplifies the shape

of his tool to its basic forms without, however, sacrificing anything that may be called essential to writing's inherent mission.

In both cases, one of the first steps toward simplification is reduction in size; it takes years of exercise and such gifts as concentration, intelligence, objectivity, and philosophical frugality to reduce one's hand to such a smallness.

For not everybody who can write legibly on a blackboard can repeat the performance in miniature size.

But simplification and reduction in size alone are not satisfactory to the *creative* and aesthetic writer. After he has simplified the individual character to its bare outlines, he cannot resist the inner urge to improve and sharpen and embellish it anew by creating certain short cuts and simplified connections of characters which he considers practical. W. H. Auden contrived for himself a useful short cut for

Repetition

"Re," while the Frenchman Romain Rolland quite naturally preferred a short cut for the combination *et*.

The creative mind, in less creative moments, or the less creative mind, perhaps, is more bent on the practical than on the creative task. In each of the following samples there is at least one remarkable short cut—not extraordinary, but practical:

Short cut for *S* plus *i*

t " *i*

s " *t*

L " *i*

t " *h*

And embellishment was the writer's aim in the following sample, which, however, is also simplified to a considerable degree. (The omission of letter connections is a step toward simplification, though not really "commendable"!)

Philosophy.

Some writers limit themselves to simplification; the creative part plays no role with them, either because they are mature and cultured but not imaginative people, or because simplicity and frugality are their life's foremost aim.

available

This simplified, unassuming, well-proportioned script may be a businessman's, whose philosophy of life is to be useful, to play his part well in his community.

it is realism.

In this woman's script simplification and reduction in size have left it not only clear and clean, but almost "naked." Only true humility, if not self-abnegation, can drive simplification as far as that.

Simplification must not be confused with neglect. In this

We all. send m

sample the script is not only simplified, but almost "decayed." Such neglect of a script (but not of the contents)

283

is characteristic of writers who are intelligent, well educated, and well read, but completely oblivious of any impression, other than intellectual, that they may make upon others. From such scripts as this, with its threads in "send" and "our," the concept has been formed that the thread as a letter connection is a sign both of neglect and even of a certain degree of moral decay, and of an intellectuality devoid of principles.

Simplification that "consumes" the middle zone in order to develop (or rather, overdevelop) the upper and lower zones to their full height and depth is very characteristic of the philosopher for whom practical considerations are of no importance and are even beneath his notice. In a person's signature such loftiness of thought assumes the meaning of a

(silent) demonstration, perhaps against the earthliness of some other people.

Simplification, I repeat, is not identical with simplicity; nor is it the natural companion of a simple taste or simple-mindedness; it is the result of much "non-fluent" writing, mature pondering, intellectual culture, and, sometimes, creativeness. As such, we look for it in every handwriting we wish to understand. And we are prepared to find that almost always the more simplified a person's script, the more complex his personality.

Chapter 20

ANALYSIS AND SYNTHESIS, INCLUDING SPECIAL INITIAL AND END ADJUSTMENTS

INITIAL AND END ADJUSTMENTS

In many of the preceding chapters, single aspects of handwriting have been treated, such as the space between words, or size of letters. But we do not write single letters (except *I* and *a*); we write words. Also, in thinking our smallest unit is generally the word, or rather the idea it stands for. And inasmuch as writing words requires a somewhat complicated procedure—first to remember, then to write, and finally to connect a number of characters—each word written on paper is a symbol of a completed act. From

Mildred

a single word, or sometimes from even one character, therefore, we may draw a number of concrete conclusions.

Again, only a few people write just words, and nothing

Jesse

but words. Many writers need an initial adjustment, and rarely can they leave a word alone when they have finished it.

285

And since inquiries among writers usually bring denials, we may assume that these initial and end adjustments are performed automatically (much as brushing one's teeth or shaving). While we adjust the pen, we think of the idea to be expressed and the word to be written, and when we have finished writing, we still think of it. These initial and final gestures (the writer's "hello" and "good-by"), particularly because they are recorded automatically, without deliberation, and are evidently part of his thinking, must be included in our analysis. I may even go further: Because these initial and end adjustments are written without deliberation, they tell us details about the personality of the writer which he himself, if asked, could not always reveal.

In the following paragraphs I shall try to analyze single words for the purpose of illustrating my methods at work, and in each case I shall pay special attention to adjustments; the reader will see that in some cases they betray personality traits which the word itself would not have revealed.

ANALYSIS AND SYNTHESIS

As a rule, words are not analyzed; but if they are, it must be done with extraordinary attention. We cannot afford to neglect anything; each detail assumes immense importance. Next to adjustments (that are so often overlooked), we must observe, for instance, whether or not the writer remains in the zone or zones in which the word ordinarily belongs. Sometimes the writer will significantly lift a letter or part of it beyond the proper zone, or let it drop, wholly or partly, into the zone below. To draw all the available conclusions a written word offers, we must take into consideration everything we see. In fact, we must apply all we have learned here to every possible aspect of every letter.

I repeat: Except where more is not available, or for the purpose of demonstration, no responsible graphologist will interpret a word or character by itself. Why should he knowingly forego the check that other words of the sample offer him? Genuinely hardened criminals, for instance, will not often reveal themselves in one page, much less one word, so why take a chance? On the other hand, letter analysis is the basis of word analysis, word analysis the basis of script analysis; we would do well, therefore, to familiarize ourselves with the general procedures in actual practice.

The writer is male, nineteen years old, a college student; went to elementary school in England.

Analysis: The first letter is written with less pressure and more right slant than the rest of the word; it is preceded by a garland as initial adjustment. The second letter is less slanted and disproportionately smaller than the first; both *t*'s consist of concealing strokes and are arched, the t-bar is a flat garland; the second *l* is more slender than the first and taller than the *t*; the *e* is more highly placed than the *i*; the whole word, "little," moves upward, in fact, so much so that the *e* is no longer in the middle zone; it is in the upper zone.

Synthesis: This is a surprisingly mature script for a nineteen-year-old boy; it actually has aesthetic qualities; most probably the style value would be positive. The initial garland and the "inclined" first letter tell us that the writer has pleasing manners, that it is his wish to court people's favor, to be popular. To reach this goal, he may be willing to play the role of the easygoing, lively, and superficial young man, which he is not (initially pressureless script changes to pressure in the rest of the word). The two *t*'s are arched: He is full of plans for his future and willing to fight for his ideas; but most of his hopes and plans are his secret (concealing strokes). In spite of this, the tallness of the upper-zone letters, the aesthetic qualities of the very legible script, the "lifting up" of the *e* into the upper zone, and the highly-placed i-dot, give us more than a hint: This young man may hope to become a journalist, a writer, or more generally, an intellectual. Of course, he still has his doubts about his qualifications: The second *l* has been written with an uncertain hand. But the *e* is clean and clear and firm, and the connecting garlands look as though they would be angles in another ten years: He is earnest, self-critical, has stamina, can work hard if need be. Moreover, to further his aims he can forego any luxury, even accept privation: The middle zone is very small. Perhaps what he cannot give up is his need and love for beauty—I have mentioned his script's aesthetic qualities. This, however, is an asset, for to satisfy his aesthetic expectations, he will work all the harder. Is he conscious of his qualities? Yes, he is; those tall letters tell us not only of intelligence, ambition, idealism, but also of pride.

The writer is male, fifty years old; went to school in Germany. The word, which to some readers may be illegible, is "reasons."

Analysis: The first letter is anything but an *r*; the following letter *e* is much smaller than the so-called *r*; but the following letter seems to be taller, and tallest is the *s*; *o* and *n* are both very minute, the latter, ordinarily consisting of an arcade, presents itself as a flat garland; the last letter *s* is again somewhat taller. A most remarkable feature is the fact that the letter connections take almost three times as much width as the letters themselves. There are no less than four unexpected "enclosures" in this word; the upper part of the first *s*, part of the *o*, and two enclosures are almost all that is left of an *n*. Pressure is light but downstrokes are well stressed. The word actually consists of two distinct parts, "reas" and "ons"; the last letter of both these parts is taller than the rest.

Synthesis: Style value is somewhat doubtful; it is a mature hand, and there are no serious excesses, but the first letter is a warning; to determine this script's style value I would have to see a whole page. Since the first letter is not what it ought to be, what is it? Something as tall as a capital, consisting of an arcade and a left-tending stroke. I might add that the *r* is not one of the easily executed letters; a simplification would be desirable, I concede. But this is no simplification; it is an evasion. The writer, unwilling to write an *r*, wrote something else instead; too bad if other people cannot read it. For these very reasons, this "private letter" that ought to be an *r* must be taken as a perfect portrait of the writer: He is intelligent, inventive, not quite sincere, selfish, also fussy, formal—and inconsiderate. As long as he is satisfied, he does not care what other people make of it. I would not say that this "private letter" is ugly: With all his less ingratiating character traits this writer has some sense of form and beauty, and perhaps aesthetic hobbies that are not very common. The following three letters are rather long and connected with very long, flat garlands: The writer is a businessman who wants to be able to proceed without much friction. The narrow neat letters add to this that he can be a concentrated, systematic worker—rather pedantic*—and again inconsiderate and little concerned either for his own or other people's real needs. In view of the narrowness of the letters, the space between them (ordinarily an indication of the writer's generosity), because of its excessive width, proves to be simulated; although we may be sure that he often has guests, the motive behind his hospitality is not friendliness; but this is in keeping with what we usually expect from a businessman, also the "secrets" that he keeps in those enclosures. The important thing is the strong left tendency of this script: In the first letter, in the *a* (attempt to imitate the writing movement), both *s* and the enclosures betray a profound selfishness. But even this inordinate concern for himself will not be able to protect him against occasional losses; for the voluntary change of an *n* into a *u,* of an arcade into a garland, may be taken as an indication that this writer, sometimes a "sucker," is not safe against a more skillful and clever businessman; he has weaknesses. And as though to make up for them, he is disputatious and even arrogant—that is what the taller last letters indicate. These are my initial "hunches" from the analysis of one single word.

Coming back to the evasion: Since it is the first letter that looks different from what it ought to be, we must expect this writer to make a first impression on us that will not be confirmed later on; he is not at all as simple as the script may seem to be. Or better, he is quite as complicated and ceremonious a man as his script. It is always dangerous to underrate a man; in graphology it is equally dangerous to underrate a script.

This advice is a warning which becomes the more urgent,

---

* The very fact that he has so neatly divided that word into two almost equal and self-contained units confirms my impression of his pedantry, but is also an indication of his individually organized and systematized thinking.

the simpler the script looks. Particularly scripts that seem to have been faithfully copied from Palmer's Method often prove on close scrutiny to be far from faithful and full of individual changes. In such cases we must assume that the closeness to the school models is planned and therefore is not only an indication of the writer's immaturity but also of his intention to utilize the cloak of genteel propriety to cover up his not so proper purposes.

The above word has a most impressive end adjustment; otherwise it looks like a copy from Palmer's. We shall see that it differs from Palmer in a few characteristic details that change the first impression of this script almost to its direct opposite.

Analysis: It is a woman's hand; age thirty-eight, American schooling. The first letter is very narrow, the garland that forms the bottom of many letters of the Latin alphabet is here depressed almost to an angle. The connection from this *o* to the *u* is irregular: In school the writer was taught to use a flat garland here; instead she writes a flat, creeping arcade. To the same extent that the *o* is too narrow, the *u* is too wide, and altogether the script is at least double the

size of Palmer's models. Also irregular is the end *r*; Palmer uses here an ordinary *r*. The end adjustment, also a digression from the school copy, flares up twice as high as the *u*, or almost half as high again as the oversized *r*.

Synthesis: Style value, in view of the closeness of this script to the school models, is negative; her mental age, by the same token, may be ten years. In case of doubt as to the positiveness or negativeness of an interpretation, she cannot be given the benefit of the doubt (see chapter on "Style Evaluation"). For instance, the extreme and increasing size of the letters, together with their primitiveness, warns us in advance of her naïve self-confidence and over-expansiveness; the left-slanted rising *r,* that she is boastful, inconsiderate, and arrogant. (Most mature writers let their

letters shrink toward the end of the word—the willingness of the considerate and civilized writer to be agreeable toward his fellow men, and to listen to their requests and claims.) But this writer has no initial adjustment, and the script is clean, very legible, with sufficient pressure: The writer can tackle any routine job without hesitation and fuss; she is a clean and useful worker who knows her business, occasionally quite frank and also open-minded; but by the same token, this frankness may be indicative of her preparedness to give advice where it is not asked, perhaps sometimes with a rather brutal frankness that may hurt. However, the lean first letter with the angle instead of a garland seems to confirm that she is matter-of-factish, clever, again quite expert in her work, but also hard and unyielding, sober, unimaginative, and socially timid—or is she? That lean *o* is closely followed by a *u* which, if measured, would prove to be much wider than it is tall (Palmer had taught her to write the *u* tall rather than wide): What a sudden expansive-

292

ness and gregariousness! A moment ago we found this writer to be sober and timid. Is she now gregarious or timid, sober and a good worker, or lazy?

Reserving our judgment for the time being, let us now look at the irregular flat arcade that serves her as a letter connection between the *o* and the *u*. Transforming a garland into an arcade was called in Chapter 14 a counterstroke, and counterstrokes are generally indicative of boasting, bluff, and pomposity, the more so when hidden within a word. The irregular *r,* with its pigheaded, left-slanted top stroke, is also too tall, and then there is that irregular end adjustment. The writer thus appears as a sufficiently good worker, the clean and fluent script well illustrating this fact. But as soon as the subject "warms up," at home and among friends, she becomes demanding and arrogant (growing letters, with last letter tallest!) and boastful. (Of course, she must have the best place in the car and the best piece of meat—the width of the *u* is most indicative of the space she demands for herself, actually and figuratively.) Her approach to life is immature and superficial; hence, she lacks deeper understanding and regard for the things that matter to others though perhaps not to her. Her working qualities must be impaired by the fact that she is impatient (Chapter 10, "Size of Letters": too wide minimum letters), hasty, and negligent, and occasionally overbearing. This interpretation is derived from that end adjustment. For, reaching far into the upper zone, quite out of proportion to the rest of the word, and turning left, this flaring-up end garland tells us that in her secret soul this writer claims and is convinced that she is highly intellectual, brilliant, talented, superior to the rest of mankind—and misunderstood!

Here the danger has been to overrate the script. For its gentility is only a mask. Far from being criminal, such writers become deceptive and unreliable (remember the timid first letter!) through the resemblance their hand bears to the modest and useful school models.

Sometimes, however, the resemblance to the school models is not so much an indication of the writer's immaturity and primitiveness as of his genuine humility. He chooses not to deviate too widely from the bourgeois line, not because he does not have sufficient strength and personality, but because his feeling of responsibility toward his community outweighs the importance of his more personal desires.

humility

Female writer, perhaps 50, perhaps older; American.

Analysis: The first letter, looking quite ordinary, has a personal note: The initial upstroke has been lifted from the middle into the upper zone. Under the magnifying glass (indispensable in view of the smallness and "muteness" of this script) the first three middle zone downstrokes reveal themselves as double s-links; the i-dots are extremely high; no pressure.

Synthesis: The first word that comes to mind when looking at this handwriting is "Quaker." The lifted initial stroke shows the writer's preparedness to discuss purely intellectual questions in a purely intellectual, almost lofty way; there is in this hand no trace of the self-complacency so often inseparable from very clean scripts. but only unselfish reserve and quiet concentration on the tasks before her. In her endeavor to "serve the community," this writer may sometimes prove too kind, too yielding: double s-form of letters (see Chapter 11) is indicative of people who are

294

inclined to lean over backward to be agreeable, who cannot say "no." On close scrutiny the stem of the *h* also has the form of an *S*: Here it is the writer's sense of beauty that expresses itself in the form of an *S*, and may it not be assumed that to some extent this writer's reserve and calm are determined by her sense of beauty and proportion? That lofty considerations are foremost in her mind is indicated by the height of the i-dots; far above the script, they seem to point to an "out-of-this-world" way of thinking which, I believe, goes well with this ascetic script. Altogether, I would say that this writer probably has many good friends and devoted pupils (there is not only a Quakerish but also a teacher-like quality about this script), who remember her true kindness and calm; others admire her truthfulness and her unassuming, almost noble willingness to listen and counsel; still others love her feminine reserve and motherly, self-sacrificing spirit. There is not one left-tending stroke in this sample; the simplicity of such a plain script sometimes has a tinge of holiness.

The writer is male, age 36; American.

Analysis: The *l* is upright, the *i* is too small and left-slanted, the i-dot extremely high, the lower loop of the *f* very wide, the *t* is right-slanted and separated from the rest of the word. The word "lift," with not one superfluous stroke, looks clean, is legible, and in most letters quite well proportioned; pressureless.

Synthesis: The style value is positive; I would not dare say how much merely on the basis of one word, but it may be assumed that the rating would be over 2, therefore this writer is given the benefit of the doubt. He seems to be an intellectual: simplified script; little pressure; the (literary) *t* printed, not written; the t-bar finely pointed (see "Mobile Axis"); the i-dot high, in fact, too high—not all the hopes and plans this writer cherishes can be realized. To start with the first letter: The initial adjustment is neither excessive nor negligible, nor is the writer very fussy or very alert; he approaches his task and his guests with appropriate preparedness. The upper, the intellectual projections of all letters are well developed, without being overdeveloped: He has imagination but is no dreamer.

The *i,* however, is different; it is extremely small. Such a small minimum letter (in the middle zone) among well-developed letters is a mute yet unmistakable witness to inferiority feelings in the face of practical everyday challenges, feelings that are half overcompensated, half camouflaged, but not forgotten. In the presence of others, or when he is given sufficient time and liberties, this writer will never admit uncertainty or depression; the breakdown is likely to come into the open when the guests have gone, or when direct humiliation or excessive pressure cause him to bolt and rebel.

That swollen *f* loop seems to fit into this picture. The writer worries over money (note the absence of pressure!), not money he owes (this clean and quick writing is indicative of a scrupulous character), but money he wants to make in the future—the loop is to the right of the *f* downstroke, not to the left. (These swollen lower loops, when executed without pressure, are "filled" with those primary, unconscious drives only money can satisfy—here, probably, the urge for security and that peace of mind a substantial savings account provides.)

After the letter *f* there is a pause: This writer cannot be rushed, even for money; before he signs his name to a contract, he takes a breathing spell to consider and reconsider the proposition. I have discussed this case in the chapter on "Space Between Letters." After a deal has been prepared with all the logic and intelligence this writer is capable of (simplified script), he quite suddenly feels the need for heart-searching; for he prefers to arrive at his final decision intuitively, not logically. I would therefore not be surprised to hear some of his friends speak of him as irrational and even unreliable. "Yesterday everything was settled, today he said, 'No.' " But once he says "yes," he sticks to it, and he carries out the agreement. Of course, in view of the literary *t,* at the end, the distinguished conclusion, so to speak, to a less distinguished beginning, I think the agreement he might like best would be one that satisfies his literary ambition.

Another detail: This *t* is more right-slanted than the *f,* and the *f* is more right-slanted than the *l,* and the *i* is left-slanted. Once the ice is broken this writer's wrath is easily aroused, and once he is excited he is in danger of losing his head. By the same token (increasing right slant), when his reserve is overcome he takes a lively interest in many things and soon seems to be really enthusiastic—with the subsequent heart-searching just described.

That minute and suddenly left-slanted *i* fits well into this picture of a not very simple intellectual who, even though he quickly becomes enthusiastic, is also worried by attacks of suspicion and doubts. With changes of slant within the word, and with his light hand, our writer is bound to waver and change his mind, and certainly sometimes exhaust himself in inner conflicts—to go any further I would need additional material. An intellectual's handwriting cannot often be satisfactorily analyzed from a complete letter, let alone a single word. But the lack of elaborate initial and end adjustments does show that this writer is neither sentimental nor a daydreamer. And the isolated last letter reveals that he is an individualist after all, that his spirit of social co-operation has limits, that, in the final analysis, he is prepared and willing to stand alone, in fact and in thought—and to enjoy it. For independence, even opposition, is his meat: The slightly left-slanted t-bar is proof of that. However, even as an opponent, he will not transgress the laws of beauty; this script strikes me as that of an aesthete.

The writer is male, about 70.

Analysis and Synthesis: This S has a counterstroke as initial adjustment; or actually that letter is one counterstroke. To produce this "terribly impressive" S with the pressure-laden initial downstroke, the writer had to start his "labor" from the bottom upwards, not as is usually done, from the left end of the character. (To determine the way a character has been written, we must try to imitate the writing procedure; even if it takes a minute or two, it will always be rewarding to feel how a character has been made.) *

We know now that this S is a counterstroke, and in Chapter 14 we learned that counterstrokes in the first letter may mean "boasting, bluff, pomposity." Why, it may be asked, would a writer choose such a strangely roundabout route? And if it is boasting he wants to do, what would he boast of? The S itself is as fine and delicate as gossamer, almost invisible, rather unimportant; he could not be so

---

* Certain Palmer models, such as the capital *I*, exhibit elaborate counterstrokes.

very proud of that *S.* But, then, there is that heavy, pressure-laden initial downstroke—what vitality, what a man!

The writer is almost seventy; his vitality, measured from the letter's stable axis, is non-existent. The interpretation in Chapter 14 continues: "Together with indications of sensuality: a seducer," and slowly we begin to see light. A frail old man juggles his handwriting in order to impress people with his virility—or what they are supposed to accept as his virility. He may be the kind of person, I feel, who must and does have everything his own way, who will boastfully delight in playing tricks on people, outsmarting the unsuspecting whom, consequently, he profoundly despises. This *S* is not artful, only tricky. It is a primitive, ordinary *S,* not the product of the creative self-possession of an artist. Yet it is very tall and very lean: haughtiness and doubtful ambition (of the senile seducer).

The most meaningful source of information as to such a reversed letter is the fact that it is performed contrary to the movement of normal, cultured writing, and the real purpose of such a "perversity" is not a good and useful letter, but an exceedingly heavy downstroke in front of the letter. This "left" spirit (as opposed to the "right" spirit), symbolizing here the joy of the successful lawbreaker, is, of course, only inadequately interpreted by the word "selfishness." A man who writes his own name by means of a trick is not merely malicious and necessarily deceptive; there is one word that satisfactorily sums up this writer's personality trait: amorality.

That old age can look and act differently is demonstrated by the following *T* that was written by another septuagenarian. The initial adjustment here also swallowed up the letter whose adornment it originally was, but the result, even though almost illegible, is something new, a creation: A new and richer *T,* or instead, a gigantic s-link that per-

mits an originally lean letter (T) to cover an unexpectedly
wide territory. Since in his native Bremen the writer (Thomas
Mann) was not taught to make a T covered with an s-link,
but with a simple horizontal stroke, the interpretations of
s-links given in Chapter 11 fit here: "People who rely on
their intelligence, instinct and intuition to guide them; who
have ambitious aims which they pursue instinctively and,
so to speak, blindly without much ado or regard for bourgeois considerations. . . ." I would like to compare this T
with a sail in a full wind, or with a shield. The wind comes
from the right. Even though over seventy, this author is full
of the modern spirit and an unshakable confidence in the
future. The shield protects his privacy. It is meaningful that
this T, although a hallmark rather than a character, and
high above the rest of the name, still reaches all the way
down into the lower zone; for no creative mind can remain
creative without steady recourse to his unconscious.

In these analyses and syntheses of short words and single
letters, I have, as it were, "let my hair down." On the
basis of only a few meager penstrokes, I have, contrary to
my own principles, attempted to paint full personality portraits. Beginning with the handmade physical facts, I have
drawn conclusions, some obvious, some bold, and I could
have gone even further. (For example, everyone can see
that the sample word "lift" contains a lower-zone f loop
that opens itself toward the middle zone; the implication is
that the writer is eager for financial security and does not

300

hide that fact, and is perhaps generally "indiscreet" about his drives and urges.) I restrained myself, for in what I had offered I had already gone beyond what most graphologists would risk in print.

Like most professionals, graphologists generally give their conclusions, not their reasoning and thinking processes. Also, they would not consent to interpret a single word, much less a single letter. And consequently, they would not have consented to do more here than enumerate a few personality traits. I have committed all these crimes. I have exposed my methods of thinking; I have analyzed single words and even letters; and in order to synthesize the personality traits, I have speculated freely, drawing tones and shades from the slightest clues. Why?

I have strayed from the path of orthodoxy in order to show that a few little penstrokes may have many broad implications, and to illustrate as far as possible that personality traits have a variety of influences one on the other. I note: While one trait influences another (for instance, envy with ambition) in only one way, two traits may join with a third in at least three different ways, and three traits with a fourth in at least six different ways! And the number of these variations must then be multiplied by the (changing) strength of those traits. It is this inexhaustible wealth of possibilities that bewilders as well as fascinates, leading to the paradox that, in character analysis from one single handwriting sample, we can be both never quite right and never quite wrong. We must gather many clues from many samples, written in the morning and at night, to friends and to enemies, and then balance the values in a coherent total picture of the personality of the writer.

A FEW CONCLUDING REMARKS ABOUT THE
PALMER METHOD OF BUSINESS WRITING

Throughout this book I have referred to the Palmer Method as a standard, for reasons elaborated in my introduction. But Palmer's is only the most recent version of earlier systems.

Many people still remember the Spencerian Penmanship; not so many may know of Lister's, Shewell's, Beers's, Curtiss', Peterson's, Falder's, Farley and Gunnison's, and Ellsworth's systems, and the Duntonian, and the Scranton schools. Of these, Spencer, Dunton, Scranton, Falder, Farley and Gunnison seem to recognize some kind of pressure pattern, but none that corresponds to the *natural distribution* of pressure. Lister and Peterson do not teach any pressure pattern. Curtis has some mild pressure pattern, but shows slightly left-slanted models; Ellsworth insists on pressure in circular, not in downstrokes.

In comparison to these writing methods, Continental

Dear Sirs,

We will thank you to ship to us per first Steamer for Glasgow, 2,000 quarters No. 2 Red Winter Wheat, at writing instruction insists, and may have always insisted, on pressure in downstrokes, and only in downstrokes. The British Foster system mirrors somewhat the Continental trend, and, at least with respect to its pressure pattern, it is, British friends tell me, still the system taught in England.

I stress the importance of a natural pressure pattern in writing mainly because of its characterological implications. A reasonable pressure pattern in a script seems to me the most evident manifestation of the *writer's acceptance of the laws of reason and order and his striving for logic, self-discipline and self-preservation* within this reason and order. Lack of a natural pressure pattern may imply lack and abandonment of these qualities and aims.

Over-all lack of pressure has been interpreted as indicative of weakness, feminineness, carelessness, and mobility, as well as peaceableness. To teach a pressureless script is not, perhaps, to teach feminineness, carelessness, meekness, or superficiality, but the feminine, undisciplined, and superficial will eagerly grasp and imitate pressureless models, and so may the perplexed, undecided and the hypocritical. The masculine, thorough, and upright among the pupils may, at the same time, inwardly rebel against these same models because they seem to hamper and contradict their striving for logical order and manliness. If then, in their childlike impatience, they endeavor to develop a pressure pattern of their own, they may arrive at such manifestations of bewilderment and aberration as the following sample.

Yet the abolishment of pressure and of the development of a natural pressure pattern is not the only shortcoming of the Palmer Method. The very way it is taught is also open to criticism.

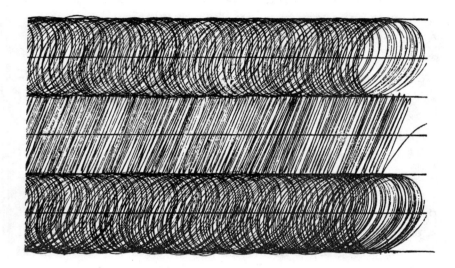

Adults still remember penmanship lessons as a source of acute discomfort and frustration.

Even with such drills Palmer's remains a tiring and slow method of writing. It is tiring and slow because it does not permit the writing hand to relax its muscles, as Professor Freeman demonstrated and explained. And this slowness is furthered through an abundance of superfluous and left-tending strokes,

of sudden changes in direction,

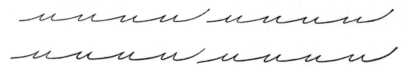

of counterstrokes,

and of elaborate, though useless and time-consuming finals.

We know very little about education through penmanship, still less about re-education, but educators who worry about juvenile delinquency might give some thought to an influence upon America's youth that lasts throughout our children's most impressionable years and, it may be ventured, leaves its imprint most deeply upon the most sensitive among them.

To this may be added that the proportions the Palmer models show are unnatural. Since handwriting is likeness it must also reflect man's *natural proportions*: a lower projection that is more extended than the upper zone projection, in accordance with the proportions of the golden section.

Equally disappointing are the Palmer models' artistic

305

qualities. Of course, not everybody wants to become an artist or an aesthete, but what harm would there be in teaching our youth an artistically perfected penmanship system? A number of British, German, and Austrian artists have striven to improve their countries' penmanship models; the names William Morris, Koch, and Larisch are internationally known. To impress all pupils with what is useful by means of beautiful models seems to me an indisputable national duty.

APPENDIX
(Pioneer Ground)

PSYCHOPATHOLOGY IN HANDWRITING

And a contribution by
ALFRED KANFER

PHYSIOLOGY AND PATHOLOGY IN

HANDWRITING

PSYCHOPATHOLOGY IN HANDWRITING

In the preceding twenty chapters I have tried to present a system of graphology that permits of the methodical interpretation of a person's personality through his handwriting. And although I have here and there shown handwriting samples of rather peculiar or, at any rate, unusual persons, I have kept pretty much within the limits of the average person's daily experience.

Some people, however, are not merely peculiar; they are distinctly abnormal, psychotic, or otherwise ill. They too have handwritings that can be interpreted. Why do I treat them in an appendix? First, because I believe it demands a reader's full attention to study and remember all the principles of everyday graphology; he will not want to take up peculiarities until he has digested the food for thought presented in the preceding chapters. Secondly and principally, because the handwriting of sick people, in spite of Lombroso,* is still pioneer- territory. No general principles of pathological handwriting have yet been evolved. Each abnormal script is largely still a problem in itself. Is this a disadvantage for the reader?

It is not necessarily one for the graphologist. He is accustomed to considering each piece of handwriting as something unique. He always looks for the individual behind the sample, not for the type. But others swear by the quantitative method alone. (Probably they are the ones

---

* Cesare Lombroso (1836-1909), professor of forensic medicine and psychiatry, and author of *L'uomo delinquente, La donna delinquente,* and other works.

who caused Crépieux-Jamin to sigh: "Today everyone who knows how to count is a scientist!") I must ask them to be patient. For in this appendix I shall continue my study of personality in handwriting, but often with new ideas, concepts, and theories.

This does not mean that here I feel less sure than in the twenty chapters. The ideas and concepts I shall present I consider "true," but in some cases I cannot offer the reader the comfort of quantity.*

For example, I have not seen many handwriting samples of schizophrenic people soon after shock treatment, yet I expect you to believe with me that the sample presented here is characteristic of at least one type of schizophrenia. The letter of a habitual liar is the only one I have at hand, but after you have read this book, you must agree that it is a quite perfect manifestation of a liar's handwriting.

It is different with handwriting seen from the standpoint of physical illness. Alfred Kanfer, who has written for this volume an exposition of his ideas on the changes that occur in handwriting through sickness, has examined thousands of cases. In the course of about twenty-five years of research, he has studied and recorded such changes on two continents, and time and again enjoyed the co-operation of hospitals and physicians; medical journals have then given him space to report on his findings.** So far, the psychological branch of medicine has not been equally hospitable. However, there is growing activity in the unifying field of psychosomatic medicine, and I feel that Kanfer's viewpoint may contribute by suggesting the physiological mechanism through which a

---

* The number of votes for or against an idea has nothing to do with its "truth." A theory accepted by 1,000 people is not necessarily truer than one turned down 999:1. "Thought and extension are qualities wholly incompatible, and never can incorporate together into one subject," wrote David Hume as early as 1736.

** "Early Symptoms of Malignant Tumors Apparent in the Handwriting," *The Review of Gastroenterology*, X, No. 3 (1943).

disturbed state (always physical and mental at the same time) actually affects the process of writing.

What uses do my concepts and findings and those of Kanfer offer the reader? Perhaps not many. But without this appendix, this book would be incomplete; with it, it has a certain roundness. That is all. And although I hope to expand this appendix in later editions, I warn future graphologists not to establish themselves as diagnosticians, not to mention disturbances when they believe they can recognize them in a script. The person who consults a graphologist does not expect to receive medical advice, but a description of a person's personality and behavior. At that moment it can be of little concern to him whether the writer is a reasonably suspicious person or a paranoid personality who is suspicious because he is mentally ill. Not the existence of a mental disorder but how it determines and influences the details of the writer's character and acts is of primary interest to a graphologist's client.*

Character descriptions are our own territory; as soon as we present diagnoses and mention specific names, we enter the realm of numbers and weights. Probably only a Freud could successfully argue his theories in the face of the violent resistance of those who measure and count, and even then it took him more than fifty years to gain adequate recognition.

This appendix is pioneer graphological territory. The reader follows me "at his own risk and peril."

---

* To provide the graphologist with these details I shall quote psychologists and psychiatrists of renown.

The Habitual Liar

The technique of lying, it seems, has at least three ways of achieving its ends. In the liar's presentation of the story,

1. one (essential) part is simply left out;
2. one (essential) part is left out and a freely invented part is substituted for it;
3. one (essential) part is left out and the gap is filled with chitchat, or meaningless or vague tales.

In all three ways the liar tries carefully not to appear as such; his story and approach must not arouse suspicion. (Essentially, the habitual liar, as a social type, is unwilling to communicate frankly; he will not express himself without indirection or hesitation.) In writing, the liar's techniques remain the same. While the first letters of words look clear and often are written with great care (to deceive us and to draw our attention away from that part of the word where the lie "resides"), the body of the word behind that first letter is, often after a visible pause, either

1. incomplete: one or more letters are left out ("ad" instead of "and," "Thankig" instead of "Thanking," "neived" instead of "received," "sicenly" instead of "sincerely"), or

2. one or several letters are replaced by letters that do not belong there ("eacl" instead of "each," "mucl" instead of "much," "costme" instead of "continue"), or

312

3. one letter is left out and instead there is a thread ("fr—" instead of "from,") or something that looks like a letter but is not ("ar—y" instead of "army").

The above samples are taken from one message, written by a habitual liar.

THE PATHOLOGICAL LIAR

These two seemingly different handwritings were written by one person, a pathological liar. She executed this writing for the doctor who had her under his care, in order to show "how clever she was," and for the purpose of having it included in this book. From the standpoint of graphology these handwritings are identical with the exception of the slant; neither contains a basic characteristic which the other lacks.

313

However, here again there is the indication of an extreme ambition (very tall capitals) together with inability to realize the hopes (low middle zone) ; the hopes may become dreams, and the writer may identify herself so much with her dream personality that she can write with different hand-writings. (Is it not striking that in one of the two personifi-cations she produces t-bars in form of arcades and a left-slanted script?)

The pathological liar, to be sure, is not merely a person who tells many lies. He is almost completely identified with the false roles he unconsciously assumes. Consequently, he will characteristically show two or more different styles of writing, rather than merely the slips of the "habitual liar." Such shifting of style is the clue to pathology which the graphologist can discover.

OBSESSIVE-COMPULSIVE TRENDS

One characteristic of compulsive neurotics is that they feel an unreasonable need to *repeat* certain thoughts or acts, often of an apparently harmless and meaningless nature. In handwriting, too, compulsion neurosis betrays itself in such meaningless repetitions.

When asked why she repeated the i-dots, the writer answered that she did not know why, but could not help repeating them.

beautiful

PERSECUTORY TRENDS

This paranoiac betrayed himself through blurred spots in his script. (They look like corrections that do not improve anything, or should I call them smoke screens?) These blurred spots may be interpreted as the visible traces of the writer's temporary *confusion* or his *unconscious* attempt to obliterate his traces. For such blurred words, letters, syllables, or figures seem to be produced during a passing loss of consciousness on the part of the writer, as I shall try to explain more fully in the following section on "Schizophrenia."

Paranoid persons may be found everywhere, in almost any office, and especially in politics. Some are merely irritable, moody, sullen; others are suspicious, overambitious, and cloaked with the pride of the deeply hurt. Very critical of the people around him, the paranoiac must suspect them of unjustified ill will, envy, and hostility toward him. For example, he may accuse them of and believe them to be communists, unfair competitors, perhaps thieves and poisoners.* In addition, he has delusions of grandeur; he may

---

* "Somewhere in this world I have an implacable enemy although I do not know him. . . . The tact that I know absolutely nothing about him makes life intolerable, for I am obliged to look upon everybody with equal suspicion. There is literally not a soul whom I can trust. . . . As the days go past I find that I am becoming more and more preoccupied with this wretched problem; indeed, it has become an obsession with me. Whenever I speak to anyone I catch myself scrutinizing him with secret attention, searching for some sign that would betray the traitor who is determined to ruin me. I cannot concentrate on my work. . . . Perhaps I am the victim of some mysterious political, religious or financial machination. . . ." From *Asylum Piece,* by Anna Kavan, copyright 1940, 1941, 1945, 1946, reprinted by permission of Doubleday & Company, Inc.

believe himself to be God and to have supernatural powers; he also is well known in every courtroom, and he will never understand that he cannot prove his case.

In the case at hand, the very light feminine script lends credence to the generally accepted notion (Freud) that homosexuality is often related to persecution mania; at the same time this writer (like so many paranoiacs*) is a man of superior intelligence who, from time to time, produces highly regarded scientific work.

As a graphologist I would like to add a few words to explain how I obtained the above sample. When I had before me the complete page, but had not yet become aware of the writer's pathological personality, I characterized him thus (from the stenographic report): "This young man is extremely ambitious, very intelligent and well educated, also literarily gifted, but sickly and often unable to carry out his plans. . . ." "Why?" asked my visitor. "Why can't he carry out his plans?"

Looking at the very tall capitals and their narrowness, the often almost imperceptible ("microscopic") middle zone, the lack of pressure, and the sickly over-all impression, I answered: "Often he cannot carry out his plans because his ambition is disproportionately bigger than his sense of reality

---

* That some of the world's greatest utopians probably were paranoiacs may be due to the urgent desire for peace and quiet the "persecuted" must feel.

316

and practicality, also because he is emotionally unstable, irritable, arrogant, particularly resentful of criticism, and timid like a little girl. . . ." At that moment, turning the sheet over, I saw the blurred word "beautiful." "And is he not very critical of other people?" I asked. "Indeed, he is!" was my visitor's answer.

Schizophrenia

The following handwriting sample was written by a schizophrenic a few days after the conclusion of a (not quite successful) shock treatment.

I shall attempt to analyze this script (without going into details) and to compare my findings with Menninger's and Noyes's descriptions of the schizoid type of personality and of schizophrenic symptoms.*

Menninger writes: "Reduced to its simplest terms, the common tendency of the members of this group is an inability to get along well with other people. This is almost too much simplified, because it might be applied to all of us at times, and to many criminals and 'insane' all of the time. But this lack of social adaptability is of very special kind. These people sometimes appear to want to mix with the herd. More often they obviously do not want to and they never do—successfully, at any rate. They may make gestures, go through the motions, even become extremists in social manoeuvres, but 'the pane of glass is always there.' They never really make lasting contacts.

"How does this make them appear? Well, variously, according to the combination of traits and reactions. Most of them are more or less seclusive, quiet, reserved, serious-minded, unsociable, and eccentric; many are timid, shy, very fine-grained, sensitive, 'nervous,' excitable, fond of nature

---

* Menninger, *The Human Mind,* p. 79; Noyes, *Modern Clinical Psychiatry,* pp. 430-452.

and books and fine arts; others are dull, apparently (not really) stupid, indifferent, often quite pliable, but more often very stubborn; sometimes 'stunty,' again morose and grouchy, and all too frequently suspicious, envious, and jealous."

Noyes says of schizophrenia: "Instead of looking upon schizophrenia as a disease entity having a definite somato-pathological basis, it would be better to consider it as a personality disorganization, an inferior type of sociobiologic reaction, an individual problem in human behavior occurring in response to the stresses of life situations, problems and experiences in persons perhaps predisposed by reason of a special constitution and personality make-up. The schizo-phrenic deals with the world in a highly distorted and sym-bolized way, the form of the distortion and of the symbols being determined by the nature of his internal conflict."

To the graphologist the over-all impression is that of dissolution and even decay. Already unable to reproduce the script symbols he was taught in school, the writer of the following sample tends to form his own writing symbols. Some look normal, some rather fantastic, unreal, infantile. In addition, there is the writer's tendency to lift or drop middle zone letters, syllables, or whole words into the upper or lower zone; the lines meander from the middle to the upper or the lower zone, and back. Another feature peculiar to the schizophrenic's script is the appearance of "split" letters.

From the writer's inability to reproduce accepted script models I infer his inability either to understand or to accept the civil conventions and social duties man has taken upon himself. That the writer executes fantastic and unreal forms of letters instead of the forms educated society has largely agreed upon, seems to me indicative of both a strongly individualistic and a regressive strain in this writer. He

318

I find New York to be the largest city world. It is however terribly overcrowded when one goes every place is jammed. It is annoying one has to wait a long time. Service everywhere is very only, ~

does not see things as we do, cannot receive our messages as we cannot receive his. In this respect the writer is in the same position as a savage or an infant: He does not want to be alone; on the contrary, he feels isolated, rejected, offended, as we would if people around us, particularly our friends, relatives, colleagues, suddenly started to speak a language we did not understand, and if, even worse, they also refused to listen to our protests.* From our side of the fence, and measured by our standards, the writer might well appear to be unco-operative, very fine-grained, "nervous."

That this writer does have a language and world of his own is indicated by the hazy and often fantastic symbols he has introduced in his writing. I refer to the *I* in "It" (second line), the distorted "res" in "restaurant" (start of fourth line), and the "and" (second word in fifth line), none of which could be easily deciphered out of context. And the same may be said of the words "overcrowded" and "terribly" in the second line. They exhibit grotesque changes and symbols that are almost illegible to us. Read "ideas" for "symbols" and you have a faint notion of what is going on in this writer's mind.

Equally noteworthy is the writer's tendency to lift middle zone letters or whole syllables and words into the upper zone, or to drop them into the lower zone. The middle zone is the zone of the "daily routine, the social relations, the habits, the conscious facts." To lift writing, which properly belongs in the middle one, into the upper zone may be interpreted as joy, elation, hopefulness, and (intellectual) ambition. (Noyes: ". . . emotional disharmony, often first exhibited by inappropriate laughter or silly giggling. . . . The patient may add that he feels he should build himself up by means of dieting and exercise . . . may become preoccupied

---

* If the writer actually withdrew from social contacts, his script would probably show disconnected letters.

with psychology or with metaphysical ponderings on such subjects as creation and causality, or with religious doubts, mysticism and meaningless problems. A young colored truck driver who had but a seventh grade education wrote an essay entitled 'The Imperative Mind.' ") Of course, since that lifting of the middle zone could be managed only by disconnecting the syllables or words from the ground line, these hopes and intellectual ambitions lack a real basis, something to build on.

The writer also drops middle zone writing into the lower zone, the zone that contains the writing symbols of our unconscious, dream, and instinctive life. From this I gather that, while speaking, acting, thinking, he loses certain essential links of his chain of thought; they vanish into the unconscious where they may continue as dreams, nightmares, hallucinations. Or his acts and utterances may have their origin in unconscious or hallucinatory impulses, as when he starts the first syllable of the word "restaurant" from the lower zone rather than from the middle zone— who can follow and understand such excursions into unreality? (Noyes: "In no other form of mental disorder do hallucinations, or the projections of inner experiences into the external world in terms of perceptual images, occur in the presence of clear consciousness so frequently as in schizophrenia.")

But this is not all. The dropping of middle zone letters or syllables into the lower zone also looks like flight. This writer may be afraid of facing reality, or does not know the difference between facts and dreams! Where does his reality end and his dreams and hallucinations begin? The lines waver, they meander up and down, from the conscious to the unconscious and back, a most bewildering stream! (Noyes: "One of the most generally accepted hypotheses advanced as an explanation of this serious disturbance in the affective

321

life of the patient is that the affect, contrary to first impression, is not lost or destroyed but is withdrawn from the conscious, perceptive aspects of the patient's life, from matter of reality, of the environment and of awareness and attached to complexes and other material in the unconscious.")

The inability to reproduce the school models and the tendency to form new and seemingly grotesque writing symbols (that look like materialized eccentricities or atavisms) appears to be common among schizophrenics. The schizophrenic writer of the following sample needed two minutes

to write his first name, "Isidore." This occurred when he applied for admission to college. He was twenty-five years old, but this script looks like a little boy's after one year of penmanship instruction. However, this is only a detail. What I am most concerned with in this sample is the almost superhuman force (pressure) the writer had to apply to produce five legible letters! He did not write, he dug into that piece of paper—unsuccessfully. For after the first five letters his effort collapsed, the last letters "re," the "sum" of his labors, distorted beyond recognition, fell into "oblivion." After a brave beginning, the writer must have understood that he could not be one with "the herd," that he could not adapt himself to "life situations," that he might "make the gestures, go through the motions, but . . . never really can make lasting contacts."

This distorted "re" is a symbol, of course, the materialization of what the writer thought when he thought of "re." It might be compared to the earliest Semitic or the most an-
322

cient Greek writing symbols, perhaps an early Greek *kappa;* or to a baby's stammer; or to a nightmare that haunts the writer when he tries to communicate with us, be sociable, co-operative. (Noyes: "Unconscious material and unadjusted tendencies break through and create sense perceptions, perhaps highly symbolized, in response to psychological needs and problems.")

The subject, on the other hand, because he can neither be understood nor imposed upon, may end by feeling both rejected and superior. As an outcast he eventually takes pride in his status, and his answer to his unresponding environment can only be hostility. In the first sample he appears irresponsible, dull, and haughty; also disorderly and moody —and so does his script. The vagueness of his writing and the up-and-down of the letters, syllables, words, and lines are particularly disturbing. In the reading one experiences a sensation of seasickness. This feeling is aggravated because of the lack of a reasonable pressure pattern, or firm and easily perceivable letter forms. I must assume that the writer also has no firm grip on his thinking, that moods and delusions play ball with him. (Noyes: "The capricious, impulsive behavior of schizophrenics is to be looked upon as due to an ambivalence of impulse, a contradiction of conative tendencies.")

The most remarkable feature may be the appearance of "split" letters in this schizophrenic's script, the *k*'s in "York" and "packed." Such a split in so great and important an intellectual construction as a letter seems to me tantamount to a split of the writers intellect from the normal environment and the world in general. It is this split that, more than the decayed, ambivalent, and meandering handwriting, symbolizes the break of his own thinking from that of other people. At least, that is what the name "schizophrenic" implies. This writer's broken intellect goes one way, the world

323

around him another way. His friends think he is deserting them; he suffers from the brutal inconsiderateness of mankind. And since his intellect can no longer follow our logical ways, he cannot but allow his emotions to take over. (Noyes: ". . . the explanation for the disorder in the thinking of schizophrenics is being found in the great extent to which associations are directed by affective processes and complexes . . . broken, led into bypaths, fragmented and joined through common affects rather than through conscious, logical connections.")

Split letters (and a broken intellect), I submit, are not necessarily connected with all forms of schizophrenia. For instance, I have seen split letters in the handwriting of people commonly regarded as normal, though perhaps a bit queer—probably indicating a schizophrenic disposition.

On the other hand, certain schizophrenics may show "split pressure" instead of split letters. Split pressure, as I see it, exists when there is pressure in *both axes of a script.* I believe such split pressure is the vitality equivalent of split letters. Pressure, being the graphological manifestation of vitality, splits into two divergent and incompatible directions (two axes): one part (stable axis) directed toward the writer himself (self-preservation), the other (mobile axis) toward the writer's environment (social contacts); the result may very well be a split in a person's vitality.

Split pressure may be observed in the following sample, which comes from a schizophrenic's hand. In the word, "oath," pressure in the t-bar and stem are approximately the same. Further, in the word, "allegiance," the *ce* is

324

blurred as it would be in the script of a paranoiac, and *the script is feeble though not decayed.* A psychiatrist, to

U.S.A., sign his men, by oath of allegiance.

(This sample is reduced to ½ of original size)

whom I am indebted for this and the following samples, told me about the writer (male, thirty-eight years old) of the above sample: "Transitory split of personality, schizophrenia attack, paranoiac trends."

My interpretation of split pressure is, I repeat, a split in the writer's drives and emotions. Such schizophrenics may be extremely capricious and bewildering, unable to distinguish between what is appropriate and what inappropriate. Alma (in Chapter 17) shows many traits of the emotionally split personality. She is both ambitious and resigned, tender and callous, sociable and retired, stupid and bright, self-forgetful and selfish. I feel that this simultaneous pressure in both axes actually divides the writer's vital force between the "I" and the "you," between self-preservation and self-sacrifice, masculine and feminine tendencies. This cannot but result in an ambivalent, unrealistic attitude of the writer who is neither governable nor predictable. (Noyes: "The other disturbance of affect is an emotional disharmony. At times experience and ideas that should evoke a certain emotional response will produce its opposite—an emotional disconnection or disassociation. States of unreality are probably closely related to thought blocks, feelings of stupidity, fugues, dream states and other involuntary withdrawals.")

However, the phenomenon of split pressure is not limited

to schizophrenics and schizoid personalities alone. The following sample was written by an epileptic. We note that pressure in the t-bars and endstrokes is as strong as in the t-stems; but the writer's pen can produce light strokes, too: the *a* and the initial stroke of the *b* in "better." Yet there

I feel a lot better to

is a profound difference between the decayed, infantile writing and this epileptic's writing. Whereas the schizo-phrenic's script is full of vague and weak forms, this script has the stiffness and jerky angles that fit into the picture of an epileptic.

Instead of split letters and split pressure there may be prevalent in the handwriting of schizophrenic writers what I like to call "clean split" or, to follow Pulver, the indication of "displaced libido." Such a clean split exists when the writer withholds all pressure from the stable axis to "pour" it into the mobile axis. Since the stable axis is the "natural" place for pressure, a clean split seems to me tantamount to the writer's anxious (or somatogenic) tendency to apply all his creative and recreative energies on sterile, abstruse,* and outward goals, abandoning his self to accidental and unhealthy forces.

My usual name

The writer (male, nineteen) has spent considerable time in institutions, was picked up in a New York park singing and shouting; as the text of the sample indicates, he has a

---

* This is the word Bernice used.

"usual name," but he believes he really is Rudolph Valentino, the late movie star. The clean split [no pressure in the stable axis ("M"), much pressure in the right-tending letter connections, particularly evident in endstrokes] is not very obvious; but it is apparent that the script is not decayed, not schizophrenic. Quite interesting is the writer's tendency to lift certain letters (*e* in "name") and whole words ("usual") into the upper zone; in this there are signs of a fugue and also of elation and euphoria. Perhaps this writer was very satisfied with his accomplishments and talents; he may have believed himself to be particularly active (pressure is directed to the right only!), enterprising, inspired, imaginative, and successful, and that others were not—the psychiatric description of this case is dementia praecox, delusions of grandeur.

The following sample exhibits a more perfect case of

clean split yet in combination with a seemingly quite healthy script. The writer is a woman of about fifty who, according to her friends, looks like a prematurely aged fifteen-year-old girl. They believe her to be very talented, ambitious, and always enterprising. (The same might have been said of Bernice and Claudia, both of whom show clean split.*)

---

* Chapter 17, "The Mobile Axis."

327

She spent two years in an institution because of delusions of grandeur.

Here, too, one would speak of a schizoid disposition rather than schizophrenia. The script is not only not decayed, it looks almost unnaturally clear, rigid, and—virgin. (But the *d* in "regards" and the *a* in "place" show a tendency to break or split up.) In an analysis of this (left-slanted!) script I would characterize the writer as a very ambitious, orderly, clean, and seemingly quite reasonable woman—but all on an extremely slender, almost artificial basis. For the "irresistible" ambition of this writer, as manifested in that highly aspiring, strongly stressed t-bar, impresses me as

Thea

directed toward futile, unattainable goals; her activity is empty, without substance, childish fussiness rather than work. I would not be surprised to find her forward as well as helpless, boastful as well as timid. The withdrawal of her innate energies (libido) from the stable axis may, of course, make the writer appear girlish in spite of her age, but it may also leave her without mission or meaning. This writer's script definitely strikes me as frigid, dried out, barren, sterile. (Noyes: "It should be said, however, that some of the world's foremost psychiatrists still believe that schizophrenia is a somatogenic, probably encephalogenic, disorder. The late Professor Mott, director of Maudsley Hospital, for example, believed that the biological basis of schizophrenia is an inherent lack of vitality in the fertilized ovum. . . .")

The following sample of clean split—pressure in the

t-bar is perhaps three times as heavy* as in the stem—appears in a handwriting which has all the characteristics of dissolution and decay. Here again the writer cannot always reproduce the penmanship models he has been taught. The word "writing" in this man's script is not the standard word "writing," to say nothing of the i-dot which is above the wrong stroke; the writer (male, thirty-five) has arrived at a writing of his own, the break with the world has been accomplished.

The psychiatrist's description of the writer is: "Schizophrenic with paranoiac attack." This leads me to another peculiarity in the handwriting of many schizophrenics. Except in that of the woman of fifty, all my samples of schizophrenic or schizoid writing show some blurred words or letters or figures. These blurred words or figures seem to be the result of a passing loss of consciousness and simultaneous rigidity on the part of the writer; for in order to produce blurred words and sudden pressure, the writer's hand must have trembled and pressed and remained on the same spot, perhaps rested there as though in a spell of vertigo. (Noyes: "Schizophrenia is not rarely accompanied by certain physical symptoms. One of the most frequent of these is a general

---

* Not always is the difference in pressure so obvious, but this holds true also for the difference between sane and insane.

disequilibrium of the autonomic nervous system. Sometimes patients in a catatonic stupor . . . persist in standing about in an immobile manner. . . . Attacks of vertigo and hysteriform and epileptiform seizures may occur. . . .")

That split letters, split pressure, and clean split have a meaning in the handwriting of schizophrenics seems also to have been observed by the psychiatrist Annelise Mandowsky.* She examined and described the handwritings of 100 schizophrenics, 15 depressives, and 50 sane writers. In the samples of 72 per cent of the schizophrenics and 75 per cent of the depressives, but in only 12 per cent of the sane she found what she described as "sharp, icy, glassy" script, which is, I believe, the same trend I call clean split: a pressureless stable axis and pressure in the mobile axis do give a script an "icy, glassy" character. Of the 22 schizophrenic samples reproduced in her booklet I found 9 with split pressure, 4 with clean split, 3 with split letters.

Magdalena Thumm-Kinzel** gives 15 samples of "psychopathic" handwritings, of which 7 show split pressure and 4 clean split. In 13 handwriting samples of criminals presented by Dr. Georg Schneidemühl*** I found split pressure in 10, clean split in 1. Out of 100 samples of the handwriting of people with "unfavorable character," which Crépieux-Jamin**** collected, I found 17 with split pressure, 20 with clean split.

To sum up: From a purely graphological standpoint, a schizoid disposition seems to be indicated if a script shows either split letters, or split pressure, or clean split. This dis-

---

* Annelise Mandowsky, *Vergleichend-psychologische Untersuchungen über die Handschrift* (Hamburg, 1933).
** Magdalena Thumm-Kinzel, *Der psychologische und pathologische Wert der Handschrift* (Berlin, 1905).
***"Verbrecherhandschriften," *Archiv für Kriminologie* (1918).
**** J. Crépieux-Jamin, *Les éléments de l'écriture des canailles* (Paris: E. Flammarion, 1923).

position may become schizophrenia when, in addition to these splits, the script shows decay and loss of zone orientation.

Graphologically I would interpret the

split letter	as indicating a break with tradition, customs, and the socially acceptable—a split in the writer's intellectual world;
split pressure	as indicating a deeper break in the natural continuity of drives and urges—a split in the writer's vital directedness;
clean split	as indicating a driven or anxious (or somatogenic) attempt on the part of the writer to redirect the natural continuity of human drives and urges into external channels leading, according to the writer's innate gifts, either to pathological demands for acclaim (delusions of grandeur) or to well-founded claims to recognition (grandeur);
decayed script	as indicating the undermining of the writer's image of the real world and the dissolution of his contact and communication with other people;
wavering lines	as indicating the writer's confusion between conscious and unconscious, facts and hallucinations.

Oversimplified and incomplete as these interpretations are, they may serve as an invitation to experimental psychiatrists to look into these problems from the standpoint of expressive gestures. As a graphologist I am not prepared to discuss the complete dynamic and genetic bases for these expressive signs and symptoms.

331

PSYCHOPATHOLOGY IN HANDWRITING

THE INHARMONIOUS PERSONALITY

A Study in Exaggeration

The inharmonious personality is not pathological, though the pathological person always has an inharmonious personality. However, when I considered in which chapter to treat inharmonious personalities, I felt that the best place was the appendix.

I have mentioned the inharmonious personality throughout this book, in "Symmetry," "Pressure," and "The Stable Axis." Whenever I drew the reader's attention to an exaggeration in a script, I implicitly dealt with the inharmonious personality. For in handwriting exaggeration is the hallmark of the inharmonious. Since an exaggeration in one aspect can be produced only at the expense of another aspect, that is, through the neglect or atrophy of that other aspect, *every exaggeration in one feature of writing betrays a deficiency in some other feature.*

There are as many kinds of exaggeration as there are factors in writing: in pressure or lack of pressure, in height or smallness, in width or narrowness, in legibility, in slant, in fluency. . . But when do we speak of an exaggeration? How do we spot it?

Two yardsticks are employed: the school model and the writer's middle zone. The qualifications of the school model as a yardstick are obvious. We all start our writing from school models; they are the standards that are held up to us through the years of writing instruction. Perhaps no social law or convention is impressed so persistently on the future citizen as the law of writing. The middle zone is probably the most subtle mirror of that instruction. This does not mean that in all or most handwritings the middle zone is preserved as a quite exact reproduction of the school model. It is, however, the most truthful manifestation of

332

how far the writer has ever accepted these models. Why is this so?

The middle zone in writing has all the characteristics of a small coin: handy and inconspicuous. This is not true of the upper or lower zones, and especially not of capitals and initials; they are most conspicuous, and since every writer is as well aware of this fact as his reader,* he embellishes them to the best of his ability—with certain exceptions! The capitals and initials are not handy either. In one hundred words there are usually:

Capitals	8
First letters	92
Lower zone letters............................	13
Upper zone letters not initials	107
Middle zone letters including initials	337

The middle zone, therefore, actually is our small coin, our daily routine, handy and self-evident, inconspicuous, undisguised, and for this reason probably the truest manifestation of what is genuine in a person's script. A law of genuineness in handwriting would state that a trait would be considered the more genuine, the more routinized its performance becomes to the writer. Since minimum letters occur forty times as frequently as capitals, we must look to the middle zone for genuineness—and for a person's routinized behavior.

Exaggeration in Size

For instance, in the following name (not legible), the

---

* After a script has been produced, we observe and judge it primarily through our eyes. To the reader, therefore, the most obvious feature in a script becomes the most remarkable. Inasmuch as every writer is also a reader of letters, the most obvious features of his script, such as size and pressure, assume extraordinary importance for him.

capital letter *J* is fourteen times as tall as the middle zone *a* (or is it *o*?). Palmer permits this capital to be only five times

as tall as an *a*. What has happened in our sample is this: The middle zone letter is only half the normal height and the height of the capital has been almost tripled. The tallness of this capital has therefore been achieved, as it were, at the expense of the middle zone letters.

Roughly speaking, we have here an extremely dwarfed sense of reality and self-reliance together with presumptuous bearing and an abnormally exaggerated desire to be and to be considered great. The result must be an inharmonious personality with both arrogance and aggressiveness and probably cycles of depression and emotional discomfort.

If, in the above case, the fact of exaggeration is very obvious, it is rather hidden in the following sample. This is

a remarkably small script that would, other considerations aside, indicate modest appearance and an objective and concentrated way of thinking. An examination of the proportions within the word "Pulver" reveals that here the capital is about six times as tall as the average middle zone letter, whereas the Palmer *P* is only about three times as tall as the *u*. The writer has reduced the *u* to one third of its standard size, the *P* to two thirds. Consequently, even though both letters are smaller than the school letters, their relation to each other is abnormally exaggerated in favor of the over-sized capital. We would find this writer seemingly rather reserved and unobtrusive, but in reality consumed with practically the same desire for greatness as the writer of the preceding sample and filled, perhaps not so much with arrogance, as with envy. Combined with this is the inability to realize his aims. Both subjects exhibit the characteristics of inharmonious personalities, the main difference being that the first writer would express his exaggerated claims freely, the second one hides them.

Exaggeration in Pressure

According to Freeman and Saudek, a certain amount of pressure is quite natural in a person's handwriting, particularly in the downstrokes. But genuine over-all pressure in a script (not simulated by means of a stylo) implies more than just vitality; it also indicates a certain amount of will power. For without the exertion of will power, we would from time to time relax the pressure, and it would not appear over-all. This is an obvious case.

To keep the writing hand suspended above the paper so that the pen barely touches it also taxes not only our muscles (secondary pressure), but our persistence as well. Therefore, both writers, the one with the heavy and the other with the small and light hand, are people of some kind of will power; the former demonstratively and obviously so, the latter rather unexpectedly and quietly; the one perhaps together with all the marks of the he-man, the other under the disguise of feminine helplessness and modesty. But if, in addition, a person's pressureless hand produces capitals that are scarcely taller than small letters, then we may be sure that this is a demonstration of modesty. For the extremely under-

sized capital is an exaggeration as well as the oversized; only this exaggeration tends toward the negative. Lack of tallness where tallness is required, coupled with lack of pressure where pressure would be natural, point to a disharmony, though of a special kind.

Exaggeration in Width

This word "iconoclast" is over three and one-quarter inches in length. Palmer would have written the same word in less than two inches. Normally, I would interpret such

an exaggeration in width as manifesting an extreme attraction on the part of the writer toward his neighbor (company, amusement), an urge toward the end of the line (laziness, lack of perseverance), a yearning for *Lebensraum* (recognition, lack of restraint, looseness, waste). But on close scrutiny the width appears to be caused by the space *between* the letters, not the letters themselves; these are, on the contrary, quite narrow. Therefore, although the writer has a desire for looseness and waste, a desire that is furthered and strengthened through pressure in the strokes of the *right-tending* mobile axis and absence of pressure in the stable axis, he is stymied and frustrated in this desire through inhibition. Add to this the yearning for the

336

very concentration, economy, and perseverance the extreme width of his script denies him, and the result is that he can neither go nor stand still, neither enjoy company nor work, a basically restless and helpless, inharmonious personality. (A similar (female) case was discussed in Chapter 14, "Concealing Strokes.")

Alfred

In contrast to this exaggerated width, this word "Alfred" is too narrow, particularly as compared to its height. Palmer requires one and one-quarter inches for A-l-f-r-e-d; this writer was satisfied with half an inch. Obviously, he does not permit himself to make the usual use of the allotted space; he tries to save, to pinch: He is not very neighborly (sociable, hospitable), not easygoing (but, on the contrary, a hard and perhaps somewhat compulsive worker), almost narrow-minded, definitely unwilling to unbend and let himself go. This is no pleasant state of mind. And to this must be added the height of the letters: a yearning for greatness, idealism, liberalism, intellectual achievement.

Inharmonious personalities, like the schizoid, the compulsive, and the paranoiac, are our neighbors, left and right. They are the people who differ in their opinions and ways of acting from the "ideal citizen," who are unusual, often original, and sometimes successful innovators. They also are the people who make different impressions on different people, who have two faces. It is one of the most important tasks of graphology to describe the inharmonious personality.

PHYSIOLOGY AND PATHOLOGY IN HANDWRITING

By Alfred Kanfer

When he said, "Handwriting is brainwriting," the German physiologist Preyer set graphology on the way to becoming a science. For Preyer proved that it is not manual skill alone, or a particular form of training, that gives handwriting the individual style which is the mark of the writer. If a person takes a pen between his toes and trains for some time to write with his foot, he will produce a writing whose peculiar forms will be consonant with those of his hand. Why does this happen? Because the hand or the foot is only an intermediary in this process. The hand or the foot writes, but the brain dictates the peculiar shape of the movement.

"Handwriting is brainwriting." No other statement in graphology has been so extensively misinterpreted. For it has been assumed that Preyer meant to refer to the intellectual function of the brain, to the psychology of personality, and not to the entire psychophysiological setup of the writer. Yet his experiments seem to prove that both man's physiology and his psychology give handwriting its peculiar form. Indeed, one is tempted to say that the physiological element is primary.

For some reason or other graphology shied away from this last suggestion. Perhaps the fact that graphology had to struggle to demonstrate the psychological bases of the individual forms of writing led it more or less to ignore the physiological aspects in handwriting. In so doing, graphology missed an opportunity to provide both medicine and psychology with a tool for studying extremely subtle change on a psychophysiological level.

That there are definite relations between handwriting and physiology, and the physique of the writer, no serious investigator would dispute. Scarcely a graphological writer on the Continent could avoid making at least some casual reference to his observations of characteristic changes in handwriting in connection with certain physical changes in the writer. But nowhere has any attempt been made to get at the root of these relations through systematic investigation.

Here a personal remark may be permitted. I have had the opportunity of examining many thousands of handwritings and case histories in hospital and private files, both in this country and in Europe, and for this co-operation I wish to express my gratitude. But if fruitful work is to be carried on in this field, the co-operation of institutions and physicians must be extended on a much broader basis.

The findings of many graphological observers would seem to indicate that a relationship does exist between certain symptoms in the handwriting and certain diseases. However, they never refer to these coincidences as determined by laws with scientific bases and consequent predictability. For example, certain symptoms in handwriting were observed to occur mainly among tuberculous patients.

Sample A: weak, interrupted loopings above the line

When the writings of these patients were examined, this

factor appeared quite often. But then it appeared in other diseases, too.

> Sample B: small, weak, pressureless loopings in both *l*'s (cancer of the bronchi)

> Sample C: weak, pressureless, uneven loopings (severe anemia with secondary heart failure)

We see, therefore, that this symptom cannot be spoken of as a specific symptom characteristic of tuberculosis. This is to be expected. Handwriting cannot give evidence of "disease." A disease is a complex affair, and the name of a disease is a label which embraces a number of pathological and physiological changes. In the case of tuberculosis, for instance, what might affect the handwriting? The fact that a certain bacillus settled down in a certain part of the organism? Or the inability of the organism to deal efficiently with this bacillus? Or the damage done to a particular organ? Or the physiological consequences, such as weakness, fever, and shortness of breath? Is it not reasonable to expect that similar symptoms may be caused by other diseases? And this has been the difficulty confronting previous observers—they found a physiological symptom that occurred with tuberculosis and also with other diseases. It is also possible that they may have observed a syndrome symptomatic of a particular change in the organism.

However elusive symptoms of disease may be in handwriting, it is nevertheless clear that physiological dispositions and functional changes in the organism determine the form of movement, and particularly the form of writing, which is the most delicate type of movement, and the type most sensitive to changes.

To understand the laws of handwriting, we must bear in mind that handwriting is a psychophysiological process. The initial impulse to write is a psychological process, in so far as a sharp separation of the two aspects of function is at all permissible. The forming of letters, of an *l, a, i,* etc., is a psychological process. But writing also involves the execution of movements, movements of contraction and movements of extension. These are physiological processes, determined in their individual characteristics by individual peculiarities of build and physiological function.

In order to make this clearer, let us forget for a moment that we are concerned with the complicated process of writing and focus our attention on the simpler, less complex movement of walking. Everyone has certainly observed that each person has a particular kind of walk, a gait peculiar to himself. One person takes long, calm, elastic steps; another, short, quick steps; and a third has a nervous and jerky or stiff and inelastic manner of walking. Now, what causes these peculiarities? You decide to take a walk. This is psychological. You intend to walk to this or that place, a psychophysiological process consisting of the psychological process that directs your steps in a certain direction and of a physiological process that carries out the orders of your mind. Your wish to see a person at this place may be strong. That would hasten your step. Or you dislike the idea of the meeting and this may slow you down. Whether you take the walk in a mood of intense anger and expectation or of aloof indifference will determine whether your manner of walking will be tense or relaxed. But apart from these psychological elements that influence the physiological process of walking, there are definite individual differences of body structure as well as of body function which leave their mark on the individual walk. Thus, a tall, thin person has a range of steps different from that of the short, stout person. Again, it makes a difference whether the legs are straight or rickety. A stout person, carrying a heavy body, may have a light, springy walk. Another person's body may shake violently at every step because of the stiff and ponderous way he sets his feet on the ground. The difference in elasticity among different walkers is a fundamental physiological characteristic, and manifests itself not only in every step a person takes, but in every form of movement he executes, and in every form of action. And here is the bridge between physiology and psychology, between physical dispositions and behavior. Yet fundamental and evident as are these differences in elasticity of movement, their deeper causes are not very well understood. What is evident is that movement is influenced by constitutional differences and subject to variation with physiological and pathological changes, such as might occur in arteriosclerosis.

There are also differences of tonicity. These are constitutional differences. One person is by nature hypertonic with high muscle tonus, another is hypotonic with slack, limp movements. Muscles with a high degree of tonus respond quickly, easily, and vigorously to a movement-impulse, require less effort to accomplish work, and cause less strain. Too high a degree of tonicity, however, would impair the flexibility of the contracting muscle and thus the controllability of movement. The innate dispositions of tonicity are likewise subject to change with functional or pathological changes. While, in some diseases, tonicity is increased, in others it is diminished.

As long as all the organs function smoothly, the process of walking is completely automatic and does not enter the

343

sphere of consciousness. The person is not aware of the enormously complicated process involved in every step he takes. It seems to be a machine-like, automatic performance in which the muscles of the right leg flex to set the foot down on the ground while the muscles of the left leg start an extending movement. This smooth co-ordination can be upset. If a tumor of the cerebellum develops, co-ordination would be disturbed. If an injury to the spinal cord were to occur, impulses would no longer be transmitted from the brain to the muscles, and the muscles of the legs would stop functioning. If the transmission of impulses from the sensory nerves of the foot were impaired by, let us say, neuritic degeneration, ataxia would result, the brain would have little or no control over the strength of muscle contractions and extensions and over timing. Movements would become uncertain and unstable.

The muscles need nourishment to function and to gain strength. This is supplied by the blood, which takes it from the alimentary canal. Given a digestive disorder, weakness of movement follows. The spasms caused by hyperacidity render taut every muscle of the body, make movements tense and inelastic. If the pancreas fails to produce sufficient insulin, the ability of the body to mobilize the food that is carried by the blood to the muscles would break down and movement would again be impaired. Nor could the muscles function well if the heart failed to pump enough blood. The rapid arrhythmic beat of cardiac cases has often been observed. Muscles cannot function without oxygen; nor can they function when waste products accumulate and are not carried away by the lymphatic system.

The endocrines must also be considered. One man walks with quick and restless steps although he has no definite goal, although there is nothing in the world to make him hurry. Another man moves sluggishly from one step to an-

PHYSIOLOGY AND PATHOLOGY

Samples 1 and 2

Photomicrographs courtesy of

Mr. Julius Weber

other though his errand be urgent. Yet the man with the restless walk may calm down after a thyroidectomy has been performed on him, and the other may become more alert after treatment with thyroid extracts. Moreover, the adrenals, the sex glands, and the pituitary all have a definite influence on the manner of a person's movement, and so on his walking, his writing, his behavior.

While the relationship between walking and the physical setup of the walker are evident and indisputable, the relationship between writing and the constitution is less apparent. This is so because the movements of writing are infinitely more complicated than the movements of walking, and consequently, observation and patient comparative studies are required to detect them. And because they are so refined, they are sensitive to even slight functional disturbances in the body.

To illustrate how complicated the process of handwriting is, I refer to the two microscopic pictures of an *i:*

In Sample 1, up- and downstrokes are of an equal and even density. Throughout the length of the strokes the width is kept uniform so that the edges of the strokes are even, sharp, and steady. At the point where the upstroke changes to a downstroke at the uppermost part of the letter, and likewise where the downstroke changes to an upstroke at the lower end of the letter, there is no thickening, no interruption visible. On the other hand, in Sample 2 the first upstroke is about half the width of the downstroke, the ink is weak, almost spotty, and up- and downstrokes seem to be composed of innumerable small, individual strokes, so that the edges of the strokes are fringed and somewhat ragged. At the end of transition from the down- to a second upstroke in the lower end of the letter, there occurs a marked thickening. The upstroke continues at about half the width of the downstroke.

346

Sample 1 shows speed, steadiness, and tension; there is a strength to the movement and a continuous transition from the flexing to the extending, from the downward to the upward movement. Sample 2, on the other hand, shows just the opposite form of movement: slow, weak, pressureless, with lateral fluctuations of the hand and frequent interruptions of movement. The transition from down- to upward movement does not proceed smoothly and continuously; the movement stops and starts anew.

These two samples represent extreme forms of steady and unsteady movements, of smooth and broken forms of transition. Between them lies a wide range of variations. Any attempt to explain these various forms of movement as accident or as merely a question of ink, pen, or manual skill, would not be adequate. The same pen and the same kind of paper were used to produce these specimens of handwriting. Nor can these differences be explained entirely from a psychological point of view. This is not to deny that there are psychological factors involved. However, the author of this book has handled these problems, and I need only mention that of course the man with a firm grip, whose movements are quick, will handle his problems in life differently from the man with the weak, unsteady, uncertain movement. The point I want to make is that weak, insecure movement comes as the result of a chain of causes, many of which are physiological.

The differences apparent in these two samples of writing reveal the basic factors: the nature of the movement, its speed, stability, tonicity, flexibility, and co-ordination. Since these factors vary widely in the handwriting of normal healthy persons, we have in these variations a possibility of studying individual manifestations and basic constitutional dispositions. Since the form of writing movement in Sample 1 changes to the form of writing movement

347

in Sample 2 when the same writer contracts a serious disease, we see that we must consider factors of movement as expressive of physiology, of individual variations in organic function. Again I emphasize the point that no such profound changes in the form of movement can be brought about by anything except profound organic changes.

There are factors involved in the writing process that are not apparent in a single letter. These are the expansion of movement, the height and the width of the letters. All these individual factors are combined in the writing process into a complex interknit whole whose elements are in turn dependent and determinant. Just as the organs combine to give a picture of the constitution, so these factors in writing combine to make up its individuality. Just as the organs are subject to particular disturbances which then reflect themselves in the total organism, so the factors in the handwriting seem subject to certain changes.

Sample 3

In Sample 3 speed of movement, stability, and tension combine with smooth transitions to up and down movement to give a picture of a well and smooth-functioning organism, of a quick and smooth response of muscles to the impulses from the co-ordination centers. The broad and regular distances between the individual downstrokes of the *m* suggest the broad, firm, yet flexible musculature of the hand, of the whole organism. These movements are like the broad and firm and at the same time elastic steps of a strong, healthy person. This is the handwriting of the German boxer Schmeling.

348

On the other hand, in Sample 4 we see delicately built features, narrow spaces between the letters; these features

wird give you my handwriting

Sample 4

are lean and angular, and the transition from up- to down-strokes is less smooth. The whole writing shows a somewhat jerky irregularity in the height of the letters. It is the handwriting of a very delicately built, tall and slim girl. Some of the outstanding features of her constitution are fine wrists, slender legs, and an uneven, inelastic, somewhat jerky manner of walking. Yet the strokes are firm and quick. Although this girl is slender, she is wiry, with good powers of resistance. One gathers she is well able to stick tenaciously to her work.

What gives a person's handwriting its characteristic appearance is the combination of the several factors of movement: speed, stability, strength, flexibility, and co-ordination. Vary one of these factors and the whole picture changes, exactly as the constitutional disposition and physical appearance of an individual vary with the proportions of the various parts of the body and the rates of functioning and different strengths of particular organs. The physical characteristics of a person are not given simply by the fact that he has limbs and a beating heart, but by the length and proportions of the limbs and the rate and strength of his heart's contractions. Similarly, in handwriting it is the individual rate of speed, strength, and so on, that make up the "constitution" of the writing. These proportions are fairly constant as long as the individual is healthy. In a healthy individual's handwriting, all the factors of movement seem to be in equilibrium with each other. For instance, there would be a disproportion if the small, delicately formed letters of Sample 4 had the strong pressure of Sample 3. Such a combination would indicate some unbalance in either the physiological or the psychological area or in both. Although all the factors of movement are closely connected, particular factors often seem to be determined in their form and extent by the functioning of particular organs.

Some interesting observations may be made which would seem to confirm the above concepts. These are based partially on experimental findings, partially on empirical material. Since the influence of various organic functions and functional changes on neuromuscular behavior are not fully understood, a medical explanation is not always possible. Nevertheless, the facts of movement can be ascertained at any time by anyone who takes the trouble to make the necessary observations. Here are a few samples, chosen because they are typical.

Sample 5

Sample 6

Consider Samples 5 and 6. They were written by the same person. Sample 5 was produced under normal conditions of health, while Sample 6 was written in a high fever accompanying influenza. There is a marked difference between these two samples: Sample 6, the fever writing, is wider, larger, faster, and weaker than the normal writing. And it is true that an elevated temperature and an accelerated pulse accelerate movement while diminishing its strength. This conclusion has been corroborated by the observation of other

350

factors: A small slow writing is generally found to coincide with a low pulse frequency and low basal temperature in the writer. This is the predominant physiological picture in the writer of Samples 5 and 6.

Sample 7 *handwriting*

Sample 8 *handwriting*

The handwritings of patients who have developed *hyperthyroidism* show a marked increase in speed and extension of movement. The writer is a woman of about thirty-five; Sample 7 was written about two years before Sample 8. The reader will have to look closely and carefully to notice the differences between these samples. The general appearance of the second sample suggests greater agitation and more irregular and uncontrolled movement. The variations in height and width within the second sample are greater (compare the low, wide first *n* with the tall, narrow second *n*). The pressure in the second sample is weaker; the i-dot is not a point but a stroke; the individual strokes are sharper and more tense than those in the first sample. These differences indicate that the second sample was produced at a greater speed accompanied by an expanded activity and reduced steadiness and control as compared with the first sample.

This is the history of the case up to the time when the second specimen was produced: Following a miscarriage,

351

the woman developed an exophthalmic goiter, a condition characterized by enlargement of the thyroid gland, rapid heart action, increased basal metabolic rate, loss in weight, and excitability. Here again we find accelerated, expanded movements in the handwriting coinciding with a raised metabolic rate and excessive nervous excitability.

Sample 9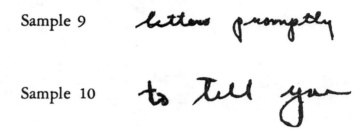

Sample 10

Both handwritings belong to the same girl. The first sample was made at twenty years, the second at twenty-three. The first is narrow, small, slow, and somewhat cramped (there is increased pressure at the end). The second is wider, more vigorous and quicker. At the time of the first sample, the girl had a basal metabolism rate of −30. She was drowsy and sluggish. Then she was treated for hypothyroidism. After three years her basal metabolism rate was up to +5: nearly normal, her behavior had changed noticeably. She was more alert, active, and self-assured. The coincidence between the acceleration of the handwriting movement and the acceleration in the basal metabolism rate is striking.

Sample 11   Sample 12

The writer, who is male, was thirty-two at the time of the first sample and forty-five at the time of the second. In the thirteen years which elapsed between the time of the first and second samples, he developed sclerosis of the coronary arteries. It may be observed that in Sample 12 the movement undergoes an increase in speed, strength, and width, while it becomes more irregular, almost uncontrolled. What causes this change of movement? No direct answer can be given. It may be related to the stronger contraction of the heart muscles, which have to overcome the resistance in the arteries, or it may be due to the irregularity of the contractions, or possibly because of the irregular way in which the blood is distributed to the muscles, causing them to work harder. Of course, a change in behavior accompanied this changed form of movement, both having been the effects of the same cause. Changed behavior and changed movement may both be early signs of a developing physical disorder.

Sample 13

Sample 13 is also the product of a patient with advanced arteriosclerosis. In this case, however, the arteries of the brain were affected. Here, too, there is a large and heavy form of movement. However, the vehemence of the previous sample is here absent. The strokes are uneven, the movement is more shaky. Moreover, there is a marked lack of orientation shown by the falling line. Failing strength and elasticity have been compensated by a greater effort on

353

the part of the writer. This is what large and heavy writing shows. (All sclerotic persons exhibit increased width and heaviness in their writing.) It seems to be a manifestation of a reduction in the flexibility and responsiveness of the joints and muscles. It may indicate what the physiological prerequisites for a smooth, quick, and elastic form of writing are.

Sample 14   Sample 15   Sample 16

In Samples 14, 15, and 16 I present another cardiac case. The subject is a forty-year-old woman. The diagnosis is rheumatic heart, more specifically, a mitral stenosis. Sample 14 is a specimen dating from 1938, before any clinical signs of a heart condition were apparent. The writer did not feel well at the time, complained about various indefinite symptoms, feelings of nervous tension, heart palpitations, and shortness of breath; but no definite diagnosis could be made. The handwriting shows quick, tense, angular movements with heavy pressure. We may assume from the later history of the disease that the heart was already at that time functioning with reduced efficiency but with increased strength of contractions, in order to maintain an adequate blood supply to the body by compensating for the decrease in the amount of blood passing through the narrower mitral valve. The strain on the heart is reflected in every part of the organism. Every muscle has to work harder to make up for the decreased blood supply. This can be deduced from the strained form of movement. Of course, there are psychological factors involved also. The strained organism is in a condition of permanent tension, and so is the mind.

354

In a defensive position the organism feels insecure, with a latent fear of organic breakdown because of diminution in the supply of oxygen. Because any change in activity threatens the organism with overstrain, the personality becomes rigid and inflexible. But these are factors which cannot be seen directly in the forms of movement. They are inferences from the forms. In this sample the movements are still regular in size and strength, though the regularity may be somewhat rigid, that is, it requires a strong effort to avoid a breakdown of control. Here is manifest the stiffness of one who is gathering his resources to squeeze the last drop of energy out of his body.

Sample 15 shows the handwriting three years later, one month before a severe heart attack occurred. Here again, as in Sample 12, we see large, irregular distances between the downstrokes. While the upstrokes in Sample 14 are straight and tense, in Sample 15 the tension of the first upstroke in the *m* breaks down. It is loose and pressureless. The increase in width coincides with more rapid and deeper breathing to gain air. There is an irregular pulse alternating between strong, tense, and weak beats.

Sample 16 was written in the hospital. Decompensation has set in. The heart is no longer able to furnish the minimal blood supply required to keep the organism going. We see the change in movement: It is weak and narrow. Notice especially the slightly blurred, roundish transition from the second upstroke to the second downstroke of the *n*. But some tension is still left in the strokes, revealing that not all the reserve strength has been exhausted.

These samples show additional cases of disorders which either directly or indirectly affect the neuromuscular system.

Sample 17: The writing shows twitching, trembling, inelastic movements. The writer has cerebrospinal syphilis, which affects the brain and spinal cord, and is usually accompanied by general paresis. Movement becomes unsteady. The ability to perform accurate movements is lost.

Sample 17

Sample 18   *for evermore.*

Sample 19

Sample 20

Sample 18: A sixteen-year-old girl. The handwriting shows stiff, sharp, angular, inflexible, and slighty jerky movements. The diagnosis was acidosis. This is a metabolic disease characterized by excessive acidity of the blood. Associated with it are headache, drowsiness, a characteristic deep breathing, and a tendency to lapse into stupor.

Samples 19 and 20: These are by two boys. One is thirteen, the other fifteen. Both are postoperative cases of cerebellar tumors. Characteristic of both handwritings is the fluctuating slant. Notice the end letters going in the opposite direction from that of previous letters. Notice also the last letter in both *give* s and the irregular, sudden increase of pressure. The cerebellum controls equilibrium and co-ordination of muscle contraction. We observe here a striking coincidence between handwriting factors and disorders of equilibrium and co-ordination.

Summary

To recapitulate, the process of writing consists essentially of two parts:

1. The act of movement itself, and
2. The production of letter forms.

The production of letter forms is a purely psychological function, and it is this aspect of handwriting analysis with which graphology deals. The act of movement, however, is primarily a physiological process, and it is here that my work has application. Keep in mind the following basic points:

1. Individual differences of movement are caused by individually different constitutional structures and individual peculiarities of organic function.
2. These differences in movement are manifested in the basic structure of the handwriting; hence, such writing may be used to infer particular physiological structures and states of the writer.
3. The truth of these statements may be demonstrated by the observation that certain elements of movement, for instance, speed, regularity, stability, and so on, are changed in a particular way by specific physiological changes.
4. The handwriting shows characteristic physiological changes which can be related to organic disturbances.
5. The forms of movement reflected in an individual's handwriting are associated with certain forms of behavior in that individual. We have demonstrated that back of changes in movement there are usually changes in physiology. Therefore, the approach to handwriting here expounded may be one means of relating behavioristic and physiological changes.

The reader will understand that the field of the relationship between handwriting and physiological processes is an immense territory of which only a negligible segment has been covered in this section. Here I intended merely to acquaint the reader with another way of looking at handwriting—with the physiological point of view.

The forms of voluntary co-ordinated movements manifested by the neuromuscular system provide access to dispositions of, and fine changes in, organic functions which are inaccessible to other forms of tests. Handwriting is both a direct and indirect record of the functions of the whole organism. Thus, handwriting can be a valuable tool for both the physician and the psychologist. Though much work has been done here, much more work remains to be done. Finally, any such effort must be a co-operative one.

FINAL REMARKS

In his contribution Alfred Kanfer has undertaken to show us on a broader scale that physiological facts and changes, too, manifest themselves in our handwriting. Graphology, thus far only the psychologist's tool, can now claim a similar role in the physiologist's laboratory.

There is, and has been, much interest in New York City hospitals in examining patients' scripts from an exclusively physiological standpoint. If the results confirm Kanfer's assertions and satisfy those who supervise these tests, promising new prospects for diagnosis would be presented to all physicians, including surgeons and pathologists—prospects unknown to yesterday's diagnosticians.

ALFRED O. MENDEL

INDEX

PERSONS

HANDWRITING TRAITS

INTERPRETATIONS

If you are unable to find any Newcastle book at your local bookstore, please write to:
Newcastle Publishing Co., Inc.
13419 Saticoy Street
North Hollywood, CA 91605

Please add $2.00 for UPS and handling to the cost of the book for the first book ordered, plus $1.00 for each additional book. California residents please add current sales tax with each order.

Free, complete, current catalogues are available upon request. Just send us your name and address and we will send you a catalogue.

Quantity discounts are available to groups, organizations and companies for any Newcastle title. Telephone (213) 873-3191 or FAX your order to Newcastle Publishing Co., Inc. at (818) 780-2007.

Thank you for your interest in Newcastle.

AL SAUNDERS
Publisher